THE
WEALTH
OF THE
AMERICAN
PEOPLE

By Oscar Handlin

Boston's Immigrants: A Study in Acculturation (1941; rev. ed., 1959)
This Was America (1949)
The Uprooted (1951; 2d ed. enlarged, 1973)
Adventure in Freedom (1954)
Harvard Guide to American History (1954)
American People in the Twentieth Century (1954)
Chance or Destiny (1955)
Race and Nationality in American Life (1957)
Readings in American History (1957; rev. ed., 1970)
Al Smith and His America (1958)
Immigration as a Factor in American History (1959)
John Dewey's Challenge to American Education (1959)
The Newcomers: Negroes and Puerto Ricans in a Changing Metropolis (1959)
American Principles and Issues: The National Purpose (1961)
The Americans (1963)
Fire-Bell in the Night: The Crisis in Civil Rights (1964)
Children of the Uprooted (1966)
Pictorial History of Immigration (1972)

By Oscar and Mary F. Handlin

Commonwealth: A Study of the Role of Government in American Economy
     (1947; rev. ed., 1969)
Dimensions of Liberty (1961)
Popular Sources of Political Authority (1966)
The American College and American Culture (1970)
Facing Life: Youth and the Family in American History (1971)

THE
WEALTH
OF THE
AMERICAN
PEOPLE

A History of
American Affluence

OSCAR and MARY F. HANDLIN

McGraw-Hill Book Company

NEW YORK   ST. LOUIS   SAN FRANCISCO

DÜSSELDORF   LONDON   MEXICO   SYDNEY   TORONTO

Book design by Stanley Drate.

1 2 3 4 5 6 7 8 9 B P B P 7 9 8 7 6 5

Library of Congress Cataloging in Publication Data

Handlin, Oscar, date
    The Wealth of the American People

    (Aspects of American life and culture)
    Bibliography: p.
    Includes index.
    1. United States—Economic conditions. I. Handlin, Mary
Flug, date   joint author. II. Title. III. Series.
HC103.H2   330.9'73   75-6962
ISBN 0-07-025985-2

Publisher's Note

This volume is part of a McGraw-Hill publishing program on Aspects of American Life and Culture.

Editorial Consultants for this program are Harold M. Hyman, William P. Hobby Professor of American History, Rice University; and Leonard W. Levy, Andrew W. Mellon Professor of Humanities and History, Claremont Graduate School.

Contents

Introduction

The year of the American Revolution also witnessed the publication of a book that profoundly influenced the modern world. Adam Smith's *Wealth of Nations* gave men the intellectual means of examining the mode of production as a system in itself; it was thus a basic step toward making economics a modern science. Indirectly it also affected the writing of history.

Until 1776 thinkers who treated such subjects as agriculture, trade or banking regarded them as aspects of political economy. Although the outcome of his studies was different, Adam Smith too had begun by inquiring into the general principles of law and government insofar as they concerned policy, revenue and arms. Attempting to describe the household of the monarch, that is, of the state, he like his predecessors focused on issues that involved the use of power for the increase of wealth. History from that point of view dealt with the measures by which princes and parliaments acted to gain riches for the nation.

But as the discipline of economics gained form and coherence through the force Smith and his successors imparted to it, the subject grew away from politics; the conviction took hold that the system of production followed its own rules of development and that therefore the sole obligation of economic historians was to add a time dimension to the forms the theorists described. Economic history, like analysis, became increasingly abstract.

Nineteenth-century social scientists, economists among them, tended to treat society as a cluster of interrelated but separate institutions, like a rope composed of numerous intertwisted strands, each of which had a traceable identity of its own. Given this premise, it seemed necessary to analyze the development of each institution as if it followed its own laws. Marxists went further in stressing the autonomy of the productive system, which they regarded as a substratum evolving of its own accord but influencing all other aspects of the social superstructure.

1

A basic intellectual assumption permeated all schools of economics. History was primarily a means of providing evidence that threw light on general laws, a body of data for the test of analytical propositions. While twentieth-century scholars surrendered the faith in rigid, immutable laws and commanded refined statistical techniques to increase the precision and depth of their work, the central concern remained the same—to build and test abstract theoretical models.

Events after 1945 increased scholarly and popular interest in the time dimension but did not alter the basic commitment of economists to theory. As attention concentrated on the problems of development, the earlier preoccupation with the condition of static equilibrium—with how a system worked in the absence of change—gave way to a concern with the dynamics of growth, for the study of which the record of the past offered attractive material. The need to make judgments about the modernization of India or Brazil drew attention to the earlier experience of Britain and Germany and produced a pragmatic willingness to concede that historical data were useful as illustration or proof of theoretical propositions.

Our purpose in this book is different. We do not challenge the worth of what other scholars using other methods have achieved; and we have labored to the best of our abilities to master their materials and conclusions. But from our point of view their work suffers from multiple shortcomings. When we look beyond the economic institutions, the analogy of the rope is inadequate; the strands are not really separate. Nor does the substratum develop independently of the influence of the superstructure. Corporations, banks and shops are factors in the system of production; they also affect, and are affected by, politics, social organization and family life. To understand how corporations and banks evolved demands an examination of changes in government as well as of changes in trade. The word "corporation" once applied equally and in the same way to manufacturing establishments, universities and churches. The word "bank" at one time referred to a currency-issuing enterprise, later to firms which made loans, accepted savings, or transferred funds. However useful it may be to isolate the economic function for other purposes, the procedure obscures the actual developments of the past. A description of the forces which shaped these institutions calls for an analysis of the whole context, rather than of a single portion of it.

Moreover, our concern is not so much with applications to present practice as with past experience. Those planning development programs in Latin America or Asia no doubt must work from abstract schemes applicable to all societies. To make investment decisions they depend on general rules and therefore on theory. In allocating scarce resources they must, for instance, choose between capital expenditures on transportation or on manufacturing; a precise measure of the past social gains and costs of railroad building might well affect the judgment of the relative contribution of various types of investment to industrialization. Such guidance would permit rational choices for development within the context of opportunities for growth offered by the surrounding social space.

The historians' problem is different. Dealing with the past, with decisions and choices already made, we must explain the inescapable fact: For better or worse, the railroad was built and many elements other than the simple analysis of profit or of social gain entered into the decision to proceed with construction. Irrational preferences, miscalculations, political pressures and intellectual and cultural assumptions were also important and those lie beyond the reach of the tools of pure economic analysis. But those preferences, pressures and assumptions are the subjects the historians must cover.

In attempting to do so, we could not center our attention on the immediate present or its problems, important as those are. Rather, we tried to describe events objectively, as does an anthropologist in dealing with a remote tribe's agriculture or an ancient historian in dealing with the trade of Sumeria or Babylon. We have sought, that is, to describe the past forms of human behavior involved in gaining and expending wealth in the United States.

To apprehend those vanished forms calls for a leap of the imagination.

Every crossroad shopping center in 1975 stocks in overwhelming abundance every sort of utensil. Conceive a situation when none was available. In 1845 a family advancing toward a new settlement in Michigan discovers a leak in the iron pot brought from the old home. There is no one to repair it, yet without the utensil they cannot prepare their food, lacking as they do the forest skills of cooking over an open fire. Wearily the father walks two days back to the town where he can have the pot mended.

Many Americans of 1975 who worry about the prevalence of hunger have in mind the nutritional deficiencies of millions of people in an affluent society. Hunger had another meaning for the critic James Huneker just before the First World War, a time of moderate well-being, when unemployment was not exceptionally high and no famine ravaged the land. Strolling along the beach at Coney Island he stumbled on a family huddled helplessly in the space beneath a bathhouse. The father, out of work, had pawned, piece by piece, bit by bit, everything in the house, while the children lived in the streets, feeding at the garbage cans. Neighbors could not help for they had difficulty assembling one meal a day for themselves. Then there was no money for rent and the family drifted, homeless, to this final refuge. Now they were hungry. That is, they had eaten nothing at all for days on end.

Once there was not enough, of pots or food or other forms of wealth. Later there was more; in time, enough. How did the change occur? That is our question.

Our task is to describe how bread and things became available. We deal not with abstract numbers but with shoes and food and machines, as well as with the emotions and ideas of producers and consumers. As well also with contracts, wages and profits, that is, with the complex of laws and customs that govern the relationships among humans in society. We must therefore embed economic in social history, treat the productive system as one element of a whole way of life and examine the total context in which changes occurred.

Our story begins at the edge of a wilderness, where men debarked to engage in a naked struggle for survival. Using transplanted crafts and skills to make and exchange goods, they slowly pushed ahead the settled area and constructed a viable society.

The economy of the Americans, like much else in their lives, was long an offshoot of Europe. The colonies depended on the Old World for the skills and capital brought over at the start and re-plenished by continuing contacts of trade and migration. The trans-atlantic relationship was colonial and in some respects remained so even after the acquisition of political independence. The Revolution was, however, a great turning point. Within the new nation dynamic individuals could assert their wills, strain against existing resources and accepted institutions, as they could not quite do while the power of ultimate decision rested across the ocean in London.

The energies thus released operated initially in the areas familiar from the past. The merchants, who continued to wield political and social influence, directed emphasis to overseas trade. The yeomen, the most numerous element in the population, responded to the magical attraction of the West; their advance along the frontier rapidly brought vast tracts of new land under cultivation in the decades after independence.

Yet the glamour of both virgin land and distant ports was transitory. The venturesome trade open to Americans who lacked the protection of an empire brought exciting immediate profits but did not endure; and the heady speculative aspects of frontier farming concealed persistent rural problems. More consequential in the long run were the industrial and agricultural experiments that laid the basis for growth in the nineteenth century. The development of transportation created a national market for the products of American factories. The plantation provided an efficient means of organization in the South until the military decision of the Civil War freed its labor force, leaving the region a complex and tragic social heritage. Elsewhere, a slow and often painful process turned the traditional family farm into a business operation.

Toward the end of the nineteenth century new types of manufacturing, organized in new types of enterprise, altered the source of the wealth of the people. Thereafter a growing percentage of the population lived in cities and drew its livelihood directly or indirectly from industry. The numerous problems created by the transition persisted well into the twentieth century and complicated the lives of the people who depended upon the factories.

Those difficulties were compounded by the failure of the global economy in the decades after 1914. The United States had never been isolated; it had always drawn strength in manpower, capital, and trade from elsewhere. It suffered as the rest of the world did from the direct and the indirect effects of war. In the 1930s the productive system spiraled downward, out of control.

Yet, despite the depression of the 1930s and a second world war, the economy acquired a new structure, scarcely noticed at the time. The realignment of productive forces in the 1950s and 1960s in the direction of increasing order, rationality and mechanization resulted not in a return to depression but in affluence which poured an abundance of goods into the society. Affluence, however, created questions about its own meaning. The millions affected by the change were scarcely prepared to deal with its consequences.

Through all the transformations that reach back from the modern industrial order of the 1970s to a few handfuls of strangers stepping ashore in a remote and unknown country more than three hundred years earlier, runs a deeply human story, of men and women seeking wealth—which for some meant no more than utensils and food, the garments and shelter to sustain life, and for others meant security, comfort, and status. The outcome of the struggle to make something of the inert resources the place afforded is the subject of our book.

1

The Burdensome Colonies

*J*ohn Holroyd's first published work was his best known. He was far from being a literary man; and the pen was not for him a familiar weapon, although the historian Edward Gibbon was his close friend. Irish-born of a well-known landed family, Holroyd was a tough military type and member of Parliament who would in time earn the title of Earl of Sheffield by services to the Crown.

He took to print for a political, not an esthetic purpose. He was something of an authority—self-taught—on economic issues, for he had traveled in Europe, ran a model farm on his estate and held firm views about commerce; and it was to expound these ideas that he became an author. The year was 1783, the American war was over and Lord North, the minister responsible for the British defeat, had fallen. Pitt's new government, seeking to salvage something from the military debacle, proposed to relax the navigation acts in favor of the now-independent United States in order to cement by trade the transatlantic ties formerly established by political sovereignty.

Lord Sheffield said no. His vigorous pamphlet *Observations on the Commerce of the American States* argued that England was better off without the ungrateful colonies. The disloyal settlements from Georgia to Massachusetts had profited from connections with Britain. Now, let them stew in their own juices. Without the links to the mother country, the former colonies were doomed. It was well to keep them at a distance. Proper, well-regulated dependencies were assets to a great nation, but not such as those which had risen in rebellion.

The argument was popular; within a year the book had run through six editions and the opinions it expressed long remained influential. Sheffield never wavered in his faith in them. A quarter of a century later, in 1809, he repeated the theory that an embargo on trade with America was beneficial to the commercial interests of Britain.

Observations on the Commerce of the American States, reprinted across the ocean, was also widely circulated in the United States, where it became the subject of warm discussion. It was not pleasing. The citizens of the new republic read it to be able to refute it. The blow it delivered to their self-esteem was also a goad to action. Their achievements, they determined, would show how wrong the noble lord had been.

Among those concerned was the Philadelphian Tench Coxe, who was no more a theorist than Holroyd. Offspring of a prominent mercantile family, Coxe had studied law, but then had entered a good mercantile firm and during the Revolution had prudently attended to his own business. A political loner who took pride in his independence, he became one of the first bureaucrats in the new republic, serving in the Treasury after 1789 and then holding various fiscal offices under Washington, Adams, Jefferson and Madison. For him as for Lord Sheffield governmental forms were inseparable from economic realities. He, too, believed that the links to Britain had significantly influenced the prosperity of the American colonies. But Coxe's calculations led to a conclusion different from Holroyd's. The Philadelphian believed that separation, far from dooming the new nation, offered it an unparalleled opportunity for growth through the development of manufacturing. Coxe's *Enquiry* into the principles of a commercial system for the United States explained that the spread of industry would create unprecedented markets for raw materials and food, thus stimulating the settlement of the interior and at the same time arming the country with cheap finished goods it could sell abroad.

Curiously, given their premises, both Sheffield and Coxe were correct. The rebellious colonies had not been worth holding by the Englishman's scale of values; by the American's, independence released a young giant from stifling ties that had too long inhibited growth.

However they added up the totals, contemporaries regarded the Revolution as a critical event in economic as well as in political development. At this point, the productive system veered in direction.

It had been the product of colonization, which had itself reflected deep strains on the traditional European ways of gaining and holding wealth. The American economy was an adaptation of Old World practices and methods to wilderness conditions. Now it cast off all imperial restraints and was free to respond to the will of the people it sustained. Or was it?

By the 1770s, the colonies were far from serving the purpose for which the mother country had long sacrificed treasure and lives. Seventeenth-century Englishmen had settled and supported these distant possessions to enrich venturesome individuals and their country as a whole. Something had gone wrong. The original plan had made sense when it was conceived; it had not operated as expected.

For seventeenth-century Europeans, whose aspirations were the seeds of colonization, the economy was not a detached activity but part of the whole life of a household. Almost everywhere in the Old World in 1600, men and women plowed and spun, traded and fabricated in the same setting within which they reared children and made their devotions to God. The family was a unit which provided its members with bread and shelter as it also united them in worship, in service to the Lord or State, and in every other communal right and duty.

Peasants, artisans and merchants differed greatly in condition, in manner of existence and in outlook; but among all of them the tasks of production centered in the household, which in turn was part of a larger community—village, guild or city. The home was the place of residence and of work in which all participated—mother, father, children and servants—all performing the labor and sharing the rewards appropriate to their condition. Tradition informed all activities. The peasants cultivated the soil less by calculation than by the ritual repetition of customs slowly defined by centuries of usage. Work was not an occupation paid for in money but an obligation incidentally attached to the status of the household; at each year's harvest, the family discovered whether it would suffer want or have enough to satisfy its needs with perhaps even a surplus to hoard against the uncertain future. Habit played a large part also in the labor of artisans, who acquired their jealously guarded skills and tools through years of training under masters who emphasized the value of accepted crafts and mysteries. The occasions for innovation were rare for those who worked to the order of customers they saw face to face. Even merchants preferred the repetition of safe and predictable routine transactions, although changing patterns of trade often forced them into unwelcome risks. Common prudence always called for caution, for the merchants brought into the local market goods the peasants and artisans could not produce, goods which were not necessities and therefore were not certain to be sold.

Everywhere, those who worked had to divert some income to support unproductive elements in the population, from the kings down through the great and lesser nobles to the local rural lords. An army of the gentry and their households lived off the economy by control of the law or by naked force. Possessors of land and of privileges drew rent and fees from their subjects; in an era when government itself was a kind of property, with office bought, sold or inherited, those who held power expected to gain from it. The legions of the church also contained numerous consumers; the priest in his parish and the bishop in his palace, as well as numerous clerical functionaries, received each his support from the same pool of riches.

The peasant or artisan or even the merchant who paid tax and tithe rarely retained a margin beyond the necessities of life; and if he did, was more likely than not to hoard it for the proverbial rainy day. Accident was an ever-present influence. Unpredictable variations in the weather determined the size of the harvest that rewarded the sower's labor. Distant gusts of wind brought the merchant's vessel to shipwreck or to a safe harbor. Brigands, highwaymen and pirates threatened the best-laid plans. No one ever knew how any venture would turn out. All therefore anxiously hoarded what they had and took only what chances were unavoidable.

Force mitigated some of the dangers of enterprise. The householder locked up his possessions and barred his door; ships and wagons moved under the protection of armed men; and many persons normally walked or rode prepared to defend themselves. In a less direct fashion, power in the form of law and custom not only enforced the obligations of contract and protected property but also created privileges that safeguarded the operations of favored individuals or groups. Towns forbade outsiders to practice crafts or trades that competed with the guild members, and in certain times and places outright monopolies reserved some types of manufacture or commerce to those with influence. The calculations of the prudent man under these circumstances focused on the means of minimizing risks and of maintaining stability and order to offset the adverse effects of accident.

The economy of the sixteenth and seventeenth centuries was nevertheless not static. Uncontrolled, dynamic factors kept upsetting the equilibrium people sought to preserve. Eruptions of war, famine and plague, changes in frontiers, and the reclamation of formerly

unusable territories abruptly altered the conditions of earning a livelihood. In some areas the population grew, elsewhere it declined; and
the changes in numbers affected the balance of producers, consumers and available land. Even when the totals remained constant, shifts
among regions or towns or even within families called for adjustments.
Always, the presence of ethnic minorities like the Jews or the Gypsies
posed a problem, because these people operated outside the closed
communities the society considered normal. The Renaissance and
the Reformation increased the numbers of those who did not fit in
and also generated unsettling ideas about man's nature, about his
relations to his neighbors and, indeed, about the world in which he
lived. One consequence in England was the appearance of numerous
placeless people, not members of any recognized household, who
thronged the cities, especially London, or who wandered the roads.

Long-term political and economic developments contributed to
the instability. With the gradual emergence of the centralized nation-
state, power gravitated toward the Crown; the intermittent little
feudal wars ground to a halt; and the gentry, no longer freewheeling
fighters, turned into administrative officials occupied with local government and with the management of their estates. The conception of
the King's household broadened to encompass the whole national
economy. The alert monarch measured his strength not by the gold
in his chests or by the weapons at his command but by the massed
riches of his subjects. His interest lay in stimulating the activities that
would increase their wealth and consequently his own. At the same
time, the European price revolution—touched off by the arrival of
treasure from Spanish and Portuguese America—and innovations
in industry and agriculture weakened the position of the traditional
households and gave an advantage to people able to respond to the
opportunities change presented.

The new conditions drew attention to the productive uses of
surplus funds. The prudent man hoarded the yield of a good harvest
or of a lucky turn of trade, of looting in war or of a treasure cast
up from the sea, against some hard time in the future; the wastrel
expended the gains from such strokes of fortune on better living for
the moment. Those choices were familiar from the past and remained
compelling when it came to utilizing the windfall of newly discovered
lands and their treasures. Well before 1600, however, another possibility had seized the imagination of the enterprising. The extra
amounts need not be consumed in luxuries or simply hidden away
against future necessity; they could go to work and bring their possessors future earnings. By 1600, many Europeans were seeking ways

to invest their capital. Out of that search grew the interest in overseas trade and in colonies, an interest deepened by the needs of the kings and by the internal changes in European agriculture and industry.

For centuries merchants had dispatched gold or goods to and from far places; and they had developed institutions to guard their investments against risk. They needed capital: lengthy voyages tied up merchandise or cash for years on end in a painfully slow and hazardous turnover. They also needed power: profits on trade with Turkey, Russia or India were fabulous but so were the hazards on the way to, or within, those far-off places. Discretion required voyagers to protect their lives and cargoes against pirates and thieves and, if they went in groups, against each other.

That the word "company" long retained both a military and a commercial meaning reflected the original union of the two functions. Individuals, when possible, pooled their resources for mutual aid and could do so spontaneously along the way as opportunity permitted or necessity required. But in the absence of some permanent organization, partners did not long stay together and internal disputes led to bitter vendettas. An institution which made the participants into a company for common defense and for financial cooperation served a felt need.

The model was the borough or guild, in which individuals participated but willingly subjected themselves to government. The English Muscovy Company, for instance, came into being in 1555, through a charter from the Crown, which made it a body politic and corporate and authorized it to enact its own by-laws in accordance with the general principles outlined in the grant. Each participant sent along his own particular bit of cargo and individually took what gains or losses resulted from its sale; the company maintained the overseas warehouses, offices and housing, called a factory or plantation, which served its members. Such enterprises were the means through which Europeans traded in many parts of the world.

In 1602, the Dutch East India Company introduced a variation that very quickly became commonplace. The company was organized as its predecessors had been, except that it possessed a joint stock. The trading goods belonged to the corporation as a whole, while the members had the right to a share proportionate to the sums they contributed. Management, risk and profit were thus common, an advantage in attracting large numbers of participants. Corporations of this sort established Virginia, Massachusetts, Plymouth and New Netherland.

By Lord Sheffield's day much had changed. The English chartered companies no longer played a role in American life, although they remained important in other parts of the world. Yet they had conducted the crucial phases of settlement and had given a decisive turn to the economy of the New World. And their failure to develop as their promoters had expected left room for novel economic developments which had much to do with the Revolution.

There were two kinds of participants in the trading corporations. Among the shareholders were both the adventurers who risked their capital, although they rarely themselves went overseas, and the planters who conducted the enterprise on the spot, guarded the magazine which held the company's goods and supervised the trading operations. The hard work the promoter left to servants of inferior status, either acquired on the spot or carried from home.

Difficulties beset such enterprises in every part of the world. The greater the hazards, the greater the expectation of gain. Communications were painfully slow; merchants who sent goods or messages to distant ports waited months for the word from Russia, Turkey or Africa that would inform them of success or failure.

Commerce with the mainland of North America encountered all these problems and additional ones as well. Between Florida and Maine there were no natives at hand for profitable exploitation, no developed society with which to deal. Nor was there readily available gold, silver, spices, sugar or any other commodity that could enter into overseas trade. The hope of remedying that shortcoming and salvaging their investments drove the planters into a continuous search for a staple—that is, for some unique, precious article of trade which would give its possessor a special advantage in international commerce. If not gold, then perhaps commodities that found ready sale in the marts of Europe—silk, glass, iron. Again and again, ill-fated experiments revealed that these would not then fill the gap.

The staples that actually did appear were of another sort, although also valuable in international trade. England had formerly paid hundreds of thousands of pounds annually to the Spanish colonies for tobacco. The same weed, raised in its own possessions, freed Britain from that dependence and also brought in the profits of resale to France, Germany and Scandinavia. The American fisheries competed with the Dutch in supplying an important element of the daily diet. The wilderness forests were an abundant source of furs to clothe Europeans and of timber for their sailing ships.

But all these riches required labor. Land was abundant; the unimaginable acres ready for cultivation, the endless forests, alive with game and thick with tall trees that ran from the very water's edge deep into the unknown interior, lacked only the men to draw forth riches. The handful of natives moved about so, they could not be induced, or compelled, to work; and the chartered companies could not persuade enough people to come or provide for the existence of those who straggled across.

The effort to attract population entirely transformed the settlements.

The first promoters had expected tightly controlled communities to earn the rewards for their investments. Everyone in the trading plantations would, in effect, be an employee of the company, nurtured from the common magazine and subject to the central discipline, toiling together for the benefit of the enterprise.

These plans never worked. The abundance of land and the scarcity of labor in this sector of America sooner or later undermined the schemes conceived in Europe. The Virginia Company early discovered, as others did later, that the inducements which persuaded people to migrate and to apply their labor to the wilderness weakened its control. Once it offered a headright of fifty acres to each new arrival, settlement fanned out into the interior. In Virginia and elsewhere, initial hopes for maintaining a common magazine, common land and common direction of enterprise collapsed. Instead, the ownership of the soil and the process of production reverted to the individual households familiar from the Old World. The needs and challenges of the North American continent drove the companies to failure and converted their trading stations into permanent societies.

As one corporation after another lost its charter, the colonies passed under royal control; and indeed other provinces, like Pennsylvania, Carolina and Georgia, with other schemes of government, added strength to the British interest in America. But the officials appointed by the monarch or by the proprietors were no more capable of imposing an economic plan on the area than the companies had been.

The Crown had always had a stake in colonization, which was a necessary means of furthering overseas trade and increasing national wealth. Spain and Portugal in 1600 had already established their empires; in the seventeenth century England, along with the Netherlands, France and the lesser European states, hastened to do the same.

An empire was essential because each country kept a monopoly of the trade with its possessions and excluded outsiders. Furthermore, each assumed that it stood in a perpetual state of hostility toward others; warfare was endemic, intermittently breaking into the open, but simmering unobtrusively in skirmishes in one corner of the globe or another even in periods of a declared peace. It was the natural posture of empires to struggle against one another, if not in war, then in commerce; and colonies were essential elements in the strategy of conflict. Since trading ships were not far different from men-of-war, each nation sought to increase its strength at sea. A ruler with possessions in remote parts of the world could exclude from the carrying business all vessels but those of his subjects. The colonies could also produce valuable raw materials and provide secure markets for the finished products of the mother countries. They thus added to the strength that enabled a nation to fend off aggression and to expand.

Later, a theoretical system justified the policies that had developed in practice in the seventeenth century. Mercantilists regarded the economy of the state as a unitary enterprise under the centralized control of the Crown which aimed to further the welfare of the whole. They measured the wealth of the nation by its favorable balance of trade and particularly by the surplus of gold which resulted from the excess of exports over imports. To improve its position a prudent government used its power, whether through general laws or through the grant of monopolies or other privileges, so that it could outdistance its rivals.

Theory and actuality pushed Britain to retain its holdings in North America after the companies failed and, in fact, to encourage every effort to found new settlements. A complex succession of laws aimed to integrate the economies of all the English possessions, wherever they were, into an empire which stretched around the globe and in defense of which Britain engaged in more than a century of struggle against Spain, against the Netherlands and against France.

In 1763, with the end of the French and Indian War, the struggle seemed to the British to have come to a victorious close. Yet by then the basis for the independence of the American provinces was already set. The colonists were headed on a course that led to independence, for the neat theories of mercantilism did not fit the circumstances of the actual population. The Americans had developed a distinctive economy, linked to the outer world though deeply rooted in their own continent. There was something new and unique about that economy, but also something with universal implications; Adam Smith, who spent the decade before 1776 writing about the wealth of nations, drew often upon the experience of the colonies in the New World for examples to support the conclusions of his great work.

The imperial interest had still emphasized the quest for staples; the Americans went their own way. In 1717 an English promoter, undaunted by a century's experience, dreamed of crops of coffee, tea, figs, raisins, currants, almonds, olives, silk and wine in Carolina; and a quarter-century later oranges joined the list planned for Georgia. After all, the reasoning ran, those provinces were on the same line of latitude as the Mediterranean. The avid search for objects of value in the imperial system long misled the ever-sanguine enterprisers by diverting their attention away from what the New World actually had to offer.

Nor were the governments any better able than the companies to hold the population together and in place. The arguments fell on deaf ears, the laws were evaded. Neither fear of the Indians nor inherited beliefs in the value of discipline, tradition, solidarity and authority prevented the Americans from pushing out to where they could best serve their own individual interests. Their households were, therefore, not identical with those left across the Atlantic. The colonial agriculturists, artisans and merchants were not the same as their European counterparts. Habits, traditions and skills were not completely adaptable to new conditions; and in the New World the villages, guilds and cities, if they developed at all, did so without the capacity for control which in England had established order among the separate households.

On the eve of the Revolution the two million or so people who lived along the Atlantic from Maine to Georgia drew their support from a thriving economy, but one which lacked central direction. Whatever the injunctions of the rulers, whatever the preachings against avarice, few restraints inhibited the head of each family from making his own decisions about how to gain his livelihood, about what to plant or make or sell, about where to reside or when to work, about what to buy or what to save. A society which had learned to make individual judgments of what was to individual advantage frustrated the policies of merchantilist statesmen, just as it had defeated the earlier plans of company promoters.

The colonies between Maryland and Georgia most closely matched the expectations of London. Their soil ultimately yielded valuable staples—tobacco, rice, indigo and some cotton. Most of that trade, as was proper, fell into the hands of British merchants. Scottish houses from Glasgow thus handled the bulk of the tobacco crop, which they purchased through factors in America and which they distributed profitably throughout western Europe. In return, these provinces took substantial amounts of manufactured goods and, since credit terms were liberal, developed an ever-increasing debt to the mother country, a nice reminder of dependence.

A long, slow course of development shaped the favorable commercial relationships of the Southern colonies with the mother country. Through much of the seventeenth century, operations in Virginia, Maryland and the Carolinas had been small in scale and primitive in procedures. There had been plenty of room; settlers had hurriedly cleared a few acres and, when they had exhausted the carelessly tilled soil, had shifted to other parts of their holdings. Some families had had the help of a few indentured servants, but labor had been scarce as long as each had been free to work for himself when his term had expired. Tobacco, furs, timber and naval stores, the commodities of the greatest value sent to Britain, were the products of small holdings.

Toward the end of the seventeenth century the situation changed. English commercial policy encouraged large-scale agriculture, colonial laws defined slavery as an institution, trade with Africa increased the supply of unfree blacks, and the Carolinians and others learned from the West Indies how to operate extensive plantations. As in the West Indies, the very term "plantation" acquired a new meaning to describe the characteristic unit of production in the southern mainland colonies. Small farms survived in many places, but the new "plantation" steadily gained economic and social importance. The eighteenth-century plantation raised indigo and rice as well as tobacco on great tracts, using hundreds of slaves who toiled under rigid discipline, enforced by the supervision of overseers.

Yet the Virginia or Carolina planter differed significantly from his equivalent in Jamaica or Barbados. The West Indians were Englishmen, absentees or on the way to becoming so; once they earned their fortunes and could depend upon the income, they withdrew to live in the mother country. Rarely was that the case on the mainland. Perhaps the Virginians were not as rich or as secluded as the island-based Jamaicans and therefore were less tempted by the attractions of London. Still, even the wealthiest Carter, Byrd or Washington considered Virginia his homeland.

The future of the mainlanders lay in the interior of the continent. The lure of the empty western lands—in the eighteenth as in the seventeenth century—gripped the imagination of discontented planters who fancied that a new start would wipe away their debts or furnish them with the effortless affluence beyond their present reach. But a similar lure also drew the attention of the wealthy, who could have lived in ease where they were or could even have made themselves comfortable places in England. Ample prospects did not hold George Washington in Virginia; he preferred in his young manhood to strike out toward the remote Ohio Valley, where his relatives and friends contemplated outposts in the wilderness.

The great western spaces attracted Southern speculators and

settlers because not all planters in the eighteenth century regarded the slave plantation as a permanent or even as a desirable mode of production. Some, of course, gladly accepted the income and status the labor of others brought them and gave no thought to the implications for their society. Enough Georgians in 1750 actually considered the bondage of blacks a positive good to effect the repeal of the original exclusion of slavery from that colony. More surprising was the extent to which many slave owners questioned the justice of the institution and expected it to disappear. Children of the enlightenment, they believed in natural rights and human improvement and had faith that this relic of a barbarous age would not long survive in the New World. Moreover, the plantation was not quite the same mode of organizing production on the mainland as on the islands. Rather than mobilizing their bondsmen in gangs or treating them in every respect as the disciplined members of a large labor force, American masters tolerated the appearance of family life among the blacks and allowed some individuals to advance toward emancipation. These inconsistencies revealed an ambiguous attitude toward slavery.

There remained something incongruous about the plantation as an institution; it did not conform to the social norm which assumed that the household was the appropriate unit of work. The effort of some slaveholders to act as if the estate was a kind of family invariably broke down at the same stubborn fact: the blacks were chattels, not children, and labored for the master's advantage, not their own. The pretense of a great, enlarged family did not hold. Some farsighted planters before the Revolution already gave serious thought to the reforms needed to bring their holdings into line with the model of a free society they considered proper for their country.

Outside the plantation South, great landed estates appeared only in a few places—in the Connecticut and Hudson valleys and on Narragansett Bay, for instance. Everywhere, South or North, the overwhelming majority of all American cultivators owned their land and tilled it with their own labor. They conformed to a type contemporaries often described with characteristics quite different from their nearest English equivalent, the yeoman.

The American farmer was independent; he worked with his immediate family and for himself; and his household, having cut away from the village community, operated on its own, set apart on its broad acres from its neighbors. Communal controls and values broke down once the immediate shock of settlement passed, for expansive opportunities and empty space encouraged men to strive for gain rather than for stability, to move about rather than to strike roots, to produce by calculation for the market rather than by habit for subsistence.

The American farmer had not been part of the colonization plans. The promoters who had encouraged migration to give worth to their empty lands had hoped that orderly settlement would contribute to the wealth of the company, proprietor or province. But sooner or later the individual households moved apart in the search for personal advantage or, as moralists charged, out of avarice. Common fields, where they existed, were divided so that each husbandman could make what he wished of them and each turned his hand to a variety of products rather than specializing exclusively in the great staples desirable in the imperial perspective.

The New World put a premium on skills different from those of the Old. The wilderness produced its own subsistence for people able to hunt and fish. Observing the Indians, men learned to hasten the clearing of the soil by girdling the trees; they planted corn instead of wheat and allowed cattle and pigs to forage for themselves. Once the frontier receded, the settled husbandmen turned to more careful cultivation of specialized crops aimed for the market—onions for the West Indies, clams dug from the shore and dried in the sun for sale to the Indians, lumber for England, flaxseed for Ireland.

Through the eighteenth century, even in areas that had long been settled, the conditions of life remained primitive. Knowing little of fertilizers, the farmer depended upon meadow grass to feed his stock; he sowed by hand, having laboriously turned up the soil with his wooden plow; and he made or improvised almost everything he used. Of necessity he developed a multitude of skills—carpentry to build house, barn, fences, and furnishings; ironwork to shoe the horse or repair utensils; and cobbling for the family footwear. Since supplies did not keep well for long, his wife learned to smoke meat; she baked shortbread on the griddle, washed the clothes by the brook, milked the cow, churned the butter, spun, wove and sewed, dipped the candles and boiled the soap in the endless task of satisfying the needs of the family which depended upon itself for almost everything it consumed. Customs officials and naval officers who acquiesced in wartime violations of the law could rarely crack down effectively when the fighting stopped.

There were fewer artisan families. But they too adjusted to the new conditions in the towns that dotted the country. Schemes for glassmaking and silkweaving came to nothing. But scores of hatters, cordwainers, ropemakers, coopers and carpenters—persons of substance who were their own bosses and possessed their own tools—turned out hats, shoes and barrels for sale to local consumers, subtly eroding the market for British manufactures. Restrictive laws enacted in London failed to curtail the output of colonial shops.

The appearance of large, powerful and dynamic groups of indigenous merchants also ran counter to imperial theory. Trade should have remained in the hands of merchants in the mother country, as indeed it did in intercourse with the plantation colonies. But a surprising share of the commerce out of Boston, Newport, New York, Philadelphia, Charleston and elsewhere fell to Americans, whose operations England could not control and whose interests sometimes ran counter to those of the empire.

At the start, the merchants had been Europeans, mostly English, of course. But as the decades advanced, an increasing proportion were native Americans. Business forms were, after all, simple. The individual, or occasionally the partners, who owned a ship loaded whatever cargo was available and dispatched it when the hold was full. Until the return of the ship the captain was in charge; he carried instructions from the owners, but was expected to interpret them in the light of changing conditions. He chose the ports of call, guided by experience and by information he picked up en route; and at each stop he made the best deals possible—selling what he had, buying what he could dispose of elsewhere, paying out or accepting gold or drafts on known correspondents. All these operations were heavily laden with risk, and chance played an important part in every outcome. The successful trader calculated shrewdly, chose a reliable captain, was ever on guard and seized opportunity when it presented itself.

Personal connections helped. A relative, co-religionist, or friend in a foreign port was an immense asset—a source of information, credit and assistance and a trustworthy correspondent for transactions at a distance. Family ties were always important in determining who could do business. Those ties brought access to capital and links to a worldwide network of buyers and sellers. Insiders could get their sons taken on as apprentices in a good counting house, knew what discounts to demand, received preferential treatment in port and could send small consignments on the vessels of friends and relatives.

Nevertheless, determined outsiders could also establish themselves, since neither guilds nor restrictive laws set effective limits on who could carry on the business of buying and selling. Small adventures could grow into large ones; and it was not hard to send to sea some damned old eelpot of a vessel that would make a start for a prospective man of affairs.

Trade with the British Isles was the mainstay of the dealings of provincial merchants, whose correspondents in London or Bristol re-

ceived and disposed of cargoes from American ports and either retained the proceeds as credit or exchanged them for goods salable in
the New World. As the volume of transactions rose, communications
with the interior also gained in importance, for it was through links in
the small towns that the products for export were collected and imports distributed.

The colonists felt themselves at a disadvantage in these exchanges, which always seemed to benefit the mother country. The
prices of goods bought seemed high in comparison with those sold,
particularly since English commercial policy blocked off trade with
other European countries. Americans usually paid their agents with
bills of exchange on a British correspondent; but often those were
scarce or the price too high and then gold or silver had to cover the
deficit, so that currency seemed ever to drift eastward across the
Atlantic. Merchants were therefore always on the lookout for alternatives to direct trade with Britain. In 1768, for instance, James Beek-
man of New York had to ship produce for sale in Portugal with instructions that the proceeds be remitted to Bristol.

Times of war, plentiful in the century after 1660, created opportunities for the venturesome. Favorites of the governors battened
on contracts to supply the British forces in America. Many colonists
found an unfamiliar welcome in the French, Spanish and Dutch West
Indies, usually closed to them but under the pressure of war open to
anyone who could get by the English blockaders. At the same time,
Americans, commissioned by their governments, could profit from
privateering raids on enemy shipping. And the habits of war persisted
in times of peace; those none too scrupulous about the distinction continued under the black flag of piracy the seizures no longer permissible
under the royal standard, or, as smugglers, circumvented the trading
restrictions of their own and of other governments.

American merchants thus had an advantage over their British
counterparts. The lush tropical islands of the West Indies concentrated on the production of sugar and purchased from the mainland
the barrel staves, timber, corn, fish, horses and even biscuits they did
not produce themselves. Such exchanges were legal among British
possessions and were profitable enough; dealing with those places,
the merchants took advantage of their position in the imperial system.
But they also felt free to disregard inconvenient restraints and traded
with the Spanish and Dutch colonies in defiance of the rules. Local
officials winked at such violations for the mutual advantage of buyers
and sellers. These freewheeling practices created annoying problems
for royal administrators who, however, had little power to do anything
about them.

An immense variety of three- or four-cornered swapping operations developed. Sugar taken on in Havana or Martinique in exchange for fish or biscuits arrived in Newport or New York to be converted into rum. Carried to Africa, the rum might be sold for slaves to be taken back to America or for gold or ivory, which could be traded for cloth, wine or cutlery in Europe. Since the shifting tides of opportunity governed these transactions, those dealers did best who were most alert to novelty and most ingenious in using whatever chances turned up.

Commerce under these terms was profitable but dangerous; shipwreck, piracy, unpredictable changes in supply and demand, and the whims of government officers compounded the risks. Therefore the most successful merchants longed for what the colonies did not afford them, the means of stabilizing their wealth. They envied the dependable established trade, the monopolies, the access to public office and the fees that gave their counterparts in settled countries some security to offset the risks of commerce. They envied also the worldwide reputation of the products of European industry and agriculture which gave English traders a market everywhere for Sheffield steel or Manchester cotton and Frenchmen a market for the wines of Bordeaux and the silks of Lyons. Few American commodities offered similar assurance of prosperity to colonial merchants who persistently sought, somehow, to develop a flow of exports that would support their business in good times and bad.

The staples produced in the Southern colonies were exceedingly valuable. Whoever took on a load of indigo, for instance, found a ready market wherever textiles were made—in Europe or in America. Tobacco also had great worth, although Scottish houses, not colonial merchants, handled the bulk of that crop. Commodities of a less conventional sort from the Northern colonies gave Americans most of their outbound cargoes. Yankees early packed the fish from their ocean for shipment to the West Indies, which could not supply themselves with food and other necessities. Grain raised along the Connecticut, Hudson and Delaware valleys found its way to the same destination, either milled into flour or baked into biscuits. Horses from the Narragansett region of Rhode Island, whale oil from Nantucket, tallow from Providence, and vegetables from Long Island added to the flow of exports handled by the merchants of Boston, Newport, Philadelphia and New York. Almost all these goods came from numerous small family farms, the total output of which would rise only as expansion into the interior increased the number of producers.

Nor could the merchants derive a great flow of exports from industry as England did, or France. The number of American artisans grew steadily, but they had all they could do to supply the needs of the growing towns. Skilled workers in cloth, leather, iron and wood who made up cloaks, shoes, shovels, and cabinets, mostly on order, produced little for export. The artisans commanded good prices on the local market they controlled, prices too high to justify shipment abroad.

Merchants were somewhat more successful in stimulating the output of domestic manufactures, that is, products made in the rural homes. Thrifty and industrious farmers did not idle away the long intervals when the chores of plowing, reaping and caring for the animals were finished. They turned their hands to tasks that might bring in some much-sought cash. If wood was abundant, if whaling was prevalent, they whittled shingles and barrel staves or made candles; everywhere, they spun and wove or else their wives did, and particularly those whose husbands combined fishing with agriculture.

Influential or wealthy farmers extended their enterprises by building mills to utilize the power of the streams. One erected a wooden-cogged wheel to grind corn, another to saw lumber, and still another to crush the oak bark used in tanning the leather he worked up from the hides of the neighborhood. Finding the flow of their stream insufficient, three such New Jersey farmers dammed a brook on the other side of a hill, planning to carry the additional needed water to their mills by a 300-foot underground aqueduct. The venture was not altogether successful, because they dug from opposite sides of the hill and, lacking engineering skill, could not get the two tunnels quite to meet. Still, it was a measure of the rural interest in industry.

Labor shortages continued to be a problem. But enterprising farmers could generally buy the contract of an indentured servant who had agreed to work for a term of years in return for the price of his passage from Europe. For the duration of the contract such a man or woman was a member of the household and obliged to contribute to its output.

The existence of these willing hands created an opportunity merchants in time began to use. Familiar with the domestic, or putting-out, system in England, they aspired to create an American equivalent so that they could distribute unfinished materials to rural homes to be worked up into saleable products. In the vicinity of Lynn, Massachusetts, the shoe industry developed in that fashion. But the merchants hoped for something more, and it was symptomatic in 1775 that Tench Coxe became a member of the United Company of Philadelphia for Promoting American Manufactures. Through this new organization he and his collaborators hoped to shore up the unsteady foundation of colonial trade. Other events interrupted the experiment.

In 1775, instability was still characteristic of the economy. The slaves were an inert mass who had nothing, not even the power of decision, and therefore were not in a position either to win anything or lose anything. The largest cities by then housed small contingents of unskilled laborers and transient seamen who lived from hand to mouth, used to taking orders and dependent on the will of others.

But most of the population was free to act and therefore open to the possibility of losing or winning. Risk was an inescapable condition of American life for the planters, farmers and artisans as well as for the merchants, and together these were the great majority of Americans. The security of Europe had disappeared along with its limited opportunities on the day when the emigrants had chosen to depart. They and their descendants had chosen to face the hazards of the New World. They could only try to make the most of them.

The willingness to venture became characteristic in the New World and was a potential source of strength. The speculator might, of course, lose everything, and ruin awaited the imprudent or incautious. But timidity was not the appropriate response; people who clung to fixed habits and followed only the safe course rarely made anything of themselves. The great rewards lay in facing and mastering dangers rather than in pretending that they did not exist. Providence or natural law doomed some to defeat and destined others for success. The blind goddess, Fortune, in the evening crowned with honors the very man whom she had in the morning loaded with disgrace— elevating one, depressing another according to the whims of a fickle humor. The individual learned which fate awaited him only through exposure. That was the lesson of experience in the New World.

The enterprisers in America could rely neither upon inheritance nor habit in coping with the inescapable yet unpredictable forces that determined their welfare. In defense of their interests they reached for privileges where they could and clutched at whatever support the ties of kinship afforded. But in the end each depended upon his own resources.

Survival called for endless, vigilant calculation. Of necessity, they were schemers all—merchants and farmers alike—for if fortune's turn was unpredictable the prudent man had to remain alert to all contingencies and had to be ready to seize whatever opportunity presented itself. Remorseless rationality overrode all other considerations, so that life was a constant process of reckoning—of prices and costs, of effort and time. Nowhere else in the eighteenth-century world was the clock so important, even in the home of the simple husbandman.

Prudence for Americans meant not only saving, but also turning savings to some productive purpose. Windfalls were not uncommon, nor confined to the merchants. The growth of population tended to raise the value of land and of urban real estate and, except for some landed aristocrats, consumption needs were simple—all circumstances which increased the disposable assets in the hands of individuals. Those fortune thus favored did not hoard the pennies but put them to work. His own storehouse no more monopolized the merchant's attention than the plow did the farmer's or the last, the cobbler's. Everyone dabbled in a variety of ventures, trading, lending, going on shares with partners in mills, forges, glass-, candle-, and brickmaking, all on the chance of some greater gain. The speculative use of capital was the prevailing feature of colonial life.

Belief in the benign feature of the country made speculation tolerable. The evidence seemed clear. Decade by decade, population grew, settlement advanced, cities spread across the open fields. So much had been achieved since yesterday, no doubt the achievements of tomorrow would be greater still. There would always be buyers— for the cargoes of miscellaneous goods brought by unexpected ships, for the lots in town on which someday great buildings would rise, and for the vast tracts of frontier lands which would in time support thousands of industrious husbandmen. Growth would inevitably reward the speculator.

Many a colonist came to ruin by adhering uncritically to these articles of faith. Prudence often demanded a willingness to borrow. Debt was therefore common among farmers, planters and merchants, incurred not only by the occasional spendthrift but also by the parsimonious to add more acres or to launch a business venture. Rising values, they hoped, would provide the means of repayment and leave a surplus besides. Disaster overwhelmed those who guessed wrong. But Americans discounted the failures and continued to seek the turn of fortune that would bring wealth.

Those who attained the object of their quest still faced a dilemma. The ship came in; the land sold at the higher price; the calculations turned out well. The clever dealer now held bills of exchange, promissory notes, sometimes gold or silver, a stock of goods. He could do little with them. Standards of consumption were not lavish; in the towns great houses, servants, carriages and elegant clothes were rare, so that the opportunities for personal indulgence were narrow. To hoard the coins or paper was unproductive and dangerous. Moneylending was common but also hazardous; in such personal transactions high interest rates exposed the lender to charges of usury and collections were sometimes difficult. Often the only course open was further investment. The proceeds of a successful venture went into the cargo for another voyage or into new speculations in land, so that risks extended indefinitely into the future.

Pervasive speculation gave everyone a stake in expansion, whether it was William Johnson among the Indians trading in furs and western lands or Thomas Hancock in Boston taking country products in return for books. Tomorrow's growth would dissolve today's problems. If this year's crop or today's sale earned little or lost, the assurance survived that the long run would right the balance as the population increased, as the interior opened, and as trade developed.

Any threat to expansion was a threat to all.

To its cost, and without deliberation, the British government learned that after 1763.

Until then, restraints on trade created difficulties and left hard feelings but caused little damage because inefficient administration permitted easy evasion of the laws.

The colonists had always resented London's pigheadedness about the currency, for instance, but had little trouble getting around annoying regulations. They had always complained that shortages forced them either to depend upon barter or to use Indian wampum, beaver skins, tobacco certificates and Spanish and Portuguese coins for money. At moments of stringency, cash disappeared and debtors unexpectedly were incapable of meeting the claims upon them. Yet every effort, such as that of Massachusetts in 1741 or of Robert Morris in 1763, to create a bank of some sort had met royal disapproval. Had each province been on its own, it could have chartered a bank; but the very idea, at the moment, was too fanciful to receive serious attention. In any case, people managed. Merchants made and received payment in paper, using personal notes or drafts on distant correspondents. In addition, the colonial assemblies issued bonds or promissory notes in denominations small enough to circulate as currency, which served for a time, until their value depreciated. The colonists had learned to live with these inconveniences. But their errant thoughts again and again returned wistfully to bank charters.

After 1763, the inconveniences became less tolerable and Americans drifted toward separation. Almost a century of war with France then came to a successful close and peace compelled British statesmen to consider an orderly form for the vast empire they now ruled. Their efforts to rationalize the colonial system soon uncovered the determined resistance of the American colonists, who resented any interference with their independent development.

The years of fighting had caused a sharp rise in the English national debt; it was not surprising that Parliament sought some reimbursement from the colonies to lessen the burden on taxpayers in the mother country. If the duties also had the effect of enforcing the acts of trade, of bringing the provinces into line with mercantilist policy, and of helping out the deserving British investors in the East India Company, so much the better. It also seemed a good time to settle many disputes among rival claimants to western territory and to pacify the Indians by halting the disorderly movement of settlers beyond the Alleghenies.

The application of imperial intentions led to no difficulties in the West Indies, where indigenous interests recognized their place in the imperial system. But the Americans on the mainland resisted bitterly. Their history had given them a distinctive cultural identity, a sense of their own nationality; and their political experience had taught them to fight infringements upon their inalienable natural rights. The royal policy which culminated in the Quebec Act of 1774 and the Intolerable Acts of 1775 would have halted expansion—territorial and commercial—and damaged all those who depended on it. The efforts to enforce restrictions on trade and manufactures and to extend monopolies for the advantage of the Crown immediately challenged a population which had grown up, unexpectedly, in disregard of mercantilist assumptions. Too many people of the wrong kind, by 1763, occupied America to make a good colony. Merchants, planters, farmers and artisans would alike have suffered from measures which closed off the West and cramped trade in a narrow dependence upon the mother country. Though many dreaded a break with England, the result was to be revolution, war and independence.

Separation was to create the opportunity for a test of theory. Lord Sheffield was all for keeping India and Jamaica British; they would remain what they were meant to be. The rebellious colonies had not. Good riddance. Thomas Hutchinson, formerly governor of Massachusetts, who was to die a Tory exile in England in 1780, expressed the same sentiment in the conclusion of his history of the colony: the inhabitants of America would never in the future be as well off as they would have been had they remained faithful subjects.

Tench Coxe, although conservative by temperament, in the end regarded independence as a blessing for it removed the impediments which restrained growth.

The future of the Republic would demonstrate who was right.

2

Trade Outside the Systems

Lord Sheffield's certainty that economic doom awaited the United States rested upon a simple calculation. Independence set the former colonies in an anomalous situation. Deprived of the sheltering protection of the mother country, they would everywhere be outsiders in a hostile world. A century of warfare had slightly altered the balance among them, but in 1783 the great empires of Britain, France, the Netherlands, Portugal and Spain remained intact. Each power would still regulate its possessions tightly and would treat American merchantmen as unwelcome intruders. Without the nourishment of trade, the cities of the United States would decay and its agriculture, deprived of markets, would cease to reward the husbandmen. The rebels soon would learn the costs of separation.

The citizens of the new republic were aware of their precarious situation. But years of improvisation before independence had left them confident. The skills developed by long experience in commerce inside and outside the rules would now serve them well. Convinced of the future greatness of their country, they expected to do more than hold their own in international competition—and without an American empire. They would not seek colonies; their natural resources and their wits would enable them to produce or procure goods others wished to buy and would also provide means of paying

27

for the goods others wished to sell. True trading power, they believed, sprang from such exchanges.

The War for Independence brought immediate hardships but also compelled the rebellious colonies to refine and improve the techniques they would need for economic survival as a free nation. The crisis that began in 1774 gave Americans a foretaste of the uncertain conditions which would prevail until 1820. The decade of struggle to confirm the separation from Britain disrupted the old ways of earning a livelihood. Commerce could not follow its former course; men laid the plow aside for the gun; prices fluctuated erratically under the pressure of the sudden shortage of supplies; and the value of the currency sank, unsettling fixed contractual relations and complicating transactions of every sort.

But the prolonged crisis was also remarkably stimulating. The Revolution generated a sense of common purpose. Only victory could erase the stain of treason and prove the rightness of the rebels' cause. Loyalists and other dissenters either departed or were excluded from the decisions of the polity. The great bulk of the population united in the face of the danger all shared.

Military defense was an absolute necessity in which all had a stake. Fighting men needed arms and munitions as well as other supplies; the economy had to procure or create them. All the commodities formerly imported from Britain now had to be improvised, as did the currency and the credit previously controlled by the mother country. As a result the role of the government expanded. The need to mobilize the efforts of the emerging nation increased its power to organize production, to ration goods and to regulate the currency.

Military and diplomatic imperatives also gave a forced stimulus to the economy. The sense of common effort in the crisis that made some men willing to die made others willing to cooperate. The disappearance in some areas of the old business and political leaders left a vacuum within which there was room for new aggressive people. Those who depended on habit or fixed incomes suffered, but dynamic, venturesome types found fresh opportunities in abundance open to them. So, Joseph Peabody, only eighteen when the fighting began on Lexington Common, rose quickly to command a privateer and thus gained the capital and experience with which he would later direct his fleet of scores of vessels manned by thousands of seamen to ports in every part of the world.

During the war, alliances with the rivals of Britain gave the Americans an additional source of strength. France, the Netherlands and Spain had no particular love for the rebellious colonies, but welcomed the opportunity to strike a blow at the English. Their willingness to help compensated for some of the inconveniences of separation from Britain, at least during the years of active fighting. Americans began to market tobacco through Paris instead of through Glasgow and looked to Amsterdam instead of to London as a banking center. The friendly attitudes of the Europeans ended once the war was over; after 1783 each empire again closed its trade to outsiders. Yet the Americans managed.

The ability to manage was a product partly of American decisions, partly of the unpredictable turns of European diplomacy. Independence gave birth to a self-consciously republican society dedicated to virtue, thrift and productivity, hostile to all imperial systems. No one lived without some occupation or trade. Apart from the slaves, there were few menial servants and rarely any luxurious distractions. All the jewels and diamonds worn by Americans, Coxe boasted, were less in value than those which sometimes adorned a single individual in the Old World. Wealth did not languish in aristocratic adornments; it was put into action as capital and multiplied itself through the free exchanges of commerce.

America remained determined that its trade should be unaligned with that of any empire; treaties of amity and commerce would open dealings on an equal basis with all nations. Neither favoritism nor special relationships of any sort would draw the Republic into the perennial squabbling of the Europeans. Distance placed the United States in a unique position from which it could trade impartially with any customers. If France and Britain were to renew their war, Tench Coxe explained in 1787, Yankee ships would carry for both sides "and our lands and manufactures would furnish the supplies of their fleets and islands in the West Indies." No more was needed than the improved central government set up by the new Constitution, which laid down uniform policies for interstate and international commerce.

It was true that some merchants favored a policy that would attach the United States to one or another of the great powers. Many believed that the safest course was to reestablish a connection with Great Britain. Once the war was over, they wished to revert to the earlier patterns of trade, only on a more equitable basis as between equals. Others considered an alliance with France, their partner in war against Britain, more natural.

But actually, Americans traded where they could and their government negotiated whatever commercial compacts were feasible without reference to the claims of empire. No sooner was the war over in 1783 than the Beekmans were importing furniture for their new mansion from Britain, which soon thereafter was buying more American goods than any other country. Similarly, the French retained the business foothold they had gained while supplying the Revolutionary forces. French investors speculated in American lands; French-manufactured goods went on sale in the interior of the United States; and French intermediaries tried to market the Virginia and Maryland tobacco crops. But neither the bureaucratic Bourbon government nor its controlled economy provided the easy terms of trade or enough of the goods appropriate for the American market. The bimonthly packet service between L'Orient and New York did not offset the slowness of communications among French ports. Then too, American merchants complained that the brandy they received was diluted with water and that there were no buyers for men's white kid gloves. Anyway, the outbreak of the French Revolution in 1789 touched off disturbances around the world which opened other opportunities for American trading skill and experience.

Well before the end of the eighteenth century, the British had again become the more important transatlantic tie. Jay's treaty, most of which was ratified in 1795, pleased merchants with close English commercial connections. But the limited trading concessions to the Americans in that agreement failed to knit the former colonies into the British imperial system. In the wars which followed upon the French Revolution and which spread from the continent of Europe to every corner of the globe, the United States remained neutral, that is, it dealt with all sides. These intervals of belligerency subjected American vessels to seizure by the combatants, whose orders they contravened or whose blockades they crossed. But occasional losses of this sort did not offset the immense gains from the usual conduct of traffic among the embattled empires. Only the embargo, an instrument of Jeffersonian diplomacy which brought all trade to a halt, produced widespread suffering in the seaport towns. William Gray of Salem then lost a tenth of his wealth at a blow. And in 1812 the United States went to war with Britain, despite the connections of trade, in order to maintain its freedom of action. Then many merchantmen became privateers and made up in prize money for what they could no longer earn in carrying profits. The fabulous gains of some individuals overshadowed the disastrous losses of others; and the cumulative effects of the striving to operate outside all imperial systems increased the wealth of the whole nation.

The growth of population was a measure of success, as from the beginning Americans expected it would be. Somewhat more than two million in number at the outbreak of hostilities in 1774, they were still fewer than four million in 1790, with a decade of fighting behind them. But thereafter rising totals were gratifying evidence of economic strength. The census showed more than five million in 1800 and almost ten million in 1820. The growth, furthermore, was largely internal, for relatively few immigrants arrived from overseas during those troubling decades. Somehow, despite the disorders of war and the adjustments to peace, Americans repaired the damage done to their commerce, expanded their agriculture and produced the wealth to support more than four times as many inhabitants in 1820 as in 1774.

The unsettled conditions of the post-Revolutionary era created openings in commerce for all sorts of people—insiders and outsiders, newcomers and old-timers, pious and free-thinking—whose sanguine temperaments and willingness to take a chance led them into a ceaseless probing of new opportunities. Restless, grasping, challenge-loving personalities thrived in this environment; and their efforts infused strength into the whole economy.

"To rest is to rust" was Stephen Girard's motto. Late in life, a wealthy Philadelphia banker, he still rose each morning determined "to labor so hard during the day" that he would be able to sleep when night came. A quarter of a century earlier, in 1795, he had considered retirement with the gains already in hand. But ambition and the "desire to keep busy" suggested new undertakings and with them new troubles and new profits. Earlier still his brother had warned him, "You will always be the same—never content." Girard had come a long tortuous way since he had left his native Bordeaux for America. Shuttling about the Caribbean had, at first, earned him little so that at one point he was reduced to peddling claret and brandy to the Revolutionary troops in the vicinity of Philadelphia. He had suffered reverses of fortune in plenty. But "the great secret," he said, was "to make good use of fortune, and when reverses come, receive them with *sang froid*, and by redoubled activity and economy endeavour to repair them." His faith was simple, enunciated in the names of his ships—*Montesquieu, Helvetius, Voltaire, Rousseau, Liberty, North America*. Reason, Freedom, National Destiny. "Let reason be at the helm of your life," was a slogan of one of his contemporaries.

Thomas Eddy, by contrast, was Philadelphia-born and a devout Quaker, willing to try anything because he was blessed with a capacity for interpreting whatever happened as for the best. Apprenticed to a tanner, he early gave up that craft and found trade his calling. In

1779, while the war tried the souls of other men, he moved to New York City, then in safe British hands, and after hanging about the auction rooms, where he learned to live by his wits ("this necessity," he later wrote, "was of great use to me afterwards"), began to import English and Irish goods from a brother in London. Eddy did well for a time, dealing with both patriots and Tories. But the misfortune of peace deflated tobacco prices just as he had launched a promising speculation. Bouncing back from bankruptcy, he took over the shop of a retailer in Fredericksburg, Virginia, was dissatisfied and returned to the place of his birth. Business there was not good enough either, so Eddy moved to New York, where he finally made it as an insurance broker and speculator in government bonds, then went on to promote schemes for a hospital, for prison reform and for a great canal to the West.

Mercantile careers in the generation of Girard and Eddy followed no neat consistent pattern but rather drifted along unpredictable currents to remote ports in every part of the world. The West Indies remained an attractive field for ingenious calculators, as it had before independence. The exigencies of war and the demand on the islands for bread and fish continued to open these colonial ports to Americans. Dealings there contributed substantially to Girard's fortune. Then too, William Tudor learned how to ship ice to the tropics and Timothy Dexter arranged more exotic exchanges still, sending off to Cuba long-handled pans made to warm Yankee beds, but useful as cooking utensils in tropic kitchens. All these deals added to the importance of West Indian commerce.

The same merchants were also aware of the opportunities for breaking into trade with the Far East, formerly closed to them. The monopoly of the East India Company barred British subjects from dealings with India and China, but those who were no longer British subjects could take their ships where they wished. Lord Sheffield had blithely assumed that Englishmen would continue to sell tea to the United States. An American gleefully pointed out that "His Lordship had forgotten that Canton is an open market, *equally accessible* to all nations."

There was, however, no simple way to arrange exchanges with Asia. Everyone in New York and Boston and Salem knew what goods from the Orient would find a ready market in the interior: tea, spices, porcelain and silk. But Massachusetts, New York and Pennsylvania had nothing of great value to send in return. Ginseng, highly esteemed by the Chinese for its restorative effects on sexual potency, for a time filled the holds of Yankee vessels. But the supply soon flooded the market so that the marvelous root lost much of its value.

In the three decades after 1790, ingenious swappers developed some profitable, though difficult, kinds of exchanges to compensate for the lack of exports. A ship from Philadelphia or New York could trade some of its biscuits and fish for cotton in Charleston and the rest for sugar in the West Indies, then sell its whole cargo in Europe for Spanish milled dollars, which it could use to buy spices, silk and tea in the Far East before returning to its home port. Alternatively, a Salem or Boston vessel might swing around the Cape and stand off the coast of California while it picked up a cargo of furs, then head for Hawaii to take on sandalwood before making for Canton, where both commodities brought good prices. There was usually a long stay at the great international emporium on the Pearl River, then the ship would head further west, either making directly for home or stopping on the way for business in Europe. Such voyages commonly stretched out more than a year and entailed enormous risks. But the potential profits were correspondingly high. Thomas H. Perkins was among those who actively worked in developing these exchanges. Perkins had first laid eyes on Canton in 1789, at the age of twenty-five. He had been six when his father died and had shuffled about in various foster homes while his mother attempted to earn a livelihood for eight children. His brother was in the West India trade and later Thomas too would send ships to pick up coffee and sugar for England and France, to bring back to Boston bolts of Calcutta cloth and specie. When opportunity was favorable, Perkins sent provisions to Spain and Portugal and wangled permission from the Dutch to take spices out of Batavia. But on first visiting Canton in 1789, he immediately perceived the possibilities of greater gains in China, especially when combined with the fur trade of the American Northwest. In 1803 he established a permanent branch in the city; and the house of Perkins maintained a preeminent position there for almost three decades.

For a time, the whole world seemed open to penetration by similar multi-pronged connections. "What shores have our ships not coasted?" boasted Americans. In 1790, twenty-two vessels came home from St. Petersburg, harbingers of the lucrative trade to develop with the Baltic. Yankees in the Mediterranean and off the coasts of Africa and India explored other possibilities for profitable commerce.

Great risk was not the most important drawback of commerce of this sort. Merchants knew how to live with risk; but they worried about the impermanence and instability of the trade in which they had to reinvest their gains. American enterprise paid off so long as it alone maneuvered freely in a world divided among the imperial systems; without that strategic advantage it would be hard-put to compete with its European rivals for the international carrying trade.

Long before Waterloo, merchants had struggled to offset their anomalous position in a world of empires. Since independence, they had taken advantage of the opportunities of war; but they realized that they would need some leverage to survive in peacetime markets. When the ship at last came in after all the anxious months of its absence, and the cargo, cleared and sold, produced its fine profit on the ledger's page, there remained the question: What to do with the gains? Simply to send them abroad again was to multiply the risk. Not every voyage had its happy homecoming; and earnings repeatedly hazarded might vanish in some alien sea. And surely someday, with the battles quieted and imperial controls restored, all those ingenious, marginally illicit transactions would become more dangerous still, or altogether impossible.

Among the penalties of success was the endless agonizing over alternative investments. Alexander Henry, a Philadelphian with extensive interests in the India goods trade, twice decided that he had had enough and twice retired. But withdrawal was no solution, for the problem of secure and advantageous disposal of funds remained. Girard put money into urban real estate and into Louisiana lands; he bought government bonds and the shares of corporations. But there were hazards in such investments, as William Duer and Robert Morris could testify from their debtor's cells.

Therefore, whatever the rewards and thrills of the great risky ventures, the merchants longed also to develop some simpler, more stable trade—preferably the direct and dependable exchange of domestic for foreign commodities. Through all the years while they sent ice to India and sandalwood to China, they engaged in a restless and imaginative search for the means of consolidating their commercial strength. The activities bred by their insecurity infused a dynamic quality in the whole economy for a half-century after the Revolution. Lacking the protection of an imperial system, they had to spur on the nation's farmers and handicraftsmen to supply goods for export and markets for imports.

There were plenty of purchasers for the goods imported to the United States. The problem was to find sufficient articles of export to pay for the English textiles and ironware, for the French wine and the Chinese tea. Again and again, therefore, the merchants' thoughts reverted to the same solution as had their seventeenth- and eighteenth-century counterparts—the development of staples with strategic value in the world's marketplaces; fish from the bountiful ocean, furs from the endless forest, and the varied yield of rapidly multiplying farms would cram the holds of outgoing vessels and earn a welcome in overseas ports.

After the Revolution, Americans became foreigners in the Newfoundland fishing grounds; and the long diplomatic and political struggle to assure their rights stretched out over a century. But in any case, the cod, once the basis of much of New England's trade, was not as abundant or as salable as formerly. The Yankees more than compensated for the loss by bringing in new and more profitable catches. They learned to take the abundant mackerel in vast quantities. They also expanded their whaling ventures; no longer fearful, as they had been in the eighteenth century of losing sight of shore, they used everlarger vessels to pursue leviathan in extended voyages to every ocean.

The scope of the fur trade also widened, even though the old trapping grounds were no longer productive. The Appalachians and the Great Lakes region were exposed to attack from the Indians and their British and Spanish allies down to 1815, at least; and meanwhile a steady westward movement of settlers was converting the forest into farms. But the source of the pelts simply shifted westward. John Jacob Astor in 1808 established an outpost in Oregon and effected an alliance with the Russian-American Company in an effort to break the Canadian hold on the business. He failed, then came to terms with the Canadians and continued to work with them even during the War of 1812. Later, his American Fur Company, operating between the Great Lakes and the Mississippi, ended the dependence upon the northern trappers and shipped pelts in vast quantities to Europe and China. The trade remained important down to the 1840s.

The spread of settlement and the rise in the output of wheat, pork, cotton and tobacco would certainly aid commerce. But in addition, the merchants hoped that increased industrial output would also add to the variety of exports they handled. Everyone knew that English success in overseas trade had rested upon its command of great quantities of cheap, power-manufactured goods. There were sites in abundance in the American wilderness which would someday be to Boston, New York and Philadelphia what Manchester, Leeds, Birmingham and Sheffield had been to the seaports of Great Britain. Besides, development was a national duty. The separation from the former mother country was both a challenge—to show Lord Sheffield —and an opportunity—to create the industry that London had long discouraged. Manufactures would give the United States economic, as revolution had given it political, independence. During the war, patriotism required the wearing of homespun and the encouragement of the country's domestic producers; and in the decade before the War of 1812, the diplomatic urgencies expressed in the embargo and non-intercourse laws emphasized the desirability of autonomy.

In this atmosphere, merchants could certainly mobilize wide-spread popular support for efforts that promised further self-sufficiency. Agriculture, which would assure the success of industry by providing a plentiful supply of raw materials, would also furnish its labor. Manufacturing would not breed horrid factory cities because it would be carried on in rural mills or in the homes of the farmers and fishermen, who would thus profitably occupy their time away from the field and the sea. Rapid expansion of the domestic and putting-out systems, which had already appeared in rural districts in the eighteenth century, would easily raise output. Coxe urged enterprising farmers to turn their barley into beer, to press tobacco into chewing plugs and to build mills for making flour, chocolate, paper, iron and nails. He hoped that they would spend part of every year producing carriages, tools, leather, hats, shoes, hosiery and silk.

The concern of the merchants was not only to increase the volume of production but also to assure a regular flow of goods to the seaports and to control the supply by dependable standards of packing and inspection so that the commodities would be salable in distant markets. To do so, they had to establish warehousing and production control centers where raw materials were assembled, given out for homework, inspected upon return and organized for export.

Secretary of the Treasury Alexander Hamilton had a still-broader vision, one which dared to cut away from the domestic system altogether. He believed that the movement westward would drain the population of the settled regions and for the time being limit the expansion of home workshops. An alternative was necessary. His reports described in theory a novel mode of industrial organization from which investors and the nation might both profit; and the Society for Promoting Useful Manufactures, in which he participated, actively exemplified it in practice.

Americans were well aware that the manufacturing techniques of Europe were more advanced than their own. It was possible, Hamilton argued, to induce skilled workmen to come to the New World, possible also to import and copy the machines in use abroad. Water power to turn the wheels was abundant. What was needed was integration of a cluster of enterprises into a coherent district or township, which could regulate the flow from the streams to the mills and provide housing for the workers away from the disorder of the large seaport cities. At Paterson amidst the New Jersey meadows, Hamilton and his collaborators laid out a model settlement with factories to produce textiles, straw hats, paper, stockings, brass and iron wire and shoes.

The more ambitious the plan, the greater the sum needed to execute it. But the Society for Promoting Useful Manufactures hoped that Europeans, and especially the Dutch, would invest; and they hoped too that the American holders of the great pile of bonds left by the indebtedness of the war would somehow turn the proceeds into productive capital rather than squandering them on immediate consumption.

All such grand mercantile designs for agriculture and for industry would remain visionary without practical measures to facilitate the exchange and movement of goods over long distances and without devices to convert the public debt into capital.

In some circumstances, the development of transportation links was almost effortless; in others, improvements called for planning and led to prolonged political conflict. Internal shipping, from which the government's commercial policy excluded foreign competitors, thrived. At the end of the eighteenth century the tonnage engaged in the coasting trade was almost as large as that which moved overseas; and the level increased steadily thereafter. Furthermore, the Hudson, the Connecticut, and the Delaware rivers became important arteries of trade; and after 1790 sizable fleets of flatboats also floated down the Ohio and the Mississippi. After 1807, when the steamboat permitted the traffic to move against as well as with the wind and the currents, this mode of travel and trade became more important still.

The trading stations at which the coastal and river craft took on and discharged cargo grew into little towns; and some, like Pittsburgh, mushroomed into cities in their own right. Here local markets developed through which the products of the country were assembled for shipment back toward the seacoast in return for Eastern and overseas goods. From these bases also a swarm of peddlers drifted out into the rural regions to tempt isolated farm families with pots and pins, with clocks, ribbons and other exotic wares. Some itinerants in time acquired the capital to stock a primitive country store, and occasionally one of them became the master of a full-scale counting house.

Town life was both a result and a cause of the growth of the interior trade. The flow of goods attracted people tempted by the opportunities for business, and they in turn became consumers for numerous goods and services. By the stage stop or river wharf a shop and a tavern or inn received the goods, sheltered the travelers. The shop became a warehouse, the inn a hotel. Now a smith appeared to shoe horses and repair wagons. Then a saddler. Competitors arrived and construction of the needed buildings called for the services of carpenters and masons. Inevitably there were deeds to be recorded, disputes to be settled in court—and lawyers appeared. In time, a church was built and the services of a minister procured. Soon streets led off the high road and wives and children occupied the houses. To bake their bread and sew their clothes, the settlers bought bags of flour and bolts of cloth. The shopkeepers increased their stocks, the boats their cargoes, the wagons their loads. A bank opened; a newspaper carried the advertisements for which word-of-mouth was no longer adequate. The interior towns—Wheeling, Pittsburgh, Cincinnati, Rochester, Cleveland—were on their way to being cities and on the way also to new problems.

The merchants took satisfaction in the spread of settlement and in the proliferation of interior towns. Their own trade gained from the growth in the number of producers of goods for export and in the number of consumers for imports. They had a stake therefore in expansion, and an interest in improving communications with the interior. Ease of access to the back country became critical to the prosperity of the seaport, as Providence showed when it supplanted Newport, and Baltimore, when it outdistanced Charleston.

Within the national boundaries, as outside them, human efforts were necessary to direct cargoes to their proper destinations. In the most wonderful country of all, nature had not been altogether beneficent. The rivers, interrupted by falls, dotted with rocks and given to inconvenient twists and turns, could not carry vessels of any substantial size. The passage of many travelers had broadened trails into roads but had not removed the spine-jolting ruts; and while the famous "Flying Machine," a speedy, four-horse wagon, could get from Paulus Hook in New Jersey to Philadelphia in two days in the 1770s, it long had no counterparts in the interior. Better transportation would bring more goods to the markets. Then, too, it would be helpful to be able to transmit funds from place to place and to be sure that the currency had the same value in New York as in Albany.

Habits of informal association and carry-overs from colonial and European practice took care of some commercial needs, particularly in the great seaports. Various methods of insurance underwriting limited the losses from disasters at sea or by fire. At the age of twenty-one, Peter Chardon Brooks of Boston was secretary to one such group that met at the Bunch of Grapes Tavern and soon thereafter was head of the enterprise, widely trusted because he was fastidious in keeping records and insisted upon prompt payment for losses without litigation. Men, meeting regularly together in coffee houses or taverns, developed formal markets for the exchange of securities and government bonds as well as for the future sale of commodities. The willingness to speculate, thus mobilized, offset some of the hazards of price fluctuations. A regular auction system permitted trade on a large scale yet reduced the risk of being stuck with masses of unwanted goods. When there were no buyers, as in 1792, panic swept through the primitive markets, destroying values and sending the recently wealthy to the debtors' jail—a foretaste of future depressions. Generally, however, these arrangements put some order into the method of doing business.

But no voluntary device could handle the public debt left by the war or convert the proceeds into capital. To effect major improvements in finance, as in transportation, called for political decisions; and while the merchants remained the dominant economic and social group in the cities, old and new, they had to take account of the more numerous artisans and farmers who shared power in the government. The methods of control effective under the colonial regime no longer applied. The favorites of the governor could no longer simply grasp at privilege; nor was the cry of royal tyranny any longer enough to unite the patriots in the legislature. In the ideology which emerged from the Revolution public office was a public trust, and only the public welfare justified grants of public power or expenditure of public funds. To take action under governments so circumscribed called for agreement or persuasion broad enough to mobilize a majority of the population.

The most difficult to bring in line with the merchants' plans were the artisans, a numerous and heterogeneous group even in the small towns, much more so in the great ones. The larger cities buzzed with the work of thousands at their different occupations. Philadelphia in 1810 housed fifteen ropewalks and ten sugar refineries, a brewery and hundreds of shops which turned out iron, hats and paper, hosiery and leather, drugs and carriages, furniture and boots. On the streets and docks, carpenters, coopers and masons exercised their callings. In this multitude, each craftsman was a case unto himself. Some were well off, employed journeymen and apprentices, and put by tidy sums to increase the scale of their operations; others barely eked out a livelihood. There were regional variations as well between the mechanics of the East and the West, of the North and the South. Yet the situation of the artisans in the economy also gave these self-employed entrepreneurs common, unifying attributes. Owners of their own tools and capital, managers of their own affairs, they commanded skills much in demand in their society. Furthermore, they had been active in the Revolution and, as a result of it, had acquired substantial political power, which they used to protect their interests. The years of actual fighting brought hard times to some, who suffered from the shortages and inflated costs of food and raw materials. But peace lowered costs and raised their standard of living and income so that they tended to contentment and defensively sought to protect what they had.

The artisan could not easily increase his output, wedded as he was to traditional methods of production based on the skill of the individual hand. Few economies of scale were possible. To multiply the number of journeymen and apprentices did not significantly lower unit costs, since there were narrow limits to the opportunities for division of labor. In any case, these assistants often seemed more trouble than they were worth, for they demanded and could get increasingly favorable terms of service and before long could set up on their own with little difficulty. Each for himself was a general rule.

Therefore, the craftsmen valued stability, resisted change and tried to gain and hold control of the local market. Unhappily, they could not employ guild and municipal regulations to do so, as their European counterparts did. While formal and informal associations occasionally set fair prices and standards of workmanship, they lacked legal sanctions and nothing prevented any newcomer from setting up his shop and seeking the custom of the town. Nor did anything prevent some meddlesome merchant from bringing in goods made elsewhere that might well undersell those produced on the spot.

Concern about these dangers tinged with caution the attitudes of artisans. They were dubious about all expensive projects for improvement that would surely take money out of their pockets by raising taxes and by stimulating inflation that damaged the honest worker. Grand schemes for developing transportation were particularly suspect; they would not benefit the craftsman, nay, would do him harm, for cheapening the cost of shipment might bring into his preserve products from elsewhere to compete with his own. Most perilous were the new processes that devalued existing techniques. The putting-out system enabled the farmers and fishermen of Essex County in Massachusetts in the 1790s to turn out shoes in their homes by the score, which the merchants who supplied the leather then exported to the West Indies. New Yorkers and Philadelphians, accustomed to having their boots made to measure, would certainly disdain the clumsy, mass-made country footgear. But the price differences were striking; and cargoes of shoes from Lynn turned up with increasing frequency in the coastal ports. The inferior wares were still disdained but when the prices were low enough they found some purchasers. Every sale of these mean wares deprived the worthy local shoemaker of a customer.

Most artisans therefore found little reason to rejoice in expansion, which destroyed the security of the close little markets in which they preferred to operate. They read their own moral into the English experience. The growth of industry there had introduced the machines that undermined the position of handicraftsmen; the threat in America was still potential rather than actual, and vigorous political action could fend it off. On every account the artisans opposed the mercantile designs, seeking to control rather than to raise output, fighting inflation and taxes, opposing new transportation plans and scrutinizing with hostility any alteration in existing economic practices.

The wealth and prestige of the merchants generally gained them the alliance of lawyers, ministers and professional people and also the support of the unskilled laborers. But the artisans were nevertheless more numerous and, in a confrontation, could take control of the urban polity. The traders tried to win them over by stressing common interests and sometimes succeeded. More often, the merchants offset the conservative influence of the artisans by joining forces on issues like transportation and industrial development with the rural majority of the population, which dominated state governments. The husbandmen who spun and wove at home objected to such great overweening projects as the Society for Promoting Useful Manufactures, which threatened to displace them. But in most matters, the interests of merchants and farmers were complementary. Both groups, although for different reasons, could not relax even had they wished to; and neither wished to. Stability was not their goal, but expansion, for American agriculture functioned on the edge of a moving frontier and whoever did not grow was left behind. The Revolution, which drove on the merchants by destroying their imperial connection, spurred on the farmers by leveling the barriers on the way to the West.

3

The Moving Frontier

*E*xpansion was the decisive factor in early nineteenth-century development. Merchants and agriculturists alike supported measures directed toward growth. Since the former were the most dynamic and the latter the most numerous element in society, together they formed a combination that the artisans, inclined to be static, could not resist.

Yet the policies agreed upon in the name of expansion rarely had the consequences anticipated. Between the expression of an idea, or the enactment of a law, or the delivery of a command and the implementation, unforeseen contingencies frequently intervened to distort the original intention. Hidden paradoxes embedded in American society sustained the commitment to growth and shaped the manner of its realization. Many who most sought change valued stability; many who moved restlessly about thought they were always coming home; and many who went into debt to gamble did so out of prudence and thrift.

People incessantly engaged in buying and selling, in borrowing and lending, in swapping and haggling, nevertheless again and again voiced their anguish about the immorality of trade. Commerce was central to the New England economy and merchants there were the

most respected figures in society. Yet the congregations nodded agreement as the clergy warned that greed, materialism and the obsession
with gain led to corruption. In other regions also, where the landed
interests were more prominent, secular and religious leaders repeatedly
reverted to the same theme.

The discrepancy between preachings and practice was not a
product of hypocrisy. Practical necessity led men into the activities
connected with trade; a powerful ideal drew their thoughts in another
direction. According to this ideal, the true American, the worthiest
citizen of the Republic, was neither a trader nor a planter, nor indeed
any man of wealth, but rather a yeoman, a simple husbandman who
consumed the fruits of his own labor in the shade of his own vine and
fig tree. Drawing his sustenance, with the aid of his family, from his
adequate but not extensive acreage, he was neither dependent upon
any master nor the master of any dependent and therefore could act
freely, rationally and honestly in all matters affecting the common
good.

The mass of citizens were indeed cultivators, independent proprietors of the soil, as they fondly denominated themselves. But even
those not within their ranks—merchants and planters, for instance—
paid respectful homage to men and women who lived in virtue on
the land. Nor did political loyalties circumscribe the ideals; although
Thomas Jefferson's *Notes on Virginia* gave the best-known description
of the blessings of agrarian society, Federalists found the identical
idyllic portrait limned by their own Timothy Dwight in *Greenfield
Hill*. Republican and Federalist, and later, Democrat and Whig, all
invoked the vision of the citizen able to act with responsible liberty
because he was independent economically as well as politically. Since
the yeoman was neither exploited nor an exploiter, selfishness would
not cloud his sense of justice, and what was good for him was good
for all.

The concept of the virtuous husbandman had deep roots in
American life. The idea of the self-contained, coherent family had
come to the New World in the seventeenth century; that its appropriate
setting was on the soil was a belief which took hold in the eighteenth
century when the Enlightenment cast a romantic glow over the simple
life of the farmer. The analogies republican political theorists drew
with classical antiquity also supported that view. Good old Cincinnatus
at his plow! But ultimately, the concept expressed the wish that the
household, as it had been, remain the unifying economic unit in the
society. To a large extent, these beliefs reflected the circumstances of
people much in motion, who clung all the more to the hope of restor-

ing old human relationships which their own instability kept disturbing.

The abstract conception of the yeoman had little relation to
actuality. There were indeed farmers who stayed put and lived
a simple, non-commercial life. In the hill country of New England,
in the North Carolina uplands and in the backwaters of the middle
states, occasional families subsisted on what they had, resisting change,
stolid, immovable. Were these the living representatives of the ideal
of contentment and self-sufficiency?

Americans shied away from the question. Every district, no
doubt, had its share of the idle, the improvident and the unfortunate.
But the failures did not count in the New World. The yeoman ideal
induced few to cut their farms apart from the business and the potential profits of the world. The dynamic elements in agriculture were
entrepreneurs producing for the market. Up early and out to the
timber to chop wood which his sons corded, the husbandman did his
day's work and more and let no opportunity slide by. He bought the
young stock of his less thrifty neighbors at low prices and drove a
hard bargain in every transaction. He rarely hesitated to abandon the
vine and the fig tree for the cash crop that would enable him to
expand. He added acres wherever he could, even though he lacked
the means of bringing them under cultivation and even though he went
into debt to do so. "My disposition," wrote a Connecticut farm boy,
"is, and ever was, of a speculative character, and I am never content
to engage in any business unless it is of such a nature that my profits
may be greatly enhanced by an increase of energy."

In the last analysis, love of the soil was less compelling than
speculation; and expansion was the dominant passion. Poverty, in-
ertia, ill health, or entangling family obligations thrust some farmers
into the backwaters, cut off from the main flow out of necessity.
But few conceived of themselves as fixed out of choice, tied to age-
old habits by preference, or attached out of sentiment to the sites
where their ancestors were buried; most were always ready to change
or to move where the best chance lay.

Given to tinkering, American husbandmen were disinclined to
caution, ready to risk innovation. All along they experimented with
scores of labor-saving devices, some of which were successful. In
the 1790s, they took to the cast-iron plow despite warnings that it
would poison the soil. They adopted Jethro Wood's improvements in
the 1820s and John Deere's steel plow in the 1840s. Very early, too,
they discarded the scythe for the cradle to cut grain. The most sig-

nificant change came toward the middle of the nineteenth century, when western growers in increasing numbers began to purchase the reapers with which Cyrus Hall McCormick, Obed Hussey and many others had been experimenting since the 1830s. Farmers who invested in this novel way of performing a traditional chore made a simple reckoning: labor was scarce, so few hands were available for hire; those not satisfied with what the family with its own brawn produced could expand output, lower costs and increase profits only through mechanization.

The hope also lingered of finding the great staple that would earn a cash reward. The plantation South took its own course; and small holders there also gave their acres over to cotton and tobacco. Elsewhere family farmers searched for an equivalent appropriate to the climate of the North and the West. In the 1790s, they were advised that the production of maple sugar would make the import of cane from the West Indies unnecessary and that planting enough mulberry trees would establish the silk industry in Connecticut. Later outbursts of enthusiasm turned some Yankees into cheesemakers, while others gave their holdings over to pasture for Merino sheep in the expectation of increasing the output of wool.

Ultimately, however, the quest terminated not in these exotic products, but in the more familiar crops which acquired salable cash value as trade developed markets at home and abroad—wheat in Illinois, corn in Indiana and Ohio, hemp in Kentucky and hogs and steers in the whole Ohio Valley. Regions close to the cities also found buyers for fruits and for dairy products. But grains and livestock remained the most important products of American farms down to 1850.

Good husbandmen who shunned idleness also found promising outlets for their efforts in industry. As before the Revolution, they invested the time they did not use on the soil in fishing or in manufacturing. In the East, they dug clams, gathered the seasonal runs of herring, or took their boats out for harvests from the sea. The take created work at home curing, pickling, and packing the fish, often in casks made on the farm. Then too, the bones and oil had a use in making whips or candles and in dressing leather. Away from the sea, the forest occupied the rail splitters, the shingle carvers and the potash makers.

The household manufactures which had originated earlier now expanded, stimulated by the markets the merchants opened. Twenty families in one Virginia county in 1790 produced 1,907 yards of cotton cloth and 269 pairs of stockings. Connecticut farmers busied themselves with cloth, hosiery, nails and buttons. The country people in Massachusetts, even the children, commonly worked small forges in their chimney corners and made great quantities of nails. Merchants supplied the rod iron and took in return the nails. In 1791, in the same state, 1,600 women and children were sticking cotton and wool cards, producing thousands of dozens for export. The shoe industry spread out from Lynn, Massachusetts, to the interior of New England, with a steadily rising output. Everywhere, busy tanning, fulling, dyeing, slitting and saw mills reflected the importance of household industry.

No doubt each individual exercised a good deal of control over the pace of his own work, lengthening or curtailing his hours as the spirit moved him or the body proved willing. Yet an inner compulsion drove many on with a discipline more rigorous than any externally imposed. Often the desire for achievement kept the husbandman from the happiness that gleamed in the stereotype held of him.

One index of discontent was the growing volume of internal migration, from Massachusetts to Maine and Vermont, from Pennsylvania to Ohio, from Virginia to Kentucky. The ability to move was the universal American asset, the assurance of potential wealth for everyone, for it rested upon space, the one great resource that justified every man's confidence.

In 1805, one of the perennial efforts to estimate the nation's riches arrived at a total of $2,500,000,000. The calculation took account of the millions of acres under cultivation, of the homes, barns, tools, slaves and livestock, of the public buildings, roads, canals, bridges, shipping and stocks in trade, all of which added up to $1,075,500,000. The balance, well over half, represented the assumed value of more than 600 million acres of uncultivated land. That ace in the hole guaranteed the future and exempted the United States from all dire Malthusian warnings. There was space for everyone. Whoever moved did so with the intent of drawing upon a share of the national patrimony.

Internal migration was not a simple direct thrust to a waiting frontier. It consisted of diverse streams carrying people of various heritages to areas as different as Arkansas and Wisconsin. The result was not a uniform West but a cluster of sections shaped by soil, climate and culture.

The movement eastward, northward and, above all, westward had been well under way in the decade before the Revolution. Once independence removed British restraints, a vast empty world lay open to the settlers, literally a thousand miles of virgin land from the

Alleghenies to beyond the Mississippi. The flow increased rapidly thereafter. In 1820, the line of settlement ran from the shores of Lake Erie southwest to the junction of the Ohio and the Mississippi rivers and thence back to the Georgia-Florida boundary, with patches of inhabited territory beyond in southern Louisiana, Mississippi, Alabama and Missouri. Thirty years later, in 1850, the line in its whole length had moved well beyond the Mississippi and there was by then already a substantial outpost on the Pacific Coast.

The disorderly outpouring of people had wasteful features. Whole communities formed in northern New England in the 1770s were almost totally deserted by 1820. In eastern Kentucky and Tennessee, settlement remained spotty, because many families which had come to the hills only in the 1780s and 1790s quickly moved on after 1800 when they glimpsed the opportunities of the plains. The endless shifting about affected both the land and its occupants. The rootless men, women and children had eyes only for the future; discontent with the present made them heedless of the place they occupied for the moment, sure that its value would in any case rise, half-knowing from the start that they would themselves soon pull up stakes. Everywhere haste for success and disregard for the long term encouraged immediate exploitation. The settlers wasted water resources, depleted the forests and exhausted the soil. The pattern of individual trial and error was open to innumerable mistakes and failures. But it miraculously recruited the necessary manpower resources to settle an immense area with astonishing speed.

It was not the empty land as such that drew the settlers onward, westward, but rather a dynamic interaction between space and people. Migration was a speculative act, a gamble on the unknown future as against the relatively safe but uninspired present. No one was crowded out by lack of space in the place of his birth; and those willing to make do with what was at hand stayed put. But people who at first aspired to adding a few nearby acres made an easy transition to calculation about the chances elsewhere in the county or state; and soon enough they were ready to think of moving west to an altogether new start. Rarely was the decision to go the product of a rational comparison of alternatives or assessment of comparative advantages. There was little dependable information about the realities of agriculture in the remote places, only romantic voyagers' tales, alluring hints in occasional letters, and a host of high-blown advertisements by speculators, all made credible by the diffuse faith that the West, still natural and unspoiled, would put within the reach of every man and woman the opportunities withheld in the East.

The decision to move on was not outlandish but usual, even commonplace; the whole context of American life encouraged it. The migrant did not move in isolation into areas totally empty and unknown; predecessors had blazed the trails. Even before the first permanent settlement sprouted, a network of paths, product of the initial encounter with the wilderness, drew families into the area. Fur traders early traversed the whole continent in search of the pelts that were still important articles of clothing and commerce. Their stories made Oregon almost as familiar to Easterners as Ohio and contributed to the romantic vision of the Virgin West, lavish in future rewards for those willing to come gather them. The trappers established contact with the Indians; other traders followed and then missionaries and government officials. Prospectors surveyed the timber and mineral resources, spurred on by an insatiable demand for fuel and for building materials and by hopes of the great strike which finally achieved spectacular realization in the discovery of California gold.

Meanwhile speculators appropriated promising territory and set about inducing the flow of arrivals which would give value to their grants. Hundreds of land companies as well as individual venturers participated in the process of subdividing tracts into manageable holdings, of providing some basic community services and of advertising the virtues of the particular area. A stream of optimistic information poured out upon the East and upon Europe as the pioneers tempted others to follow.

Political changes also stimulated the flow of population. The new regime created by the Revolution exerted a positive effect on migration. In 1781, the states which had held conflicting claims to the West ceded their rights to the Confederation, thus eliminating one source of future disputes over land titles. Ordinances enacted by the Congress in 1785 and 1787 put together an institutional framework that quickly opened the frontier to settlement. Those measures promised stable government, easy terms of acquiring freeholds and precise methods for guaranteeing titles; they assured people who contemplated a move that they would enter territories soon to be sovereign states, in which the rights of citizenship would be at least as ample as in the homes they left.

In the nineteenth century, frontier government grew more stable and national land policy further favored the small settler with little or no cash in hand. In 1820, a change in the law made possible sale of a half section or eighty acres at $1.25 an acre; and in 1832, the minimal amount sank still lower to forty acres, so that $50 was then enough to acquire a clear title. In fact, determined squatters disregarded even that obligation; they cleared desirable plots without regard to the deed book and then counted, usually successfully, upon a preemption law to give them an option to buy when they had the cash. A general statute in 1841 regularized the practice; thereafter a settler could take up a vacant site without payment and with the assurance that he would have the right to purchase when he wished. A consistent pattern in legislation and practice had thus emerged since independence; government, while refraining from any effort to direct migration to one area or another or to control the type of movement, did what it could, short of actual subsidy, to speed the process of settlement.

A strong, independent national government also removed the Indian barrier in the way of expansion. The prospect that the British might shield the aboriginal inhabitants vanished as a result of the wars of the Revolution and of 1812; and the Redmen themselves were unable to develop a political or military system strong enough to defend their ancestral hunting grounds. A chain of United States forts, built along the frontier between 1816 and 1822, applied pressure to the tribes disposed to argue that solemn treaties allowed them to remain where they were. Usually they saw the logic of power and agreed to removal beyond the Mississippi; desperate uprisings under Chief Red Bird in 1827, under Black Hawk in 1832, and under Osceola in 1842 demonstrated that resistance was futile. Even the Cherokee of western Georgia who, with the aid of missionaries, had developed an orderly agricultural society and had established their own republic were compelled to depart despite a ruling in their favor by the Supreme Court of the United States. President Andrew Jackson and the Congress had by then determined that the Indians were not to impede western settlement.

The men and women who climbed the still mountains or floated down the lonely streams, whether on foot or in wagons, whether by boat or, later, by railroad, faced dangers known and unknown. In leaving Connecticut or Virginia, they turned their backs on friends, churches and schools. But they had some assurance that the government had erased the greatest hazards to the journey, that at the terminus a society of schools, churches and friends would re-create what had been left behind. A constant faith also buoyed the spirits of the migrant, the expectation that expanding internal and external markets in the growing cities and abroad would provide a good price for the commodities he produced and would also raise the value of the land he brought under cultivation. Therefore, even at the risk of going into debt, he took on as many acres as he could and invested in any machines to help increase his output.

The urge to go West, to drag women and children off to the wilderness, most often appeared in social settings in which upbringing and family life generated aspirations the economy could not fulfill. The internal impetus to departure required both the acceptance of separation and danger and also the lure of an image of what arrival at the destination would be like. Down through the first half of the nineteenth century, the types of personalities tempted by migration sprouted luxuriantly in two sections of the country, out of which distinct lines of settlement pushed the frontier westward.

Some men seemed just restless, made so by family histories of recurrent migration, of alternations of disappointment and renewed hope. David Crockett, for instance, found it easier to increase the size of his family than that of his fortune; and rather than harness himself to the drudgery of feeding his yammering brood, moved west where food was available for the hunting. Always in debt, he stayed in motion, thus escaping immediate obligations and sustaining the hope of a stroke of luck that would solve all problems. Meanwhile, fighting the Indians and the British gave meaning to his life. It was not uncommon for such a man to make four or five moves between the kindling of the dream in youth and its extinction in old age, illness or violent death.

Crockett was a Virginian, one among many Southerners who drifted toward the setting sun or led along wives as tough as they and broods of hard children already preparing for their own departures. They refused to stay where they were because they refused to settle for what they had. The ability to live by hunting and fishing freed them from dependence on the crops of the old place, fenced in as it was by past defeats, old debts and limited horizons. The wilderness, attractive for its chance of a new start, could also provide them subsistence. They moved out of Virginia and North Carolina across Kentucky and Tennessee, then north of the Ohio River into the Lake Plains, where they established a band of settlement through southern Ohio, Indiana and Illinois and on into Missouri.

E. Lakin Brown was also a moving type. His grandfather, Nathaniel, had left his native Lexington for Lunenburg, Massachusetts, then had come north to Plymouth, Vermont. Thomas, the eighth of his eleven children and Lakin Brown's father, had taken up a small farm nearby from which he painfully extracted a livelihood, slowly adding strips of land by purchase from neighbors, annually dragging a load of pork, cheese and poultry for sale in Boston, operating a lime kiln in winter and squeezing out a little extra cash from maple sugar and cider.

Lakin, twenty-one in 1830 and habituated to labor from early youth, nurtured the dream of college, for he had been to the Academy, had taught school when the rhythm of seasonal chores permitted. When the old man said no, the young man decided to make out for himself. Big families were an asset—Lakin had ten brothers and sisters, twenty-five uncles and aunts, an army of first cousins. A chain of relatives had earlier established themselves across New York State. They provided him with shelter and information on the journey from Vermont to Schoolcraft, Michigan, where he settled down to farm, bought land, went partners in a succession of stores and purchased shares in banks and railroads—all on credit. From time to time, he did a bit of surveying and held public office, which kept him where he was although on several occasions he prospected the situation in Iowa and farther west. Never a smashing success, he managed to make ends meet and in his eighties was still on the watch for a deal or a swap by which to better himself.

Brown was one of many New Englanders who left the stony hills of the old towns in a sober, steady, westward advance. For these people, too, migration was an accustomed feature of life. An English visitor in the 1840s noted: "If you ask a Connecticut Yankee in any part of the world how he is, he will, if not 'sick,' answer 'moving, Sir,' equivalent to saying 'well'; for, if well, he is sure to be on the move." They were already in motion in 1780. The Genesee fever in the 1790s drew them into the state of New York. By 1820, they had come along the Mohawk Valley and on into northern Ohio. Completion of the Erie Canal in 1825 and the railroad building of the 1830s and 1840s eased their journeys and by 1850 brought the Yankee farmers through Illinois, into southern Michigan and across the Mississippi to Iowa.

The people who left Connecticut and Massachusetts were less individualistic than the Virginians, more concerned about settling in communities with schools and churches; now and again, they bought land in groups to be sure of being with others like themselves. But the same restless discontent pushed on the Northerners as the Southerners. The hill country of upper New England, which had only just been settled in the last quarter of the eighteenth century, had quickly revealed its shortcomings. While some men accepted the meager harvests and clung fiercely to their stony fields, many more of their neighbors refused to make do and moved off in search of greener western pastures.

The Virgin West was thus an instrument of providence which enabled men and women to make themselves better, if they willed to do so; and, in the regions where aspirations far outdistanced resources, the will was there.

But the American West was also the heritage of Europeans, for centuries the promised land that would make good the deficiencies of the Old World. Never was the distant transatlantic continent more alluring than in the era of the American Revolution, when a new kind of man seemed to be bringing forth in the New World a new kind of society. It was precisely then that thousands of husbandmen in England, Scotland and Ireland and on the Continent felt the need of a refuge. Despite war, the population of Europe just about doubled in the century after 1750, lending substance to the fears of overpopulation and overcrowding. During the same hundred years also great factories and the consolidation of large landed estates upset the traditional forms of industry and agriculture. Artisans and farmers, unable to compete or to provide inheritances for their sons, increasingly fastened their hopes on an American solution. Across the ocean, skilled hands were at a premium and limitless tracts of fertile land welcomed those willing to till it.

Until 1815, however, the longing for America remained latent. Long periods of war prevented its fulfillment. The return of peace that year finally restored stable conditions of transatlantic travel. The trickle of emigrants from Britain swelled rapidly and by 1830 was joined by streams of like-minded families from Ireland and Germany and soon thereafter by the first Scandinavians.

Lacking the skills for survival in the wilderness, unfamiliar with firearms and with the frontiersman's ruthless speed in clearing the forests, the transplanted European preferred a dependable, stable setting for his labor. Moreover, he wished to strike roots rather than remain in motion and aspired to create a home that would pass down the generations to his descendants, a home in a community like that which he had lost. The Pennsylvania Germans of the eighteenth century had already demonstrated their resistance to change; the peasants who arrived later also sought to reestablish a total pattern of familiar daily activity in a traditional household.

The movement of immigrants from Europe was therefore complementary to the migration of Yankees and Southerners. The Europeans generally brought some capital with them or, if they were lucky, accumulated what they needed by work on the way. They followed along behind the advancing line of settlement, buying out the native frontiersmen, filling up the empty spaces and turning the pioneer clearings into permanent agricultural enterprises. Meanwhile, the purchase price they paid enabled the Americans to move yet further west.

Immigration from overseas and internal migration invigorated American agriculture as a whole, brutally eliminating inefficient producers, buoyantly bringing new areas under cultivation. The men, women and children suffered, paying a cruel physical price in harsh conditions of life, endless toil, unrelenting illness and insanity for every acre cleared, paying also a less precisely measurable emotional price in loneliness and isolation. But the return was substantial. The number of farms, of animals, of machines and of capital invested went steadily upward. In the thirty years between 1820 and 1850, the population of the country rose from 9,638,000 to 23,191,000; and while the percentage in cities had grown somewhat, well over 80 per cent were still rural.

European immigrants who brought to the land old values, buttressed by firm family and community sanctions, resisted the commercial pressures which played upon other farmers in America. But after a time, even the peasants from Swabia or Yorkshire—and certainly their sons—reappraised their economic roles. They began to conceive of agriculture as the restless natives did, not as an end in itself rewarded in the stability it provided the household, but as an enterprise yielding an abstract cash income.

American farmers bought or sold land, plowed and reaped, hunted, fished or trapped, traded, and speculated out of calculated preference rather than out of ingrained habit. The West was their chance for success. Less concerned with the present than with the future, they put stocktaking off from year to year. Buyers and sellers of property as well as of corn and hogs and of anything else they raised, found or took, they were never satisfied, forever set themselves new goals. The man who acquired 80 acres aspired to 160 and then to 320. A nagging compulsion to reject today's conditions, whatever they were, drove such people to expansion. Their objective was not the solitude of unexplored places, but conversion of the wilderness into real estate of ever-increasing value. Therefore, they pushed ahead as individuals. Even when speculators or land companies directed the flow to favored regions, each household was on its own.

The few exceptions, notable chiefly for their singularity, were experimental societies held together by the vision of a secular or religious heaven on earth. New Harmony, Indiana, Amana, Iowa, and Bishop Hill, Illinois, were among the sites of such settlements, where individual goals were subordinate to communal ones. The Church of the Latter-day Saints, the most durable and most powerful of these groups, attracted numerous adherents to its colonies, first in Kirtland, Ohio, and then in Nauvoo, Illinois. Along the way, as they moved west, the Mormons picked up converts from among people who lived in isolation in the woods, each family by itself, seldom seeing any other person. Men and women for whom every new voice was a charm and every new face a revelation were drawn to the warmth of the intimate communal life of the sect, and joined the migration. When riotous non-members in 1846 killed the prophet, Joseph Smith, a new leader guided the Mormons to Utah, where they again demonstrated the cohesive discipline that made them successful colonists.

Apart from exceptions such as these, the western settlers, like other agriculturists, held to individual objectives. Each made his own way to his own tract and sought his own fortune with little regard to others. Hastening onward toward a receding frontier, uncontrolled by external reference points, driven by personal impulses rather than by social imperatives, the thousands of men, women and children who speeded the process of settlement took the risks of migration as a matter of course. Win or lose.

Their speculative temperament injected a significant commercial component into American agriculture. Farmers drifted inexorably into debt in their eagerness to seize the opportunities of the future. Even the frontiersman of modest ambition, in the 1820s, required a stake of no less than $1,000 to purchase forty acres and to carry his family through until the first harvest. But few ambitions were modest; most settlers grabbed for the largest possible tract their cash and credit permitted, counting on the sure rise in land values that would someday permit a profitable sale. The speculators who retailed holdings of various sizes were accommodating enough; heaps of mortgages dotted the trails of settlement. The government too was quite willing to accept payment on time. Once established, the farmer usually could easily find institutions or rich neighbors willing to honor his signature. Borrowings born of need, hope or greed developed a complicated credit system, and the moneylender or banker became a familiar rural figure. European immigrants, more cautious, more traditional, less speculative, were not as likely to take the risks their native counterparts did. But the frenetic take-a-chance atmosphere intoxicated all who breathed it deeply enough.

Since the westward movement was geared to speculative ends, the heavy employment of credit was a normal feature of settlement. As a result, migration was subject to violent cyclical fluctuations with expansion, boom, crisis and depression following regularly upon one another. Everything was just fine in 1830 and finer still in 1831; the price of wheat and corn rose, as did the price of Ohio and Kentucky land; plenty of bank notes circulated and loans were easy to get. Everyone borrowed to buy more, which thrust prices higher still in '32 and '33 and '34, which encouraged further borrowing and buying. People flocked in so that demand increased and '35 and '36 showed the same upward trend as the years before—as no doubt the years to come also would. But they did not. The federal government asked for payments at the land office in gold or silver. Doubts about the value of paper money crept in and individuals also demanded payment in specie, which now became scarcer than ever. To lay their hands on cash, men hastened to sell whatever commodities they could and also their surplus of land. Now there were more sellers than buyers. Prices dropped. Panic struck. In the rush to unload, values spiraled downward as creditors demanded payment, foreclosed mortgages and threw more land on a market already sated. Creditors, unable to collect the sums due them, defaulted on their own obligations. Scores of banks closed their doors. The velocity with which fortunes vanished matched that with which they had earlier appeared.

The panic of 1837, like earlier ones, was an incident in the speculative cycle, which in the 1840s was ascending toward another era of boom. Whatever deference American farmers paid to the agrarian image of a contented yeomanry, the vision that drew them on was success measurable in wealth.

The products of agriculture passed through towns which sprouted promptly wherever settlement developed along the frontier. Sometimes an old military post on a strategic river or lake was the nucleus for a future city, as Fort Dearborn was for Chicago. Or else merchants set up shop at a junction point where roads, canals or rivers intersected, as at Pittsburgh or Wheeling or Cincinnati. At these entrepôts goods, assembled and arranged for shipment to the East and overseas, were exchanged for manufactures and cash. The growth in the number and size of such places was evidence of the intimate links between American agriculture and commerce.

The orientation of the farmers toward the market again and again made them conscious of the problems of credit and of internal improvements. If only there were more money in circulation! People whose hopes fastened upon the rise in prices of commodities and land believed that only the unnatural dearth of coins and notes inhibited potential buyers. And if only one could reduce the expense of getting crops from the harvested field to the city, the same increase in incomes would result. The costs of inland freight sank consistently after

1816, but never fast enough to satisfy the desire for still-lower rates. Goods would more easily flow eastward and additional settlers, prospective land purchasers, would swiftly move westward once charges fell. Rising values would then quickly pay for improvements in transportation.

Credit and communications depended upon the action of the government, which determined the character of the currency and of the roads and the canals. Political decisions also directly affected the pace and cost of settlement, for federal law set land policy. Necessarily, therefore, the desire to protect and advance their interests involved the farmers in politics. As voters and officeholders, they struggled for control of the machinery of the state. In the political arena they sometimes worked with, sometimes clashed with, other groups also seeking power for ends of their own. In particular, the farmers shared with the merchants a commitment to expansion, although interpreted in a fashion of their own. The interplay between the differing interpretations held by farmers and merchants of the role of government in an expanding economy profoundly influenced both the politics and the productive system of the Republic.

4

The Role of the State

*E*xpansion, whether agricultural or commercial, operated without effective social controls; each family settled where opportunity or preference took it, each trader made his own estimate of where to find the best deal. But the individual, endlessly probing the unfamiliar places, again and again arrived at a stream and wished a bridge were there. It took little effort to blaze a trail for those who might follow; it took strength and skill to build a bridge and no single traveler could do the job—nor was any likely to expend the time for the sake of the unknown others. The thousands who stumbled across, each by his own efforts, knew that all would gain by the improvement. Therefore, they believed, all should participate equally in making it; and, in their culture, such communal arrangements were effected by government, which commanded the labor and funds of its citizens.

The developing economy frequently seemed to require the intervention of the state. But while Americans generally agreed on the desirability—indeed inevitability—of expansion, they divided sharply over its purposes and over the means of bearing its costs. The divisions rose to the surface at every occasion for decision. Everyone objected to taxes and tolls which brought them no direct benefits, for each made the judgment of benefits in his own terms.

Differing as they did over money, taxes and roads, the merchants, artisans and farmers struggled among themselves to control the legislators, judges and executive officers who made the important decisions. Since numbers and strength varied from place to place, and

57

since force in the Republic was dispersed, not concentrated at any single point, the outcome of the contests was uneven, reflecting marked local variations. Federalism and the separation of powers divided authority among the states and between them and the national government, and also among lawmakers, judges and administrators. Furthermore, the whole complex structure was loose and imprecise in operation, guided not by experienced bureaucrats but by citizens who rotated frequently in and out of positions of responsibility. The effect of a statute depended generally upon on-the-spot interpretations and upon the willingness of those it affected to accept it. Sanctions ultimately lay in the hands not of the standing army or of paid policemen but of citizens' posses and militias. The effort to use government to mold the economy to men's will, therefore, rarely ran according to any general plan. More often it produced untidy and unexpected results. Disturbing as the process was, its very disorder was also stimulating. For if the weakness of the political system prevented the state from acting consistently to implement any design, it afforded the citizens enough flexibility to improvise and to utilize unforeseen opportunities. In the end, the discrepancy between what people wanted and what they got transformed the whole conception of the role of the state in the economy.

Americans inherited from Europe well-defined techniques for using government to foster economic development. Independence gave them control of the political apparatus, with which they could increase the wealth of the nation. Republican rhetoric stressed the importance of citizen participation, persuasion and education. At last, free of British domination, they were sovereign, eager to use the weapons withheld from them when they had been subjects. The numerous privileges formerly lodged in the hands of the monarch were now at their disposal. They confidently expected to use for their own ends the mercantilist methods once under the exclusive control of the empire.

Almost at once, however, modifications crept in. The theories that legitimized government action in the United States subtly altered the familiar techniques of sale of office, licensing, monopoly and other forms of privilege.

The founding fathers called their government a republic, a term which reflected their intention to do without a monarch. But the word also conveyed something more to them—the exact meaning of the Latin roots from which it was derived. The republic was a *res publica*, that is, a commonwealth. Its wealth was the property not of the Crown but of the public, not royal, but common. The purpose of the state was to protect and advance the common wealth, from which it followed that it had an interest of its own, above the particular interests of the individuals who were its citizens. The state could use all the familiar techniques for stimulating the economy if they contributed to the common wealth. It could bestow privileges not to benefit the recipients but to further the common welfare.

These ideas about the structure and purpose of government gave measures borrowed from the Old World a fresh appearance in the New. Americans had to discard the European view of governmental power as a kind of property at the disposal of the Crown which could sell privileges and officers to enrich its exchequer. The wealth of the sovereign, visible in the person of the monarch, was not the proper measure of social utility in the Republic.

Moreover, much of the struggle against Britain had grown out of hostility to mercantilist practices; the dumpers of tea, the protesters against arbitrary, restrictive trade practices, could not promptly turn to grasping monopolies and privileges of their own. As avid for favored positions as the European, the American could not demand them as the simple concomitants of status and wealth.

Citizens of the United States could justify government action on their behalf only by arguments consistent with republican ideas. In the new nation, sovereignty, in a way not precisely defined, was said to rest in the people, whose welfare alone justified the grant of a privilege—a slippery concept readily enunciated in political oratory but difficult to apply in practice. At once the questions arose about vestigial practices: whose interests did licensing, apprenticeship, price-fixing serve? These devices would wither and all but disappear after independence, for there were few with a stake in them and with enough political power to revive them. But other forms of state action—to control commerce and currency, industry and transportation—certainly involved the welfare of thousands of people and certainly remained vigorous through much of the nineteenth century, although in forms that were far from traditional.

Political imperatives modified even the most familiar methods. Every citizen in the 1770s had thought about the navigation acts and their economic effects, and few doubted that similar measures were useful if enacted by legislatures responsive to the will of the people. A well-contrived commercial policy would confine the coastal trade to Americans, reduce the wanton consumption of imported luxuries, protect native farmers and artisans against foreign competition and produce a revenue besides. At independence, the thirteen states promptly and enthusiastically set about framing laws on the subject, with near-chaos the result. New Jersey and New York, Delaware and Pennsylvania, Rhode Island and Massachusetts, each making its own regulations and setting its own levies on exports and imports, plunged into conflicts that canceled out the positive effects of their statutes.

In 1789, the new federal constitution transferred jurisdiction over these matters to the central government. Thereafter discussion of commercial policy unfolded sporadically and monotonously in the halls of Congress and, more widely, during some presidential campaigns. Having eschewed any aspirations to empire and having espoused the cause of freedom of the seas, the United States made no effort to control the trade conducted by its merchants or to channel the flow of commodities in one direction. Only rarely did the requirements of foreign policy dictate an exception, as during the embargo of 1807 and during the collaboration with Britain in stamping out the export of slaves from Africa.

Generally, down to the Civil War the debate over commercial policy focused on the tariff—whether to set rates low enough to permit imports and yield revenue, or high enough to exclude foreign goods and protect American producers, though that might diminish the yield at the customs houses. The argument tended to lofty emotional abstractions about the virtues of protection and free trade; but Congress never voted on those alternatives as such. The actual legislative process, which defined specific rates, simply arrayed against one another the concerned interest blocs searching for the greatest advantage. Artisans generally wanted high levels, merchants low ones, unless they held investments in industry as some did after 1820. Cotton planters in the 1790s and wool growers in the 1840s feared competition from abroad, but most agriculturists did not, and rather preferred rates that kept down the cost of the goods they bought. The outcome was a succession of inconclusive compromises, interrupted by an occasional fluky high tariff as in 1828 or by an exceptionally low one as in 1846. In practice, down to 1861, the tariff probably made no economic difference whatever. It was not an effective instrument of protection because no group of producers exercised enough leverage to secure what it wished.

In every effort to grasp the traditional forms of state aid, eager citizens discovered that there were two aspects to the exercise—both difficult. First, they had to lay hold of the favor sought; then they needed additional power to make something of it.

Standing in the way of any direct grant or expenditure of public funds by county, state or nation was the unfailing plea of poverty. Faith persuaded Americans that their country was rich, for the future; prudence told them that it was poor, for the present. The ambiguous condition was not fixed, immutable, but rather a product of decisions —even if not explicitly made. The governments had few debts and hastened to extinguish those promptly; and their current accounts frequently showed a surplus. Public penury reflected the unwillingness of the citizens to allocate any significant part of their wealth to communal purposes.

There were many demands for expenditure, few enthusiasts for taxes; those who sought grants for their own benefit resolutely opposed grants to others, and everyone united to fight off demands that might raise assessments. Schemes for bounties, subsidies, public construction and even education—no matter how laudable or how ingeniously defended—faced skeptical scrutiny and generally came to nothing.

Privileges which called for no outlay of public cash were more easily granted. But then the recipients required additional force to rake in the profits. A monopoly, for instance, certainly seemed worth having, for it exempted the possessor from the penalties of the old common-law prohibition of forestalling and of conspiracies in restraint of trade. Individual efforts to control the market were criminal. But the legislatures could grant the right in order to further some communal purpose. Employed for the welfare of all, according to legal procedures, the privilege was then a justified use of state power. And ingenious entrepreneurs were rarely at a loss for phrases to show that the monopolies they sought served the common wealth.

The difficulties were not abstract but practical. It took no little effort to line up the votes needed to get an act through the state legislature or Congress. Then, despite the law, it was a formidable problem to make good a claim to rewards from the privilege. The government was not strong enough to act against interlopers, poachers and infringers. The pre-revolutionary experience had left a deep-seated popular prejudice against monopoly; and juries raised on stories of the East India Company's tea would not convict violators of rights granted even for worthy purposes.

Robert Fulton, for instance, earned the gratitude of his countrymen, but little more, for designing the first practical steamboat in the United States in 1807. Vessels thus propelled replaced the sloops and rafts on the inland waterways and, after 1820, also carried a growing share of ocean traffic. Their speed, convenience and freedom from dependence on winds and tides lowered costs for everyone. For a generation or more, mechanics had strained their ingenuity to devise a way of making steam move a craft across water; and investors had backed them with hard cash. Fulton, working for Chancellor Robert R. Livingston and his partners, had succeeded where others

had failed. But though the Livingston group was politically powerful, it never enjoyed the fruits of the twenty-year monopoly of steam
transportation on the Hudson River which New York had promised it.
New Jersey objected, outsiders intruded and the Supreme Court ultimately decided that the state's grant was an unconstitutional interference with interstate commerce.

The question of state as against federal jurisdiction complicated
Fulton's situation. But no such problems arose in the case of inventions recorded under the national patent law. Yet inventors who followed all the proper procedures nevertheless found it difficult, expensive, time-consuming, and frustrating to attempt to assert their
rights. Eli Whitney gained little from his work on the cotton gin, and
Cyrus McCormick met endless difficulties in validating his claims to
the harvester. In fact, the more important the innovation, the slimmer
was the likelihood of reward from it. The Commissioner of Patents
in 1861 lavishly praised the worth of McCormick's device but denied
an application for an extension on the grounds that the reaper was
"of too great value to the public to be controlled by any individual."
The government could bestow the privilege of monopoly but lacked
the power to make it profitable in the face of popular resistance.

The technique of incorporation borrowed from the Old World
was also transformed in application to American conditions. But the
new features acquired in the process proved unexpectedly valuable
and made the device ever more popular. The colonies before 1776
had lacked the authority to charter companies. In 1800, twenty-five
years after independence, there were more corporations with business
functions in the United States than in all Europe.

Incorporation was a privilege with medieval origins. The traditional charter created a body politic, a governmental entity using a
share of state power for a particular public end. It could elect officers
and make rules that applied to its members and to others over whom
it held jurisdiction, and it could employ a common stock, a common
name and a seal.

The grant of a charter was therefore a serious matter. Parliament
retained the prerogative for itself, so that colonists had to resort to
subterfuges when they applied the familiar technique to communal
functions. Churches, universities and the New England towns were
among the agencies the colonial legislatures thus created before 1776.

Occasionally in Britain the corporation had appeared also in
fields in which economic and political interests overlapped—the
seventeenth-century overseas trading companies, for instance, or later,
the Bank of England. But those instances were rare and justified only

by exceptional circumstances. In the whole of the eighteenth century, the Parliament chartered fewer than twenty business corporations.

Revolution gave the Americans the power and the opportunity to use the privilege without external interference.

A bank, like that of England or Amsterdam, thus seemed the reasonable way to end the perennial shortage of currency which had long inconvenienced Americans and shackled their economy. The colonies had always suffered from lack of an adequate circulating medium and independence in itself had not solved the problem. The states and the Continental Congress had experimented with the issue of paper money; but since people had no confidence in the government's ability ever to redeem them, the notes had tumbled in value and soon were practically worthless. That experience confirmed the lesson of a century's history: paper printed by the government was not trustworthy because its worth in gold or silver fluctuated wildly and unpredictably. And a holder of a Continental or any similar note had no recourse if the issuing authority refused or was unable to pay. The federal constitution of 1787 therefore forbade the states to issue any paper at all.

A bank seemed more reliable. It was free from political control and it was responsible; the holder of its notes could sue if it did not sustain their value. Stockholders who had invested their own funds and were liable for its debts would assure prudent management in their own interest. At the same time, it commanded respect by virtue of its charter and seal, the signs of the communal service it rendered in issuing the currency on which the nation's economy depended.

The Continental Congress had established the Bank of North America with the expectation that it would perform that function. In 1791, the new federal regime assigned the task for a period of twenty years to the Bank of the United States. Its charter, like that of its predecessor, provided for investment by the government as well as by individuals and for control by a board of directors, some appointed by the national president, others elected by the shareholders. The Bank, through branches in the chief cities, issued notes, received, held and paid out government funds and made what loans it considered prudent. Like other corporations chartered in Europe and America, it was an instrument of the state, combining political power with private capital.

The ties to the state speedily disappeared; well before 1860, the corporation became simply a means of private enterprise and lost all connotation of public interest or control. The transition occurred in every area of the economy but was earliest in banking.

The inexperienced first promoters did not foresee the complications of federalism and therefore drifted into innovation. Not one, but fourteen governments, all sovereign, had the power to charter banks in the United States. The federal Bank of North America had scarcely gone into operation when the Massachusetts Bank opened its doors (1785) and New York soon followed. By 1791, six states had established banks which issued their own notes. Yet the nation was one and its economy one, so that the currency thus printed circulated throughout the country. Paper issuing from many presses now became abundant.

No one envisioned the speed with which banks would multiply. Governments too weak to say no reluctantly but repeatedly yielded to petitioners for charters. The earliest institutions, as a matter of course, had their seats in the capital cities or at least in the largest mercantile centers—Boston, New York, Philadelphia. Local merchants held the shares, served as directors and used the facilities. Soon, however, businessmen elsewhere demanded banks of their own. If Boston had one, why should not Salem? Or Newburyport? Or Pittsfield? A republican society responded permissively to the question. In almost every state, the alliance of local traders and speculators had power enough to secure the same privileges. By 1800 demands within the same city for second or third banks had become irresistible. Ignorance, skulduggery, or political pressure further diffused the right to print notes. Ingenious subterfuges enabled determined entrepreneurs to circumvent legislative recalcitrance, as when a vague clause in the charter of the Manhattan Company, set up to bring water into New York City, allowed the promoters to operate a bank.

But legislators were not usually recalcitrant for long; and the process of multiplication continued. In 1811, in scores of places throughout the country, 88 corporations turned out paper money and made loans. In that year, the charter of the Bank of the United States expired and no controversy developed over the issue of renewal; the privilege had little value and there were more than enough state banks. Indeed, in the five years that followed, the number rose to 246.

Currency was plentiful, but of uncertain value. Everywhere in Britain any pound note had the same value because all issued from the single Bank of England, which stood ready to redeem them in specie. Americans could count on no such assurance. Many notes passed only at a discount. In every transaction, the buyer and seller, the debtor and creditor had to use gold and silver or else calculate the worth of each bill from published tables of current quotations.

Each bank emitted as much as it could, subject only to the obligation to pay in specie for notes presented over the counter. If the paper never came back or stayed out in circulation for a very long time, the bank could cheerfully take the risk of printing more to its own great advantage. Bankers in remote rural areas, ever hopeful that the drift of their notes to the large Eastern cities would be one way, yielded repeatedly to the temptation to expand output without reckoning reserves. If some hard-hearted, big-town broker drove up with a pocketful of notes, bought at discount, then the game was up. Or a collapse might follow simply on a run touched off by fear, rumor or loss of confidence.

A far cry, all this, from the Bank of England! The privilege, effective when bestowed on a single recipient, lost value when scattered among many.

The European technique of incorporation in every field assumed grotesque forms once transplanted to republican soil. The reports of Alexander Hamilton, which had urged the charter of the Bank of the United States in 1791, had also recommended the development of manufacturing. The Secretary of the Treasury had in mind the dual objectives which then excited mercantile and agrarian interest; nurture of an activity which would supply articles for export and utilization of the raw materials and the labor of American farms. The Society for the Promotion of Useful Manufactures chartered in New Jersey, in which Hamilton was an active participant, was a model of the kind of corporation which he believed would stimulate industry. It proposed to turn out paper, brass and textiles, using where needed the water power at a site in Paterson. Its mill housed those operations best performed by machine; from its central warehouse it distributed the materials to be worked up at home and assembled the finished products for marketing; and it set uniform rules and standards to earn the confidence of its customers. Similar factories sprouted hopefully in the next two decades, especially when the embargo stopped the flow of manufactures from Europe.

Little came of these efforts which assumed that the corporation could control production, either through communal discipline or through political power delegated by government. Both were in fact inadequate. The seal and the prestige of the charter counted for nothing. Uninhibited, freewheeling traders made their own deals, and the smiths, weavers and spinners accepted the arrangements most to their personal advantage.

The inability to apply political controls also affected transportation. The early republic urgently needed internal improvements to make its roads passable and its rivers navigable, to clear harbors and build wharves. Before the Revolution, these had been the tasks of towns and counties which, however, lacked the resources to perform them. Independence brought into being a federal government that could act; and expansionist merchants and farmers expected it to do so. Indeed, the first steps toward the Constitutional Convention of 1787 had come out of efforts at cooperation among the states bordering on the Potomac, which sought to improve the navigation of the river. Talk of a great federal transportation program thereafter ran into the impenetrable obstacle of lack of funds; the diverting legal discussions of congressional power were less important than the sense of fiscal feebleness. Not until 1802 did Congress authorize a national road to the west, to be built from the proceeds of the sale of Ohio lands, and it took sixteen years to stretch it from Cumberland on the Potomac to Wheeling on the Ohio.

State legislators voiced the plea of poverty as readily as did congressmen. The prevailing unwillingness to raise tax levels, which reflected both the weakness of government and the unwillingness to subordinate individual to general interests, dampened enthusiasm for expensive projects. Merchants who vociferously endorsed closer links to the back country, farmers who petitioned for better access to urban markets, fell silent when the awkward question arose: who would pay for the communal efforts to develop the roads and waterways? The convenient response was to persuade corporations chartered for a particular purpose to bear the expense in the hope of remuneration and profit from tolls charged the users. Privileges such as the right to take land by eminent domain or the monopoly of a particular route added inducements for entrepreneurs.

European experience had shown the utility of turnpikes, bridges and canals. Americans hoped to do as well or better, and a good many entrepreneurs in the quarter-century after 1790 responded to the challenge.

Conditions in the United States were, however, different from those in Europe and the number of successful projects was small. Any effort to build transportation before the development of the traffic to be served was subject to miscalculation. Even a well-articulated and carefully planned system would have been open to error so long as it depended on wild guesses of future needs. But, in any case, construction before 1815 did not proceed according to any central scheme.

The states lost control when they delegated the responsibility to corporations. Governments were no more capable of confining the privilege in transportation than in manufacturing or banking. Applicants multiplied—and grants. The speculative possibilities attracted investors, and local interests mobilized in support of ventures that promised to bring urban markets closer to the agricultural heart of the nation. Anyone could take a fling through purchase of a share. Merchants hastened to forge links to the back country, lest their rivals in other cities gain an advantage; the importer Thomas Pym Cope of Philadelphia thus spent much of his time after 1790 guiding the Chesapeake and Delaware Canal to completion. Farmers, eager for closer links to the buyers of their produce in town, willingly collaborated in pushing proposals through the legislatures. There was no denying the requests. As a result, bridges, pikes and canals proliferated, some actually to be built, others started but unfinished, and still others never progressing beyond the paper on which their charters were engrossed. The improvements actually effected were not integrated into any comprehensive plan; on the map they appeared as spokes radiating outward from numerous hubs, that is, from the cities in which their sponsors did business. In effect, the states transferred the power of decision to local investors, each group making its own appraisal of prospective traffic.

Few enterprises thus launched did well. Shareholders, in for a penny, soon were paying out pounds as repeated calls reflected rising construction costs. Local juries set high prices for every strip of land taken. Competition from free roads and alternative routes kept the level of tolls low; and the users who had, not long before, clamorously supported the petitions for incorporation began to question the justness of the charges they grudgingly paid over to the soulless monopoly once the road, canal or bridge was open.

The situation was ironic. Privileges were useful as long as they were exceptional and exclusive. But, in transportation as in banking and manufacturing, every increase in numbers drained away their value; and in the United States government was not strong enough to fend off competing applicants, nor was any social group powerful enough to retain a favored position. The more Americans employed the old techniques, therefore, the more remote was the possibility of attaining the ends anticipated.

People in pursuit of wealth, however, were slow to give up; since personal experience, not history, was their guide, they often repeated the miscalculations of the past. The revival of nationalism during the War of 1812 rekindled the determination to do something to demonstrate the economic greatness of the nation. After Waterloo, the end of the cycle of wars in Europe and in America opened a period of rapid growth everywhere. In the United States westward expansion and the rise of manufacturing stimulated the process. Fresh opportunities for trade attracted merchants, budding industrialists and entrepreneurial farmers; and the concern with developing markets created a general sense of impatience with the limitations of existing facilities for doing business.

Political power after 1815 rested in new hands. The great figures of the Revolution and of the early republic had passed, or were about to pass, from the scene. Their successors vigorously assumed the burdens of office, confidently expecting to complete what still remained undone. Old party lines faded; and, while fresh ones in time appeared, they continued to shift sporadically down to the Civil War.

For a few years, Henry Clay, John C. Calhoun and the other young congressmen of the coming generation achieved surprising unity both in the rhetoric they employed and the willingness they displayed to utilize any techniques, old or new, that promised to advance the national economy. There was a star-spangled attractiveness to the American System they espoused. They would use the continent, open the vast Louisiana territories acquired from France and now made safe by a second war for independence. The people were ready, would pour in once the means of communication were adequate, and it was the duty of government to provide those. The question of costs was still troublesome. But a tariff could pay for many internal improvements and if it were high enough would also protect industry. Then would follow a beneficial internal exchange of the agricultural goods of the West for the manufactures of the East.

This tidy solution rang plausibly from the rostrum. But citizens accustomed to sniff suspiciously at any increase in government revenue still insisted on asking: who pays? A tariff high enough to protect domestic manufactures would exclude imports, lower receipts and leave nothing for internal improvements. No stretch of oratory could altogether conceal the contradiction or wish away the inescapable account someone would have to settle.

Nevertheless, for more than a decade after the War of 1812, hope of a great federal effort persisted. The idea of a national road, now to reach St. Louis, gained new strength; and Senator Martin Van Buren in 1824 suggested a constitutional amendment to resolve earlier doubts by explicitly giving the United States authority to build roads and canals. President John Quincy Adams, who considered the amendment superfluous, proceeded shortly thereafter to sketch the outlines of a great federal transportation program.

Meanwhile, the states hastened also to get into action. Some of them tried to work out well-thought-through plans for developing communications within their boundaries. Virginia produced a notable scheme, much discussed throughout the country and influential as far away as Pennsylvania and New York. In most cases, the approach was eclectic, using all available means. There was still a preference for assigning the tasks to corporations, but if they would not do it, then the governments themselves were willing to launch, construct and operate the desired improvements.

In the postwar confidence of 1816, with national feelings strong, Congress also chartered a second Bank of the United States upon terms very similar to those of the first. The task of establishing some central control over the currency, at which its predecessor had failed, was now to receive another trial. Nicholas Biddle, who became president of the Bank in 1823, was a Philadelphian, born to wealth, something of a scholar—a type far removed from the merchants of an earlier generation. Certainly he was interested in economic growth, but of an orderly, predictable character, nicely regulated to prevent excessive booms and panics. He was far from ignorant, indeed knew a good deal about financial institutions in England and on the continent of Europe.

The key, he believed, was the currency. Paper money still flowed freely from the presses of hundreds of state banks. The notes served a useful function, so long as they rested solidly upon adequate reserves of specie; detached from that base, they depreciated in value, lost the confidence of the public and unsettled all commercial transactions. Biddle made the Bank of the United States guardian of monetary probity. Its branches in various cities assembled the notes of banks everywhere, sorted them out and arranged to present them to the issuers for redemption in gold or silver. The Bank of the United States thus applied a brake to the unlimited expansion of the money supply. Immense resources and the deposits of federal funds freed the Bank of any comparable restraint so that it could expand or contract its own currency outstanding as its managers deemed fit.

Biddle nevertheless stumbled over the same political forces that defeated other efforts to guide the economy by the grant of privilege. The Bank of the United States lacked the support to withstand attack by those whom its policies confined.

By and large, the great overseas merchants accepted the wisdom of maintaining a moderate supply of paper currency—enough to lubricate the internal business of the country but not too much to cause the flight of specie required to settle accounts in complicated international financial transactions. A proper balance would permit foreign trade to follow its own course without inhibiting the internal expansion in which many invested directly and which indirectly increased the business of all. While some merchants disliked Biddle personally or were jealous of Philadelphia's preeminence or held shares in rival state banks, most believed that the Bank of the United States was a worthy custodian of the nation's monetary system.

The opposition was far more numerous, consisting as it did of two powerful groups, both hostile to Biddle's policies although for contrary reasons. They would not in the future be able to unite on an alternative, but they could for the moment join forces to bring the Bank down.

The decades since the Revolution had persuaded the artisans that the whole practice of passing off paper as money was a cheat, part of the pattern of privilege which enriched the few at the expense of the many. All too often, the bank notes the craftsman took in payment sank in value by the time he passed them on; and inflation raised the cost of his food and materials by more than he ventured to increase his own prices. Puzzling over the tricky bits of paper, the artisan concluded that banks—like the other monstrous corporations which had fastened themselves on the Republic—were soulless, devoid of the personal responsibility expected in business as in other transactions, and somehow implicated in large speculative schemes which upset the stable order of trade. The solution was an end to all charters and other forms of government meddling, and the use of a solid currency only, gold and silver, not susceptible to twists in value by sharpers. That plea evoked the support of some conservative Southern planters; John Taylor of Caroline (Virginia) expressed their hostility to the commercial monopolies which oppressed the honest agrarians and workingmen.

Speculative farmers in every part of the country and those with whom they dealt—local merchants, lawyers, and land-swappers—opposed the Bank, but not banking. Far from it. Biddle, they charged, unnaturally restrained the increase in currency in order to halt expansion. Out of the Easterner's jealousy of the West, he barred the path to wealth of deserving men so that a financial aristocracy could control the nation. Speculators wished to liberate banking from the shackles of the Bank. Anyone should be free to issue notes, subject only to the requirement of redemption in the normal course of trade; supply and demand would set the value of bills. A plentiful money supply would ease credit to the great advantage of people prone to sliding into debt in the risky process of expansion. Optimists also believed that abundant bank notes would raise the prices of crops and land and thus benefit all who looked to the future.

A powerful, if somewhat incongruous, alliance of hard-money and soft-money elements rallied behind President Jackson in his war against Biddle and the monstrous monopoly of the Bank. The issue that held these uneasy partners together was centralization of control—in the first instance of the currency, more generally of credit and of economic policy. The outcome was never in doubt; the gradual removal of federal deposits after 1832 sapped the institution's strength, its charter expired in 1836, and efforts to keep it going under Pennsylvania auspices failed. For thirty years thereafter the federal government abstained from any effort to control the nation's currency or credit. It minted some coins. But it collected and paid out its funds directly through sub-treasuries and remained aloof from the banks and all their problems.

Although the individual states continued to issue bank charters, they too refrained from attempts to direct the monetary system. Free banking became the rule—in effect, anyone who conformed to broad general conditions could secure incorporation; the charter became merely an instrument of registration. Once having complied with the simple procedure for doing business, the bankers alone made the decisions about the amount of paper to put into print and to hand out as loans, and they were guided solely by their own estimates of what was profitable. By 1860, fully 1,500 of them issued their own notes. Indeed, the only effective limit on the flow was through voluntary associations set up by bankers in metropolitan centers such as Boston to take paper back to its issuers for redemption. Government after 1830 stood aside, treating the banks as it did other enterprises which operated primarily in the interest of the owners of their stock. Not until after the panic of 1857 was there thought of serious regulation.

With few exceptions, developments in transportation also slipped away from political management. The federal government speedily and decisively pulled out, just a few years after J. Q. Adams sketched his ambitious proposals. The national road languished incomplete, and Jackson's veto of a bill to provide funds for the section to Maysville not only killed the project but also proclaimed that all such ventures were really in the province of the states. Grudging support for lighthouses and for some river and harbor improvements was the extent for federal involvement until 1860.

The states could not as easily shirk the responsibility. Their citizens clamored for improvements and yet adamantly fought increased taxes or tolls. Everywhere the turnpike corporations, tiring of the losing battle to make a profit, surrendered their privileges and relinquished their roads, such as they were, to the public authorities, to be maintained as other highways and bridges were by the counties and municipalities for the free use of travelers. Local tax considerations, always preponderant, did not encourage large, venturesome and expensive schemes.

The unfavorable outcome of efforts to improve transportation by land turned attention to the uses of water. The great designs in the 1820s pivoted on canals. The failure of the corporation to earn its way operating turnpikes did not dim the hope that it would do well in canals. The imagination of promoters fastened upon the idea of new links between the West and the Atlantic seaports. The merchants of Baltimore, Philadelphia, New York and Boston as well as their rivals in lesser, but nonetheless aspiring, cities believed firmly that their prospects for future growth depended upon the ability to tap the vast new areas of settlement beyond the Alleghenies. Plans and pleas toward that end filled the columns of the press and generated monotonous enthusiasm in meetings of the chambers of commerce.

New York's Erie Canal, the great success of the era, was something of a sport, built directly by the state at a time when the corporation seemed the best means of getting such jobs done. In fact, a corporation of the usual type had initiated the effort to link the Hudson to the Great Lakes. The project had originated back in the eighteenth century, and the Western Lock Navigation Company was already in financial difficulty by 1800. It floundered along for another decade, then in 1811, *in extremis,* called upon the state for help. War a year later was an excuse for denial of the plea. The company expired, and the project passed into the reluctant hands of the government. The revival of interest in internal improvements after the restoration of peace in 1815, and the forceful leadership of Governor George Clinton, churned life into the moribund enterprise; and the spread of settlement into the western counties weakened the usual inhibitions against the expenditure of government funds. Any means served to make the cash available—taxes, tolls, lotteries and the sale of public lands. Topography provided a lucky gap in the mountains through which the canal passed at water level, minimizing engineering problems and costs both of construction and operation. In 1825, the ditch, 350 miles long, was open.

New York's success stirred its rivals into action; the Erie carried 13,000 boats in its very first year of operation, an irresistible challenge. Other states dusted off old plans or devised new ones. In some places the government tried its hand at construction, elsewhere corporations and still elsewhere a mixture of the two. The result was a rapid increase in the mileage available to carry the nation's freight over long distances.

But the achievements of the Erie were beyond the reach of its imitators. Formidable natural obstacles, such as those surmounted in Pennsylvania, raised costs to the bitter regret of stockholders and taxpayers. Some projects were never finished at all; on many that were, the passing barge but rarely summoned the locksman to his gates. Canals which drew traffic from existing waterways, such as those linking the Great Lakes and the Ohio River, paid their way, but even they were not parts of a coherent state system. Ohio, for instance, built two competing north-south systems, one from Cleveland to Marietta, the other from Toledo to Cincinnati, each weakening the other. As a result, when a miraculous new mode of transportation appeared in the 1830s, the states, although sometimes willing to aid, shied away from the involvements of planning, construction, direction or management.

In transportation, as in banking, the role of the government shrank. The openhandedness of the state, whether in the grant of privilege or the use of its own funds, meant that the recipients of its favors gained little. Neither Toledo nor Cleveland did as well as if either had been the sole terminus, just as the right to print notes lost value when anyone could do it. Increasingly, both the winners and losers in the political contests questioned the worth of positive state action. The Jacksonians became spokesmen for the view that enterprise functioned best uninhibited by central controls of any sort—in currency, credit, communications, manufacturing and agriculture. Every assertion of common interest disguised a grab for private advantage; there was no *common wealth*, only an aggregation of personal wealths, and therefore government served no transcendent unifying purpose, only the multifarious competing purposes of its individual citizens.

Where all were rivals—actual or potential—the state stood by the side to enforce the rules so that the race would be fairly run. The law it administered—outcome of a complex and subtle process of defining what was just—had the unintended effect of sustaining faith in the worth of the competitive struggle. Slowly, between the Revolution and 1860, local variations faded; in frontier Tennessee as in tidewater Virginia, in rural Wyoming County as in metropolitan

Philadelphia, similar rules of a binding character sheltered alike the merchant who shipped his goods to a remote purchaser and the farmer who bought land at a distance, reducing somewhat the hazards of all transactions. Men jostling for the prize of wealth could concentrate on their work in the assurance that the regulations governing contract and debt gave none an unfair advantage.

The great full-dress judicial issues of the nineteenth century, those argued by famous advocates and resolved by decisions of the learned justices of the Supreme Court, dealt with constitutional problems of national and state power. But in their day-to-day business, the same attorneys and judges pondered other shirt-sleeve questions. When they came into the county seat, often riding circuit together, or when they chatted in the corridors of the urban courthouses, their minds searched for ways to apply the power of government to resolve conflicts to the advantage of their clients.

Every case presented its own problem. Litigants could not demonstrate how the law applied to a particular case simply by reference to an accepted, defined code—although there was now and then talk, particularly in the 1830s, of producing such a code. Nor could the law simply be discovered by a search for precedents, for there was by no means agreement on how far the common law—distant, English, feudal—was binding on free Americans in a different, rapidly changing society. The lawyers thumbing through the pages of Coke, for want of other information about past cases, twisted the old rulings to fit new conditions, for precedent alone was not authoritative.

In a republic, it was appropriate to let the people decide. Their consent had given effect to constitutions and had brought government into being; they elected the legislators who produced the statutes and, in most jurisdictions, the judges who interpreted them. And the people as jurors rendered the verdicts. The process of adjudicating disputes required no technique or knowledge not possessed by every man. All were equally eligible to be judges, jurors and legislators; and admission to the bar was so slight a formality that almost anyone could enter the practice of law. In any case, caution kept the courts from deviating from the popular view of justice. The people offended could take the law into their own hands, for theirs was the power in reality as in theory; efforts to evict squatters or to collect debts or taxes against the will of the populace produced frequent outbursts of violence, memories of which remained vivid for decades after the events.

Marked differences therefore persisted among laws of the several states and in their application from county to county according to local circumstances. Nevertheless, tendencies toward uniformity gained steadily. A deep distrust of arbitrary power created a desire for rules; religious precepts and social experience taught the most independent-minded that they had better do unto others, lest they someday be done in themselves. Men and women continually moving about understood that there was greater safety in adherence by all to an abstract standard of justice than in hazardous, each-for-himself defense.

Furthermore, those lawyers and judges traveling, dining, drinking together, developed a sense of fellowship, partly from having read the same Blackstone, increasingly in the nineteenth century from having drudged through similar apprenticeships and drowsed through similar law lectures, but mostly from the tolerant accommodations of extended rivalry. Trying to win them all, each knew that every man had his own fall coming, and tricky tactics that might earn a favorable verdict here might boomerang there. It was more advantageous to everyone, and more interesting, to play by rules, despite the temptation to evade them.

A sense of professionalism helped counteract the effects of localism. In 1860, there was still no uniform legal code in the United States; each state made its own laws. But within each, an appeals process offset, to some extent, the prejudices and eccentricities of juries. On some crucial points also litigants could resort to the federal courts, which applied identical standards to cases originating in every part of the country.

Appeals were expensive and time-consuming; experienced attorneys rarely advised their clients to have recourse to the process. It was better, in marginal matters, to work out an arrangement among brothers at the bar, pushing neither party to his knees, getting an approximation if not a full measure of justice. Deals thus worked out became increasingly common. Shaped by the lawyers' estimates of what the outcome of a trial of strength would be, they were evidence that American law was acquiring uniformity. The outcome of proceedings was likely to be the same in one place as another, was therefore dependable and predictable.

Increasingly Americans discovered that government rendered a more important service when it created conditions that enabled all the people to do business with confidence than when it granted privilege to some. Strangers in motion, ever haggling in their purchases and sales, could not depend on faith in a handshake to seal a bargain. Sharpers all, buyers and sellers had to beware, for few restraints of family, status or informal relationships operated in the marketplace.

In this world of strangers, law alone established order, set and enforced the terms and forms of negotiations. The legal system was not prescribed by constitutions; nor was it ordained by legislative enactments; nor was it even the product of plan or forethought. It evolved through procedures that were not wholly rational but that were sensitive to a rapidly changing economy.

The developing understanding of the concept of contract thus freed business transactions from dependence on personal relations. The sense, in ethics, of a binding force to agreements had ancient antecedents; and English law, since medieval times, had explored its implications with reference to land and other property. Furthermore, Puritan theology which linked man to God and men to society through covenants nurtured a general respect for all compacts. Nevertheless, while everyone accepted the general principle, doubts about the application to particular cases persisted. Questions about the proper evidence of validity or about the effects of fraud or misrepresentation could throw an issue into confusion and the more so when resolved in a distant courtroom. Hence, down through the eighteenth century, prudent people sought personal reassurance to back up the abstract mark on paper; they preferred to deal with relatives or co-religionists in the hope that the sanctions of family or faith would strengthen those of contract.

The need for a more general assertion of the rights of contract was urgent under the Republic. The Revolution ended the authority of the Crown and of the justice which had previously emanated from it. The velocity of movement through the country increased, so that business deals more often involved strangers and informal personal obligations therefore lost their force. Tenants refused to pay rent, journeymen and apprentices broke their contracts at will to leave for more attractive fields, and purchasers went back on their bids when better buys turned up. John Adams in 1792 recognized that honor, fidelity, punctuality and respect for property and for the moral obligation of promises never did and never would of themselves prevail in any populous nation. Only a decisive government enforcing the law could develop the habits essential to economic growth.

In the half-century after independence, the law reaffirmed the principle that a deal was a deal and also acquired the machinery to compel adherence to it. The federal constitution of 1787 forbade the states to abrogate the obligations of contract, thus taking care of the immediate crisis in which stay laws in some places protected debtors against the claims of their creditors. But in the decades which followed, the negative injunction became positive; the government assumed the duty of enforcing contracts and thus reduced some of the risks of impersonal business transactions. Certitude—to some degree —about how the law stood brought with it some assurance that the bargain struck here and now would be valid there and later.

A society of plungers, prone to borrowing, was particularly solicitous about the rights of contract. Many loans used for speculative ends were bound to go wrong; and the lender all too often presented his demand for payment only to learn there was nothing to collect. There was no profit to squeezing blood from a stone, from forcing the debtor to sit out his days in jail. But the breach of the agreement was unjust to the lender; and without faith in reimbursement, the credit upon which expansion depended would dry up.

All the maxims Americans cherished warned against the perils of debt. The Bible, Poor Richard and McGuffey drilled into their readers a positive horror of the usurer and the wastrel, archetypes of the participants in a transaction considered somehow illicit. The prudent individual, like the prudent government or the prudent organization, hastened to get rid of obligations, for whatever reasons incurred. The mortgage on the homestead, the national or state debt, were to be paid off as soon as possible.

Experience nevertheless seemed to confirm theories suggesting that there was economic utility to the horrid practice. Hamilton's report on credit had urged the United States to do as England did, to fund the national debt as a permanent arm of government which provided flexibility in its own fiscal operations and also in those of its citizens. People with excess cash could then buy interest-bearing bonds, secure in the knowledge that they could always sell when necessary. Their money would thus be safe, available and at work. Although the older belief persisted that solvency meant debtlessness, the governments, state and federal, occasionally assumed obligations, particularly as an alternative to increased taxation.

Borrowing by individuals also seemed prudent sometimes, and the practice became usual in many commercial transactions. During the post-Revolutionary decades in New York City, for instance, leather dealers customarily made sales without receiving cash; they kept an account in a book for each purchaser and got a single settlement once a year. Along came Gideon Lee, a Massachusetts Yankee close on to thirty in 1807, who had not yet done well anywhere but would someday be mayor of the city. At the moment his problem was to sell at prices lower than those of established firms because, lacking connections, it was only thus that he could break into the business. Lee decided to cut his charges to purchasers who paid cash, hoping thus to eliminate the cost of all that capital tied up in the account book. This was careful management. But Lee also offered the cheaper rate to those who gave him short-term notes, which he then assigned to his bank at a small discount. He came out ahead because the ability to expand his operations more than compensated for the reduced price and for the discount; his customers gained from lower costs; and the bank earned interest on its loans. Fine! But all the participants in these deals thereupon became enmeshed in credit relationships.

Through hundreds of specific transactions of the same sort, American banks learned that making loans in this fashion was as profitable as issuing currency, which they still regarded as their primary function. By frequent and regular renewals they converted short-term into long-term credit and, in effect, added to the capital available to enterprise. Merchants and farmers bursting to expand formed a pool of ever-willing, interest-paying borrowers. In time too, corporations of various types also went into debt, not only through the issue of bonds but also through the discount of commercial paper. They, like individuals and the state, borrowed without qualms when opportunity was abundant and their own capital scarce.

When expansion slackened and panic struck, credit showed its darker side in foreclosures and in the swift loss of invested savings. The sanctity of the contract, which had formerly put loans within reach, now exacted its toll as creditors called on the courts and the sheriff to collect their due. The law was the law, just as a deal was a deal; and any breakdown in confidence would cut off the supply of further funds upon which future expansion depended. (The few Southern states which repudiated their debts in the 1830s learned the costs when they were thereafter starved for capital.)

The enactment of an equitable bankruptcy law created an orderly procedure for resolving disputes involving insolvency. The courts then stepped in to assure a fair division of assets among creditors, while permitting the debtor—released from past obligations—to make a fresh start. Bankruptcy was a regular, calculable process in which the state, as impartial intermediary, assured both borrowers and lenders of the limited risks of extending or accepting credit against the pledges of the future.

The law, which settled disputes and upheld contracts among individuals, also applied to corporations. These bodies after 1830 were no longer the instruments of state policy they had been fifty years earlier. The distinctive attributes that had then given them value had disappeared. Occasionally promoters still troubled to secure charters by special acts of the legislatures, but more usually general statutes allowed any applicants to incorporate through a simple step of registration.

Nevertheless, corporations not only survived but increased rapidly in number. That they had shed their privileges mattered little; the development of American law endowed them with new characteristics which turned them into convenient business devices.

As the corporation ceased to be a body politic or state agency, it became an artificial person brought into being by legislation but, once in existence, endowed like natural persons with private rights. The power of the government was scarcely greater over it than over individuals. True, the state created it; but, the judges held, incorporation was a contract, no more subject to abrogation or unilateral amendment than any other. Furthermore, the stockholder was responsible only to the extent of his investment. He might lose the price paid for his shares through mismanagement or ill fortune; but that was the limit of his liability for the debts of the corporation. Numerous ventures in manufacturing, transportation and finance would attract large amounts of capital by the assurance to investors of limits to the risk of loss and of security against capricious interference from the state.

On the other hand, the charter was a contract, no longer a privilege, and, in any case, it carried no guarantee against damage by changes in the future. The builders of a bridge or a pike laid out the costs of construction in the expectation that they would profit from the collection of tolls. The state could not deprive them of that right; but neither could it guarantee their profits, in the event that new developments diverted traffic elsewhere. The bridge had displaced the ferry and would, in turn, be replaced by still-newer means of transportation. The government might, in its wisdom, someday even decide to build alternative free bridges and roads for the greater convenience of travelers. Tough luck though for the ventures which depended upon tolls; their interests were secondary. So ruled the Supreme Court in the Charles River Case.

The law protected existing rights but it did not allow any vested interests to impede the development of the economy. Individuals often suffered as a result: the innkeeper who had a good thing on an old highway, until a new one was built; the carters and coachmen who enviously watched the barges haul goods and passengers along the canal; merchants stranded in Newport or Alexandria, while Providence and Baltimore grew. At any given moment, improvements—

newer means of transportation and of doing business—constantly threatened those unwary enough to relax in the belief in their own entrenched positions.

No one could sit still. It was necessary to keep up, look ahead, as Cornelius Vanderbilt did. He could have maneuvered through politics for a favorable place in the trade around New York harbor, or he could have sought a monopoly of some part of it, or he could just have tried to hold on to his schooners, which did well enough for a young man whose father had, after all, been only a poor boatman in Staten Island. But in 1818, Vanderbilt smelled steam in the wind, sold his sailing ships and went to work for the Raritan River Ferry. It took him ten years to amass the capital, then his steamers captured the lion's share of traffic on the Hudson and on Long Island Sound. Go-ahead promoters did not wait for licenses or guarantees; they set up stagecoach and express wagon lines, took the steamship into the inland rivers and lakes and worked out ingenious combinations of road and water routes to reach the farthest parts of the country.

The pay-off was to the shrewd entrepreneur. Moses Brown and a group of canny Providence enterprisers set about to circumvent British restrictions on the export of machinery and the emigration of skilled artisans. They contracted with Samuel Slater for a carding machine similar to those used in England, hoping to get ahead of rivals by the new labor-saving device.

Many decisions were faulty, based as they were on guesswork, unsubstantiated hopes and greed. But since the investments were personal rather than political, the cost of each mistake fell upon the individuals who made it rather than upon the whole society. The failures fell by the wayside, forgotten. The successes shoved ahead, remembered and rewarded.

A society which stressed development, valued change and was averse to all static forms refused to be fenced in by plans already out of date before they were realized. The state could not control either the pace or the direction of expansion; it could only regulate and police the multifarious activities of people who now sought from it not privilege but an equal-handed application of the rules of the game.

Some literate Americans read the works of Adam Smith and David Ricardo with respect, particularly when the economic theorists provided subtle support for what the citizens were in any case doing in practice. But the state, in the New World, did not wither away nor did laissez-faire doctrine win many converts. The old restrictive mercantilist measures, ineffective, were discarded; to that extent enterprise was uninhibited. But Americans continued to call upon government to act for numerous desirable ends—to promote the health, the temperance and the education of the people and otherwise to improve or reform each other. The public welfare, advanced by the liberating effects of expansion, justified measures through which the state contributed significantly, if indirectly, to nineteenth-century industrial growth.

5

Industrial Experiments

Steam slowly made a difference. For a century almost, men knew what women had long before observed—that heat applied to an enclosed body of water generated energy, in the kitchen to lift the lids off kettles, in the mines to drive the pumps which emptied the sumps. That this wonder of nature could also power a ship was certainly clear after 1807. Yet it was almost forty years more before the development of transportation made steam widely available to industry. Then the swift seizure of opportunity transformed the economy.

In 1870, manufactured products had become an important component of American wealth. Yet in 1812, the promoters who took the first steps toward the modern factory did not foresee where their road would lead. Well into the 1830s, they operated cheerfully and profitably under the mistaken assumptions that their society would not change significantly, that they themselves would do business as merchants much as before, and that the great value derived from their investments was to increase the commodities available for their trade. They certainly did not desire—they could hardly conceive—the actual outcome of 1870. Their efforts brought into being large-scale enterprises, conducted in great plants which harnessed complex machines to power. The new industry depended upon heavy investments of capital and required the recruitment and employment of great armies of wage labor. The pressure of these changes transformed the whole country.

In 1812, the early industrial experiments in the United States were fizzling out. Americans still depended on Europe for many manufactured goods and would continue to do so for a half-century more. Self-sufficiency remained an elusive goal despite the prevalent belief that communities which most completely supplied their own wants were in a state of highest political perfection. Furthermore, nothing since the Revolution had shaken the assumption that the household would remain the basic productive unit. Corporations and societies moved by patriotism, by Hamiltonian nationalism or by the opportunities of the embargo had organized, had collected money and had tried to increase output, but had envisioned few substantial changes in the modes of production. The collapse of more ambitious experiments, such as that of the S.U.M., had a sobering impact. Merchants, willing to invest in manufacturing, concluded that, given the cheapness of household labor, improvements in the existing structure of domestic industry would most effectively increase the volume of the goods they handled. The number of spindles which supplied yarn to home weavers increased; most entrepreneurs believed that more radical innovations had to await favorable circumstances, for artificial stimuli could not hasten the time, in any country, when manufactures would spring naturally out of necessity.

The more venturesome promoters who continued to experiment with the possibilities of making salable articles in factories still chose sites in the countryside. The insistence upon a rural location was the product partly of habit and partly of the dependence upon water power. But fear of the effects strengthened the wish to keep manufacturing out of the cities. Americans, while eager for the wealth industrial growth would bring, dreaded the consequences it had had in the Old World. England was a standing reproach, its Manchesters and Birminghams cast under the permanent pall of that smoky nuisance, the steam engine. Life in their slums was altogether incompatible with citizenship in a free republic; the replication of those conditions in the United States would be intolerable.

An undercurrent of distrust tinged the efforts to recruit factory workers. Entrepreneurs assumed that people who had fallen so low as to accept this employment rather than move to the free lands of the West had something inherently wrong with them: they would be intemperate, feckless and disorderly. Swayed by visions of agrarian virtue and fearful of the European pattern of assembling hordes of impoverished wage-laborers in the towns, Americans preferred to establish factories in the countryside. The S.U.M. had thus planned to provide all its employees with adequate housing in a newly settled tract away from the big cities—a decent environment readily subject to policing.

The countryside, furthermore, had the practical advantage of distance from the artisans, who opposed any tendency threatening their command of their own markets. American mechanics, aware that industrialization in England had depressed the status of craftsmen, were determined not to suffer a similar loss. The newfangled mills, able to offer lower prices to customers, able to pay more for raw materials and in a position to lure away skilled journeymen with higher wages, were a standing menace. In the cities the artisans could retaliate, through their strength in municipal government and, as British examples showed, through their power in mobs to lay waste expensive machines. Plants situated miles away from existing centers of population were relatively secure against such pressures.

In the early nineteenth century, apart from a few eleemosynary efforts to employ the idle fingers of women and children, Americans regarded industry as a rural activity. Their dislike of manufacturing in an urban context helped shape the form of the factory when it did in time appear in the United States.

Merchants retained a consistent interest in manufactures, and their concern steadily deepened after the War of 1812. The romantic voyages of old to distant corners of the globe shrank in importance; and the glamorous clipper ships designed in the vain hope of holding the Asian trade were not long profitable. Moreover, steam and the more efficient organization of traffic by sail forced ocean freight rates down, and before the Civil War the American merchant marine had already begun its long decline. Traders discovered that it paid to let vessels of other registries carry their goods, while they themselves acted as middlemen, pure and simple, in the direct exchange with Europe. Gone were the days of the ingenious triangular transactions worked out from port to port by the enterprising supercargo acting on behalf of the merchant shipowner. In 1860, more than 70 per cent of the exports from the United States, and more than 60 per cent of the imports to it, simply shuttled across the Atlantic. The vessels of a few large lines, operating on regular schedules, carried most of that traffic between a few great ports—New Orleans, Baltimore, Philadelphia, Boston and, above all, New York in the west, Bremerhaven, Le Havre and, above all, Liverpool in the east.

The merchants who sent cotton, tobacco, flour, wheat and meat eastward and received in return textiles, pottery and iron consistently sought to strengthen the internal economy which made these exchanges possible. They supported efforts to improve transportation and they helped create an infrastructure to ease commercial operations. Trade became more specialized. A network of jobbers, wholesalers, retailers and peddlers took shape to distribute the goods merchants imported, while the same, or other, intermediaries assembled the commodities for export. Long-term credit facilities reduced the need for cash; and insurance, freight and financial services of increasing effectiveness speeded and safeguarded the exchanges.

Merchants, especially those with surplus capital, itched to exploit the opportunities created by a growing market for manufactures. The textiles brought over from Britain yielded a profit; but the gain would be greater still were they produced locally. The channels of distribution were at hand, for domestic goods as for the imports. It was only necessary to make the most of a market already in existence.

The potential investors were merchants, moved by the trader's calculation even after they were deep in manufacturing. The evolving business corporation offered them an instrument through which to put money into industry without involving themselves directly in management and without interrupting their primary pursuits. The early factories reflected their thinking. Almy and Brown accepted stockings in payment for yarn, then shipped the stockings to Philadelphia in exchange for starch, cotton, dyes and flour, which they in turn swapped elsewhere. The Troy Company sold its yarn for fish, which it sent south for cotton. Often, too, payment to employees was in kind. The mills, for a time, were thus adjuncts of commercial operations.

In 1812, an experiment had solved the problem of matching the English methods in efficiency. Francis Lowell and a group of Boston merchants built a factory which brought together under a single roof all the stages of cotton manufacture, from the spinning of the thread to production of the finished cloth. They located the plant well outside the city in Waltham, where the falls of the Charles River supplied them with water power. Lowell, fresh from a tour of British mills, understood the requirements—unification of the process of production to include weaving as well as spinning, adequate power to operate the machines, a sufficient supply of capital and a dependable labor force drawn from the countryside and housed in facilities provided by the corporations. The outbreak of war, which interrupted the flow of imported cloth, assured the factory's immediate success. But war or no war, the experience was promising enough to persuade the promoters, within the decade, to undertake a still more extensive manufacturing project, one which they expected would be able to stand up against any foreign competition.

The Bostonians responsible for the venture at Waltham repeated the experiment on a larger scale when peace returned. The capital amassed in privateering and trade again turned their thoughts to manufacturing, and renewed competition with Britain demanded a bold response. There were more than enough machines at Waltham; but power was lacking to turn them all. A scheme set in motion in 1821 created a new manufacturing community in the rolling countryside of northern Massachusetts. The key was a corporation, The Proprietors of the Locks and Canals on the Merrimack River, which developed and controlled the flow of the stream. The corporation allocated water power to potential users who built and operated the factories, around which a town appeared, named Lowell, after the most prominent investor.

The most important Lowell plants manufactured cotton goods. The shareholders were merchants who had handled English cloth for years, knew the channels of distribution in the United States, and knew also that the growing population filling out the West was raising demand for the product, while the spread of cotton cultivation in the South was lowering the costs of raw materials. The merchants were aware, too, that in this branch of production they faced no competition from entrenched local artisans. The conditions were propitious; and the investors put in enough capital to build mills large by the standard of the times, to equip them with modern machines and to harness adequate sources of power. In 1839, eight corporations in town, each capitalized at between $500,000 and $2,000,000, operated twenty-four mills with 158,784 spindles and 4,894 looms. Since shares generally bore a par value of $1,000, the participants in the corporations were few in number—mostly known to one another, linked by family or business ties, and actively engaged in other mercantile pursuits. They left the day-to-day conduct of the factories in the hands of superintendents, while selling agents in Boston conducted the business affairs.

Girls from the farms of northern New England ran the machines. Plenty of young women were willing to spend a few years at this work before going on to marriage or to teaching or to some other occupation. Since at first they thought of themselves as transients, out on their own, away from their isolated farms, and earning cold cash as well, they eagerly accepted the wages offered. If something remained above costs of living, so much the better; it could help pay off the family mortgage or send a brother to college. Pleasant conditions of life in communal boardinghouses under quasi-parental supervision kept them content and left them time to publish a little magazine of their own. The entrepreneurs gained from a docile, flexible and cheap labor supply. In flush times the girls themselves recruited relatives and friends from their native villages; in hard times, the girls had a place to go back to. The system thus, for a while, avoided the slum-dwelling proletariat of the English type. Lowell was not amusing, a French observer noted, but it was clean, decent and peaceful. It thrived; and in imitation, other merchant groups formed the Cocheco Company of Dover, New Hampshire, the York Company of Saco, Maine, and the Amoskeag Company of Manchester, New Hampshire. In 1850, some 50,000 young women worked at the machines in such places.

Cotton mills south of Boston, shaped by their eighteenth-century origins, took a somewhat different form. In the vicinity of Providence, Slater, Brown and others continued to improve their machinery and expand their operations. As earlier, they confined themselves to spinning and sent their products out for weaving. In time, some firms employed hand weavers inside the factory. But not until 1828, after Lowell had shown the way, did a Rhode Islander bring in the power loom. Meanwhile, competition increased as various outsiders entered the business and as former employees and partners split away to set up enterprises of their own. In the decades after 1815, new mills dotted the countryside of New England and the middle states, with notable concentrations in Fall River and Utica. These too were rural, located at the water power upon which they depended. But from the start, they drew upon a more traditional labor supply. As on the farm, the family was the unit of employment; the household as a whole went to work, only within the factory rather than in its own home—father, mother and children serving together in return for a flat lump sum, with sometimes a dwelling supplied as part of the payment.

The increase in the number of plants and their gains in efficiency steadily raised the output of cotton goods. Establishments became so numerous that none could be content with a local market; and the larger the enterprise, the more aggressively it had to seek customers throughout the nation and abroad.

In the interest of economy, the Waltham mill had refrained from weaving the usual stripes and plaids and instead had concentrated on a plain, coarse white sheeting; and its imitators did the same. High-quality cloth made abroad continued to find buyers in the United

States; but the cheaper textiles in which the domestic mills specialized not only commanded the market within the country but also found places in export cargoes. The overseas connections of the merchant shareholders were helpful, at first in South America and Mexico, later in China and the Levant. In 1840, more than 7 per cent of the total output went abroad, and the potential for further growth attracted still newer entrepreneurs and investors. A rising population throughout the world was ready to purchase the products of Yankee mills. The demand would thrust the American factory beyond the first rustic forms shaped by conventional mercantile and agrarian visions.

Tinkering had long been a New World trait. Ignorance of accepted procedures, haste, or lack of the customary materials forced craftsmen to rely upon common sense rather than habit or practice. The frequent need to improvise and perennial shortages of skilled labor drove on scores of mechanics in the quest for ingenious devices to compensate for the backward productive system. The number of inventions, measured by applications at the patent office, increased steadily. An incalculable loss of labor and money was the result of most experiments in the search for new devices. But the gains from the few successful deviations from the beaten path far outweighed the costs of the many failures. All these efforts at innovation dealt with specific problems; the sum of them would transform American industry.

Everywhere in the United States, on the frontier as in the East, in the South as in the North, the smiths supplied their neighbors with the tools and implements necessary for the farm, shop and home. Each produced for a local market in a quantity limited by what he could turn out by hand, alone or with the aid of a helper. In each vicinity, plenty of customers were ready to buy axes, nails and muskets, and aggressive merchants could find more purchasers at a distance. But the restraints of supply were more irksome than those of demand. The mechanic simply could not increase his output significantly. The requirements of the growing western population for household and agricultural implements were met not by established Easterners but by smiths who moved out to the spot.

Eli Whitney faced the problem of increasing output in 1798 when he took on a contract to manufacture 10,000 stands of guns— an enormous undertaking, given the scarcity of competent artisans. The long tradition of metal-working in the Connecticut valleys running south to Long Island Sound was no help to him, for it depended upon the individual craftsman. He therefore gambled. He organized his factory near New Haven after a quite novel fashion. He did not assign each employee to the task of producing a whole gun. As he regarded the finished product, he perceived that it was divided into a score of component parts, each replaceable by others precisely like it. Each could therefore be produced by a laborer who specialized in it and who could learn the task quickly and do it well through repetition. The separate parts, then assembled, formed the whole weapon.

The method was not altogether novel; there were antecedents in France; and Adam Smith had certainly understood the principle. Yet production through the technique of replaceable parts became identified with the United States, where it helped compensate for the perennial shortage of skilled labor. It spread steadily. The Colt works in Hartford much later adopted the same organization—and more successfully than Whitney had. The economies of stamping out the parts for later assembly enabled Chauncey Jerome and others to produce cheap clocks for thousands of time-conscious citizens, although Americans produced few fine watches. Other entrepreneurs improvised similar techniques to increase output when they decided to concentrate upon a single, cheap line for sales in quantity. The need for precision in processes in which each part had to be identical so as to be replaceable created a market for lathes and for other machine tools. Yet, though great industrial enterprises later grew out of these rude beginnings, down through the 1830s only the seeds were there.

The output of American manufactures rose at a gratifying rate, by perhaps 50 per cent in the 1820s, by 45 per cent in the 1830s and by 80 per cent in the 1840s. Growth came primarily in rural areas. In the cities, glasshouses, ropewalks, distilleries and the shops of furniture makers operated on a limited scale very much as they had in the eighteenth century. But outside the cities systematized household manufacture, as in the boot and shoe industry, and factory organization, as in textiles, largely accounted for the total increase in output. The opinion of a knowledgeable observer in 1829 remained valid for years thereafter. Industry, Zachariah Allen explained, operated in little hamlets, which sprang up in the bosom of the forest at the waterfall that turned the mill wheel, dispersed therefore from Indiana to the Atlantic, from Maine to North Carolina, instead of collected together in great urban places as in England. Manufacturing was still rural, its capacity for growth limited by the fact that existing supplies of labor and power could not expand indefinitely.

The men, women, children stood awkwardly at the machines, their places in the plant not yet precisely defined. Following the practices of agriculture, they signed up for the season or year but then often moved restlessly from job to job; high turnover rates kept managers on the edge of uncertainty, for the force on the shop floor was not long the same. That was an advantage in depression; in 1837, when most of the Lowell mills closed, the unemployed girls seemed to rejoice and regarded return to the farm as a time of recreation. But in expansive times, a labor force with durable rural connections was inconvenient, for it was not totally dependent upon factory earnings. Wage payments were part of every agreement. But cash rarely changed hands, for to hold its workers in the isolated villages in the North or the South, where no other services were available, the firm had to provide some combination of housing, of produce and of credit at the company store.

Employers in the first third of the nineteenth century were unable to break their traditional communal relationship to the employee, incapable, that is, of treating him in the abstract as a profit-producing integer without consideration of his human quality. Even the advanced metal-working plants depended upon inside contracting, a modified artisan system in which a master craftsman, paid by the piece for what he produced, in turn hired on his own account less-skilled hands to work for him within the factory. The paternalism of the Lowell firms, whatever its numerous drawbacks, involved a personal link through the community between the girls and those who hired them. South of Boston, too, the scale of the mills was still intimate enough, the habits of the past still intact enough, so that the corporation could not be altogether soulless or the wage-earning families simply proletarians. The factory owners did not wish the savage conditions of European industrialization repeated in the New World. Nor were the hands totally helpless, retaining as they did some freedom to choose among jobs, freedom, too, to move elsewhere if terms were unsatisfactory. The inhibiting sense of the requirements of decent treatment complicated and restrained the entrepreneurial urge to expand.

Contrary to early expectations, there were limits also to the power available to keep the wheels of industry turning. In the 1830s, the best sites in New England and the middle states were staked out; and ingenious as was the use made of canals, intricate as were the systems of pulleys and belts, the weary streams were doing just about all they could. Without some breakthrough to increase the supply of power and of labor, manufacturing might spread to still more hamlets as the nation expanded, but growth would come to a halt.

In the 1830s, a revolution in the nation's transportation revealed the full dimensions of the problem.

The promoters of transportation schemes in 1830 still focused on the familiar methods and objects—harbor and navigation improvements and canals to reach into the back country, as the Erie had. Water was dominant and, indeed, continued to carry a heavy volume of freight as steamships of increased capacity moved into the inland rivers and lakes.

Carriage by land was distinctly less favored. The builders of the Bunker Hill monument near Boston had increased the efficiency of the horse-drawn carts which carried their granite from Quincy by setting the wheels on rails. But that seemed a special device to meet a specific need.

News of the success of George Stephenson's experiments in England altered all calculations. At once interest in the United States shifted to railroads. Baltimore, the fastest-growing city in the country, which had planned a canal to the Ohio, in 1827 turned its attention to a horse-powered railroad and in 1831 finally fixed on steam. Other coastal cities quickly decided to seek the same way to the West; and soon many inland towns also sought iron links to their markets.

For four decades, construction continued, the pace rising in flush times, slackening in depressions. Americans pitched into railroad building as feverishly as they had into other forms of speculation.

The schemers and investors hoped to profit, and some did. But however rational they considered their projections, they invariably gambled on the future. An expanding economy did not confine improvements in transporation to present felt needs, but always reached ahead to anticipations of what was yet to come. There were doubters: Had God wished men to move at such dangerous speeds, He would have manifested some earlier sign of it; and it was unhealthy to cover in two hours the distance naturally traversed in two days. But such warnings fell upon ears deafened by the new mode of locomotion. Steam was itself dramatic, demonic and fascinating. Americans—always in motion—had, like people everywhere, connected movement on land with animal force, with the plodding push and pull of beasts and men. Now the great wheels, turning through some hidden agency, the great machines gliding with dizzy speed through space, evoked visions of enormous, pent-up, secret power worthy of the continent to be conquered. Romantic impulses moved promoters and investors as much as any rational calculation of profit or advantage. The daring and the dreaming that once had shipped Yankee ice to Calcutta now thrust rails through the western forests. A wild hope took hold of sober politicians and business leaders that the new device would somehow overcome all the problems that had earlier plagued canal and turnpike builders and would somehow span all the country's distances.

The artisans still hung back. Rarely did they see the prospect for gain in the bustle and hustle generated by speculation; all too often, they understood, change would weaken their own local position. The flood of paper, the rising prices, the piled-up debt and the increased taxes—inevitable side effects of the new developments—frightened people who valued stability above all else.

Farmers, by contrast, expected the improvements to bring them closer to markets, to lower transportation costs and therefore to raise their incomes. They might hassle with the corporations over compensation for lands taken for the right of way. They might complain about charges. But they nevertheless took a favorable view of the railroads that would ultimately carry their freight.

Above all, merchants had a stake in the spread of the rails. As investors they hoped to draw dividends on the stocks they purchased and, in addition, anticipated indirect gains from the effects on their own enterprises. Those already involved in manufacturing expected a fall in the price of raw materials and a rise in the price of the finished products once the lines reached the factories. Others believed that reductions in transportation costs stimulated trade by widening the sources of goods for export and the markets for imports. Intense rivalry among the seaports heightened the concern of their citizens; Boston, New York, Philadelphia and New Orleans, along with lesser competitors, all aspired to serve the rapidly settling interior. The city with the best connections would do the best business.

Citizens, informed by political rhetoric and newspaper puffery in the euphoric years down to 1837, now understood the inadequacy of the previous generation. Earlier plans had failed because they had been too timid. A go-ahead nation would not repeat the same errors. Allow any venture to proceed where it would. Entrepreneurs with the means to do so had the same right to lay out railroads as to open banks. The state could not fence them in with any unitary plan or require them to do more than conform to general regulatory laws.

The government did not take a directing role in the construction and development of the railroads. Although some states and municipalities supported favored ventures by subscribing capital, guaranteeing bonds or providing other forms of subsidy, the initiative, the control and the potential for profit and loss were private. By 1830, the techniques of incorporation were sufficiently well defined to apply without question to the new mode of transportation. The states issued charters to private promoters, who laid out the routes they imagined would be most advantageous. The emerging network thus took a form dictated by the self-interest of the groups with access to political power.

In the grab for advantage, the promoters in each town aimed primarily to extend its hinterland, laying out lines like spokes from a hub, just as the turnpike builders earlier had. The prevailing aim was to strengthen and extend ties with the countryside rather than to link one big city with another. The results appeared on the map as numerous jagged, discontinuous stabs out of the seaports and other trading centers, reaching away into space.

The panic of 1837 had a momentary sobering effect; many a grandiose venture then disappeared into the thin air whence it had been conjured. But the pause was soon over and the builders at it again. In 1850, about 9,000 miles were in operation in the United States, more than in all of Europe. Nor did either depression in 1857 or Civil War in 1861 long retard the pace of construction. In 1870, almost 60,000 miles of rail served the country. A year earlier, the Central Pacific had met the Union Pacific in Utah; the bands of steel reached from ocean to ocean, symbols of the conquest of continental distance.

As important as the sheer increase in mileage was the gradual evolution of a safe, speedy and efficient transportation system. Everything had to be devised afresh; the techniques of the stagecoach simply did not apply, and the Old World was no more advanced than the New when it came to railroad management. No organized body of knowledge instructed the promoters nor was there a trained corps of engineers to help. Improvisation was the rule and trial and error the costly method, with many steps sideways and some back, for each step forward.

The rickety wooden coaches, lengthened and entered through vestibules at the ends rather than from the sides, held increasing numbers in the seats arranged along an aisle instead of facing each other. Set upon trucks capable of maneuvering around curves, these and the wagons built to carry freight moved along roadbeds improved by experience and in time across iron bridges rather than timber trestles. More powerful locomotives, guided by intricate signal and braking systems, drew the heavier loads up the steep mountain grades at gathering speeds. Schedules took form, capable of withstanding inclement weather and unexpected delay. The passengers paid for tickets, the shippers for bills of lading, and a small army of agents, clerks and superintendents directed a large army of trainmen and maintenance workers.

As these innovations hardened into practice, the multitude of little lines jutting out of each city acquired a more coherent order.

Vanderbilt early saw the opportunity for consolidation. His boats had done a thriving business, but in the 1850s he pulled out of a brief venture into transatlantic shipping when he discovered how meager the profits were. For a while he did well on a sea route from New York to California with a land crossing at Nicaragua. But then he grasped the future in railroads, not in building new lines but in buying up and combining early, poorly built ones on the verge of bankruptcy. The New York Central, formed in 1853 by a merger of ten little roads between Albany and Buffalo, became the main piece of an imperial route from New York City to Chicago.

In the competitive world of railroading, integration had great advantage, not only in easing the carriage of goods and persons over long distance, but also in establishing control over the flow of traffic and over the rates charged. Emphasis therefore shifted to the development of through routes, from New York to Boston and Philadelphia, from Philadelphia, Baltimore and New Orleans to Chicago, and from Chicago and St. Louis to San Francisco. Trunk lines linking the chief centers of population replaced the spokes reaching out from each of them. In 1870, the railroad system was no longer local, but regional—even national—in character.

The development of the system called for vast human and financial resources. Where did the people come from—and the money?

Recruitment of the builders, administrators and operating personnel was haphazard. Thomas Canfield left a Vermont farm to become a country storekeeper, moved on to wholesale business in Burlington, Vermont, invested in railroads out of that town and then brought together a syndicate to build the Northern Pacific. Ross Winans was a trader from New Jersey who came down to sell horses to the Baltimore and Ohio. He stayed on when the projected line switched to steam, became an engineer and designed its rolling stock. Andrew Carnegie, bobbin boy in a textile mill, then telegraph messenger, was still a youth when the superintendent of the Pennsylvania Railroad made him a section manager. In the shifting American population, numerous men with training of sorts as artisans, clerks, salesmen, eagerly grasped the chance to pull ahead on the rails. Connections established by family or religious affiliation, a pleasing appearance, the willingness to work, or a glib line of talk gave some their start. Many never went very far, remained ticket takers, brakemen or freight-handlers for years on end. Others moved up—or out. No one had experience to begin with; everyone learned by doing and the system was resilient enough to suffer the shocks of errors, to make the most of innovations. Only after the Civil War did a more stable bureaucracy take form.

The recruitment of capital was complex. At the beginning, most projects sought broad community support. But local and state governments, shackled to narrow tax and borrowing bases and always strapped for cash, generally responded to calls for aid only through guarantees of securities or petty grants of privileges. Nor did the federal land grants in the 1860s provide substantial assistance in the actual process of construction.

Most of the money came from private investors; and the chief value of state aid lay in the appearance of assurance it afforded. From the very start, when Thomas H. Perkins bought shares of the Granite Railway Company in 1826, merchants were in it both for future dividends and to develop trade. From the very start also, hopeful small fry put in their savings, pressed to do so by appeals to local pride and avarice; and institutions and banks likewise responded.

Heavy construction costs, and operating expenses that mounted up before any return came in, sooner or later exhausted the supply of risk capital. Promoters then turned to borrowing. By 1855, the bonded debt of American railroads stood at $300 million and the sum outstanding continued to rise, creating a burden of interest payments that thereafter was a first charge against revenue.

Ultimately, a sizable and indispensable stake came from overseas. English commission merchants, of whom the best-known was the firm of Baring Brothers, usually allowed Americans to make purchases on credit of fifteen months, time enough to allow the goods to move into the interior and the payment to pass back to London or Liverpool. The sum of such short-term debts outstanding rose through the 1830s, leveled off in the next decade, but then climbed to a total of $155 million in 1857. It was an easy transition to acceptance of long-term bonds to finance the sale of rails and engines to companies in the United States, for the British merchant-bankers then profited both from the commissions and from the interest. Much of the structure, financial as well as physical, was therefore speculative, subject to repeated strain from alternations in the cycle of boom and panic as well as from the wastefulness of spasmodic construction without any unifying plan. Put together in haste out of ill-assorted pieces, the rails nevertheless held and the trains ran. A day's journey from New York City in 1820, with luck, might take men and goods as far as Philadelphia or New London; in 1870, to beyond Bangor, Maine; Cleveland, Ohio; Pittsburgh, Pennsylvania; or Richmond, Virginia.

The new pattern of transportation, unfolding gradually in the four decades after 1830, subtly affected the character of American industry. By an abstract, twentieth-century hindsight calculation of social costs and benefits, the gains resulting from construction of the railroads were slight. Alternative methods might have achieved equivalent results. Some canals remained in use; they might have developed further and new ones might have been built had investors' sights not shifted elsewhere. So too, later commentators might judge, also in the abstract, that the nation invested too much in transportation of every kind, that a more leisurely, more localized, expansion like that of Europe might have been better (in what terms?). A nice game, but irrelevant! Nineteenth-century Americans could not conceive of expansion at a leisurely pace and framed their visions in continental not county boundaries.

Calculations between 1830 and 1870 were not abstract. Men of flesh and blood, not computerized investors, made the decisions; and romantic visions as much as prudent reckonings determined the outcome. So, as between the railroad and the canal, there was no contest. So, too, the persistent preference for east-west routes was not entirely rational. Imaginations quivered to the bold westward thrust across space; despite the profits earned by the occasional north-south line, such as the Illionis Central, the idea of the transcontinental retained a fascination inexpressible in dollars and cents.

The parallel lines reaching away into the distance bore a symbolic as well as an immediate practical significance. The costs of moving goods sank when the mills received their bales of cotton and sent forth their bolts of cloth in wagons pulled by steam rather than by horses. But in addition, the spectacular change opened the minds of the mill managers to the possibilities of what still other changes might achieve. Steadily the market expanded, no longer limited to a city, soon not even to a large district, but increasingly national in character. Express and fast freight companies took the responsibility for effecting transfers, and word sped across the nation by the dependable postal and telegraph services the railroads made possible. New opportunities for specialization and for economies of scale tempted producers who served the expanding populations of expanding territories. The first phase of industrialization had already created an infrastructure of selling, marketing and financing arrangement. The drummers were on the road, the clerks were at their counters, the bankers and brokers, ledgers open, were ready for business and bold displays of advertising in the press were beckoning buyers to sellers.

Manufacturers subject to the pressures from the expanding market created by changes in communication could no longer depend upon the water wheels and the rustic hands of the countryside. Their aversion to the British factory towns vanished. They turned to steam for power and to the proletariat for labor. Come what may.

The alternative to water was steam; and the improvements in transportation, which cheapened the cost and increased the supply of coal, freed new plants from dependence upon the seasonal flow of already-burdened streams. Factories powered by steam did not have to be in the countryside where the falls were. They could function as well or better in the city, where the railroads and the docks gave easy access to supplies and to customers.

In the cities, too, an immigrant labor force waited, ready in almost limitless numbers to enter the service of the factory. The movement of Europeans to the United States had resumed after the restoration of peace in 1815 and for three decades had grown steadily in volume. Then it had consisted preponderantly of English, Irish and German peasants and artisans with resources enough to enable them to settle either on farms of their own or in growing towns where their skills found employment. But in those years there were already some immigrants who landed with neither skill nor capital, with only the capacity to labor. Their adjustment was therefore more difficult than that of their more fortunate brethren. They lived from hand-to-mouth by casual work in the seaports, where the ships left them. The women went out to domestic service or took in laundry or sewing. The men toiled with the pick and shovel of construction gangs either on the streets and buildings of the growing cities or on the canals and railroads of the countryside.

The great famine of 1846 sweeping through Ireland and Germany raised the number of immigrants for whom starvation was the alternative to departure. Steadily the entries increased, reaching a peak of 427,000 in 1854. To the total population of the United States, which had risen from 9,600,000 in 1820 to 31,400,000 in 1860, immigration contributed almost 4,000,000 persons. Wherever along the routes of travel the wanderers rested, they formed a pool of helpless, utterly dependent workers, willing to labor at any rates, under any conditions. Due in good part to their arrival, American cities swelled in size. In 1820, only New York and Philadelphia held 100,000 inhabitants. In 1870, they were up to 942,000 and 674,000 respectively, and nine other places had gone above the 100,000 mark. Chicago, unknown to the census takers in 1820, in 1850 housed 29,000 people; in 1870, 298,000. A larger proportion of the total population was urban than ever before. Moreover, the percentage of persons employed in nonagricultural occupations leaped from 28.2 to 47 between 1820 and 1870. Americans ceased to be either agriculturists or self-employed.

The new immigrants challenged the innovative entrepreneur, just as the expanding market and the prospect of using the power of steam did. Labor, until 1830 relatively scarce in the New World, became relatively cheap—and usable as never before. The employer could hire individuals without responsibility for whole families and could discard the apparatus of lodging houses and social welfare. Labor was becoming a simple, faceless unit in the cost of production.

The availability of a seemingly unlimited fund of willing workers tempted people with money to invest. All the elements for growth were at hand: a spreading transportation system, power from steam and the coal to generate it, and scores of inventors with promises of new technology. Shareholders in earlier enterprises tended to plough their dividends back into new ones, merchants tended to shift capital from trade to industry, and land speculators who made out well tended to put their returns into factories, as did the men who profited by windfalls like the discovery of California gold and the exploitation of other mineral resources.

The mill towns mushroomed into cities. Lowell had 6,477 residents in 1830, 33,383 in 1850. The expansion of a single enterprise there measured the growth of these decades. The Middlesex Woolen Mills in 1830 employed 185 hands, twenty years later, 1,500. In that interval also it had shifted the source of its power from water to steam and had replaced wood with iron in its machines. The change involved not simply an increase in number of inhabitants but also a transformation in the quality of life. As Irish hands took the places of the ladies of the loom in Lowell, employers shed the obligation to worry about the literary tastes, the morals, or the housing conditions of their employees. The relationship narrowed to the exchange of wages for toil in the plant. The new city founded in Lawrence, Massachusetts, in 1850 clearly demonstrated the shift. Given over to the manufacture of wool, its factories, larger than those of Lowell, were equipped with elaborate iron machines powered by steam and tended by a working force consisting largely of men. The trend continued on through the second half of the nineteenth century.

The new scale of manufacturing after 1850 did not, however, alter the preponderant emphasis upon production of goods to satisfy the immediate wants of a society which lacked and desired many commonplace objects. The merchants who organized the first successful factories kept their eyes on the customers and invested first in products for which markets already existed. Cotton and woolen textiles were the most modern of American manufactures, that is, the most advanced in mechanization and in number of workers and capital invested per plant because they met a widely felt need. The yards of cheap cloth for sale on the shelves of the crossroads shop relieved housewives of the domestic drudgery of spinning and weaving as neither the local artisans nor imports from Britain did.

Manufacturing cities in time generated their own impetus toward still further industrialization. Mechanics and artisans clustered there, some to serve the mills, others to serve the burgeoning population. Little enterprises in Lowell fabricated bolts, screws, carriages, belts, boilers and files, their proprietors on the constant lookout for the chance to become big, their journeymen eager to strike out on their own. Elias Howe, Junior, a boy of sixteen, came to Lowell in 1835 to help build cotton machinery; he left after two years, carrying an idea with him which in 1846 bore fruit in the lock-stitch sewing machine. At about the same time, James C. Ayer, employed in an apothecary shop in the same town, invented a machine for the mass production of pills; in 1868, 150 men and women in his firm shipped almost 2 million healing bottles and boxes to every part of the world.

The effects rippled out. The sewing machine permitted entrepreneurs to use thousands of unskilled Irish immigrants, male and female, in new ready-made clothing industries in Boston, New York and Philadelphia. Ayer's innovation had more subtle consequences. His laboratory consumed hundreds of thousands of pounds of drugs, spirits and sugar, more than half a million square feet of packing boxes and cardboard, which in itself churned up activity in the city. In addition, to make the merits of his pills known and to sustain the volume of his sales, he distributed, free, millions of copies of an annual almanac printed on his own presses in English, French, Dutch, German, Norwegian, Spanish, Portuguese and Chinese. His continuing concern with publicity made him the largest stockholder of the New York *Tribune*.

Swift mechanization also transformed the process of making other consumer products. In the 1860s, the manufacture of shoes moved to the large urban centers as machines permitted the factories utilizing cheap, unskilled labor to replace the craftsmen of the domestic system. In Cincinnati and Chicago, efficient slaughtering and packing plants supplied the country with cheap beef and pork, lowering the price through the utilization of by-products—everything but the squeal of the pig, it was said. Flour-milling developed on a large scale in cities where economies of scale were possible. By 1870,

even manufacture of furniture had begun to move out of the craftsman's shop into the factory.

The outpouring of products put within the reach of the many,
possessions which had formerly been accessible only to a fortunate
few. In the past, only people of means bought the products of tailors
and seamstresses, of cabinetmakers and pastry cooks. With rare exceptions, men and women then consumed what their own families
produced—had made their own utensils, had raised and prepared
their own food, and had worn the garments stitched at home. In
1870, Americans adorned in store-bought coats and shoes and shirts
supped on store-bought bread and ham off store-bought tables.
Machines made the goods available; and industrialization shifted
habits of consumption away from the household to the market. Swell-
ing purchasing power sustained the demand: agriculture, always directed toward the salable staple rather than toward self-sufficiency,
put cash into the hands of an army of farmers, who joined thousands
of city clerks and mechanics and business and professional people as
buyers. The factory workers alone lacked the income to participate
fully in the bidding. But they were not pauperized natives, as in
Europe, who either never had the ability to pay for goods or lost it
in the move to the mill. The proletarians in the United States were
foreign-born and their lack of means did not seriously limit the expansion of the market among purchasers already in it.

Manufactures aimed not at immediate consumers, but at other
producers, were only in their infancy.

The railroads generated a demand for locomotives and coaches
as well as for rails. Factories needed equipment and the massive new
machines could not be knocked together by any ingenious mechanic
out of whatever timber was at hand. Only iron could sustain the power
of the steam that coursed through the new devices. At first in the
gears and cylinders, then in the frames, metal replaced wood, a change
which called for the services of numerous engine makers and ma-
chinists. The larger firms set up foundries and shops of their own, but
ambitious artisans of varied experience also seized the opportunity
for independent enterprise. Phineas Davis, once a clockmaker, Peter
Cooper, once a glue maker, and Erastus Corning, once a nail maker,
were among the craftsmen who turned their minds to machine-
making.

The factories and railroads created a rising market for fuel
and for metals. The iron industry was, in a sense, as old as the first
smithy in the colonies. Everywhere, hundreds of little rolling mills,

forges and furnaces strove to supply local customers with nails, locks, horseshoes, agricultural implements and shovels. Typically, in 1850, these were small enterprises employing from one to fifty hands; the largest that year used one hundred thirty.

Some unfinished iron in pigs or bars came from Europe; but 80 percent of the total consumed came from native sources, at first from the coastal bogs, later dug from mines, but in either case processed with charcoal drawn from the receding forests. The thinning timber supply limited the ability to satisfy the expanding demand and spurred a search for new methods. George W. Scranton, for instance, a Connecticut boy, in 1839 put the savings from his farm into an iron furnace in New Jersey. A year later, he was experienced enough to form the Lackawanna Iron and Coal Company to operate in Pennsylvania on a site where soon would rise the city that bears his name. The enterprise developed a technique for smelting iron with the abundant, nearby anthracite and grew steadily. People concerned with the fabrication of metals began to experiment in the haste to catch up with the more advanced Europeans. David Thomas, for instance, was imported from Wales in 1840 to try to use the abundant anthracite of the Lehigh Coal and Navigation Company to smelt pig iron; and many a village smith had caught the fever of experimentation. In 1870, in the United States as a whole, less than 25 percent of the output of iron still depended upon charcoal and upon proximity to the forests. By then, too, the techniques were in hand for still more startling developments later in the century. William Kelly, who had stumbled into the iron business in Kentucky, had hit upon the idea of somehow using a blast of air to convert iron into steel. His own efforts led to bankruptcy in 1857; but a decade later, others were beginning to use his patents successfully.

A half-century had taken the United States from one stage of industrialization to another—from the rural mills operating with water power and a provisional labor force to the urban factories manned by a proletariat and driven by steam. This transition revealed the persistent characteristics of American industrial experience. A high technology, receptive to innovation and invention, reflected lack of experience and the weakness of custom. Orientation toward the consumer passed products quickly on to their users. A cheap, fluid labor force replenished by immigration freed entrepreneurs from concern about manpower costs; and the fact that the factory hands were foreign-born rather than pauperized natives expanded the market for consumer goods. Finally, frequent blasts of windfall capital, available for investment, fired the impulse toward experiment, speculation and growth.

These characteristics explained why manufacturing located where it did. Necessity made New Englanders receptive to innovation. Generations of struggle to swap fortunes out of trade had thrust ingenuity upon them. That region, too, was close to the great consuming markets, and it was the unwitting destination of numerous immigrants, ready to labor. Here too, the precarious commercial position after 1815 forced merchants to take chances to preserve and increase their capital. Every sector of Yankee society had learned from *waste not, want not* that underconsumption was a means of saving and saving a means of investment; wastrels were damned in this world and in the hereafter. The habits of early life and the diffusion of knowledge through free schools, an observer noted, produced in the mechanics of New England a vivacity more prone to invent new plans and machines than to operate upon the old ones. Joseph Dixon died in 1869, only a few years after he hit upon his most profitable contrivance, a wood-planing device for shaping wood to form pencils. The patent granted in 1866 lay at the terminus of a circuitous route: he knew about graphite through his efforts in the 1850s to use it in making crucibles for the steel and pottery industries, and those in turn grew out of his efforts in the 1840s to devise an anti-friction bearing-metal, and that from still earlier experiments with stove polish and colored inks for photolithography, and those from inventions in the 1820s of a machine for cutting files and of a matrix for casting metal type.

The middle states shared some of the same characteristics and passed through some of the same experiences as New England. Desperation was less a factor there than toward the northeast, for agriculture and commerce both fared better. On the other hand, here the immigrant labor force ready to work was even more numerous than elsewhere. Traditions of craftsmanship and entrepreneurship stimulated men in the middle states also; in Hoboken, New Jersey, for instance, three generations of the Stevens family tried their hands at improvements in engines, plows, boats and rails. Furthermore, an army of transplanted Yankees such as Scranton and John Flack Winslow, the steel promoter, made themselves at home in the region, joining local types in the thrust toward industrialization.

Even the trans-Allegheny West by 1870 had felt the effects of the new modes of manufacturing. There also the Yankees exerted their leavening influence; and there also migration brought access to a willing labor force. Furthermore, in these western regions the closeness to the raw materials provided a cost advantage—distilleries and meat-packing plants drew upon the abundant supplies of corn and hogs raised in the vicinity. Later, the discovery of sources of coal and iron provided an incentive to new industries, which had originally taken root sheltered by the relative isolation of their markets.

Least receptive to the new economic trends was the South. Occasional factories appeared in Baltimore, Richmond and elsewhere. But the transforming effects of industrialization passed the region by. It had labor in abundance; it was close to many kinds of raw materials. But it suffered the handicap of a system of production that was not congenial to the requirements of manufacturing.

6

The Plantation and Its Consequences

*I*n the South imaginations veered away from industrialization toward a rival goal. Young men below the Mason-Dixon line dreamed not of the helms of China ships or of the ledgers' figured columns or of gears and cranks and driving shafts, but rather of the pastoral plantation's ample acres through which they rode gallantly mounted. As American as any, they too longed for success, which however they measured by standards other than those prevalent where manufacturing flourished. They turned their backs upon the grubby railroads and grim factories of the North and strove toward a different, gentler social order.

A generation of popular writers in the 1840s and 1850s most clearly expressed the aspirations of plantation culture. But the forces that would separate the South's experience from that of the North were evident long before. Back in the 1790s, Eli Whitney's cotton gin had simplified and cheapened the processing of short-staple upland cotton; steadily, the cultivation of the fiber spread, relieving the expanding factories of England and of the continent of Europe from dependence for raw materials on Asia, North Africa, and South America. Two decades of intermittent warfare had throttled the trade until 1815. But then, pent-up overseas demand for cotton evoked a rising flow of exports from the United States and provided a firm foundation for further expansion of the areas devoted to the crop, which became the mainstay of the Southern economy.

In the 1820s, however, there were still troubling questions about the kind of labor force which would raise the cotton. The doubts of the Revolutionary generation about the future of slavery and therefore about the future of the plantation were still unresolved. Jefferson was still alive and John C. Calhoun still a nationalist at the beginning of the decade; and the contradictions between the bondage inherited from the past and the republican rhetoric of liberty still troubled Americans in 1820. The United States had outlawed the slave trade in 1808, as soon as the Constitution permitted; and, although some Africans continued to be surreptitiously and illegally smuggled into the country, in 1818 the law declared the traffic a form of piracy, further to discourage it. Public condemnation of the practice reflected the widespread assumption that the system of bondage would in time disappear or at least cease to expand.

As late as 1828 Governor Brandon of Mississippi argued that slavery was "an evil at best," because it destroyed "that mutual dependence which would otherwise exist between the rich and the poor" and thus discouraged the settlement in his state of a free population. Like most Southerners at the time he hoped that the region would follow, even if slowly, the same general line of development as the North. Faith survived in a South peopled by yeomen, especially since immense additions of land through the acquisition of Louisiana and Florida guaranteed the availability of space for all. Cotton, by these expectations, would provide the cash crop of family farms, as wheat did in the North.

But the established labor system did not dissolve simply through the pressure of good intentions. In fact, the unfree population of the country had mounted from 750,000 in 1790 to 1,777,000 in 1820; and in rice- and sugar-growing areas the plantation was as strong as ever. Elsewhere, uneasiness about future relations between whites and blacks strengthened resistance to change; often discussion of emancipation wandered off into speculation about what the freedmen would do—how would they earn a living? would a race war follow?— and became entangled in chimerical hopes that the former slaves would vanish by emigrating to Africa or to the remote West. The conflict in 1820 over whether to admit Missouri as a free or a slave state and the discussion of abolition in the Virginia constitutional convention of 1831 showed that while Southerners were unwilling to contemplate the consequences of an immediate end to slavery, they still professed an attachment to the ideals of free labor.

After 1830, however, profound economic and social changes settled the issue by reversing the Revolutionary commitment to ultimate emancipation. In the three decades which followed, slavery did not disappear. Emancipation ceased to be even a distant objective; and the Southern commitment to its peculiar institution deepened. The number of bondsmen grew, without significant additions from abroad, from 1,770,000 in 1820 to 2,328,000 in 1830 and to 4,441,-000 in 1860. Meanwhile the geographical area of unfreedom expanded rather than contracted. Intellectual, social and economic forces fortified one another to create a system permanently grounded on unfree labor. Slavery, no longer regarded as a necessary evil, was justified as a positive good; the image of the planter replaced that of the yeoman as a model; and the plantation thrived by specializing in cotton culture.

New doctrines in defense of slavery erased from the minds of Southerners the glittering platitudes of the Declaration of Independence. A traditional line of argument reverted to scriptural and classical sources to prove that bondage was a universal human relationship, assuring patriarchal oversight for the dependent and civilizing leisure for the masters. Negroes, within that scheme, occupied the place they did in accord with God's judgment upon Ham, the son of Noah, their original progenitor. More important were the scientific ideas which emerged from efforts to classify the various breeds of men and which made the blacks an entirely separate and inferior species. The Biblical account of a single creation had left all men brothers, descended from a single pair of ancestors a few millennia back. Religious faith assured the continuing acceptance of that account; but pioneer geologists nevertheless hinted that the earth was far older than supposed; and pioneer anthropologists and sociologists argued that blacks were biologically different from, and inferior to, other people. Slavery was therefore a necessity, as beneficial to the bondsman as to the master. The agonizing doubts of the past were needless; citizens of good conscience could accept the institution as a durable part of the Republic's future.

For the petty farmers who remained the most numerous element in the white population of the South, the racial issue posed a cruel dilemma. Ever more deeply they came to believe that the blacks about them were degraded, degrading, beings. Self-esteem demanded distance between the free and the slave, that is, between the white and the black; color was the identifying mark that separated the poorest citizen from the chattel, that united the dirt farmers with the masters. In the presence of the engulfing blackness, the image of the yeoman lost relevance; for to conceive a society composed entirely of cultivators of small landholdings demanded the unimaginable—either the total removal of the Negroes or their acceptance as equals. The Jeffersonian goal having faded, the white farmers drifted in search of an alternative. Hinton R. Helper's *The Impending Crisis* (1857) offered one line of escape through an extension to the South of an idealized vision of Northern industrial society. But most whites yielded to the attractions of the plantation image, aspiring themselves to ascend to a big house, or at least to retain the social advantage their color brought them.

Economic considerations strengthened the intellectual and social supports for slavery. The area of unfree labor expanded and the value of its products zoomed.

The removal of the Indians from western Georgia and Florida in the decade after 1829 leveled a barrier that had impeded the spread of slavery to the southwest. The tribesmen not only held lands their neighbors coveted, but also provided a disturbing refuge to runaways. The removal opened the way into the Gulf Plains—into the fertile black belt of the Mississippi delta and into the Tennessee Valley. "Lord, Lord," exclaimed a planter accustomed to the poor eastern soil, as his eyes opened on "the golden view" of "the rich lands of the new counties." The migration of masters and slaves from the seaboard to Tennessee, Alabama, Arkansas, Louisiana, Mississippi and Texas had already begun in the 1820s; it soared in the 1830s once the Indians were out of the way. Thereafter, the great plantation utilizing unfree labor developed without impediment in the rich soil of the lower Mississippi Valley.

In these years, too, the demand for cotton soared. The market for the fiber in Europe had grown steadily since the resumption of transatlantic trade in 1815. But after 1820, and even more so after 1830, the requirements of American mills in the North added substantially to the demand. A symbiotic relationship developed in which the availability of the raw material encouraged the spread of factories and the rising output of machine-made cloth encouraged the spread of the plantation.

Cotton became king. The older staples—tobacco, sugar and rice—retained some importance; but cotton was by far preeminent in output, value, hands employed and capital invested. The United States had raised some 335,000 bales in 1820; the size of the crop grew to 732,000 in 1830, to 2,136,000 in 1850 and to 3,841,000 in 1860. Cotton yielded planters a return on their investment of 10 to 12 per cent annually. It provided a steadily rising share of all

American exports down to 1840, and in the next two decades fully kept pace with the expansion of other products sent abroad. Pyramiding profits helped the plantation masters finance expansion and also attracted the funds of outsiders. Prosperity spread from those directly involved in cultivation to the whole region and produced a heady sense of confidence that endured until the Civil War.

Concealed within the general process of growth was a subtle, regional shift in cotton cultivation. In 1821, 117 of the 177 million pounds raised had come from the Old South—Virginia, the Carolinas and Georgia; only 60 million from the newly settled southwest. In 1834, the balance had tipped; 297 million out of the 457 million pounds raised came from Tennessee, Louisiana, Alabama, Mississippi and Florida; 160 million from the Old South. While the output of South Carolina had continued to rise, that of Virginia and North Carolina had actually declined. The westward trend continued on through the nineteenth century.

The expansion of cotton culture created an insatiable demand for slaves which outran the natural increase of black population. Since the law against imports cut off supplies from abroad, the value of the bondsmen rose steadily. Hands worth $300 to $400 in the 1790s sold for about $1,000 in 1830 and brought close to $2,000 in the 1850s. A regular internal slave trade shifted the surplus stocks of the older East to the newer West. Mississippi, between 1830 and 1860, imported from other states well over 200,000 bondsmen at a total cost of more than $100,000,000.

The process of extending slavery westward made the recently opened areas the preeminent sites of the great plantation. Everywhere, in Mississippi as in Virginia, there was a mixture of large and small holdings; for in growing cotton as in growing tobacco there were few advantages of scale. No one used expensive machinery in planting and picking and the gins were independently owned and operated, as available to the family farmer as to the planter. But in the areas opened to settlement after 1830, the man who brought substantial capital with him, either in slaves or in cash, had the choice of the best acres; he could drain swamps and build levees; and he therefore made out better than the marginal producers who were forced into the least desirable tracts. The very large plantation dominated the life of Alabama, Mississippi, and Louisiana through the wealth and political power of its master and through the attractiveness of the model it offered the whole society.

The great plantation also linked the interests of the Old and the Deep South. Increasingly the planters of Virginia, Kentucky, Tennessee and North Carolina depended upon sales of their hands to the expanding areas of cotton production. Thus the human commodity became an attractive investment both in the old and in the new areas. Indeed, the invigorating impact of the crop raised the value of all property, human as well as land. Many a master in Virginia or Kentucky, whose exhausted acres had long since ceased to yield a profit, learned to balance his books with the gains from the sale of surplus slaves. The deference still accorded in the South to the first families in their grand tidewater houses was shadowed by the consciousness of dependence upon the exploitative plantations down the river. By the 1850s the political, economic and social center of gravity in the region had shifted from Virginia westward toward Mississippi.

The rapid spread of the plantation widened the distance between images and reality. In the old established regions, the masters grasped at tradition and retained practices and soul-searching doubts that reached back into the eighteenth century. A strong sense of family extended in an attenuated fashion even to the slave, even to the slave sold off by force of circumstance. No such guides to action inhibited their counterparts in the recently settled regions. Landowners there were new men, sometimes Northerners. Brash and uninhibited by Jeffersonian ideals, they regarded their holdings in a businesslike way, to be judged by profit and loss statements. In time they abandoned the rude shacks thrown up at arrival for homes which recalled the stately lines of tidewater mansions. Chivalric rhetoric replaced the rough frontier idiom in their reading and talking. In time too, they looked down upon the crude newcomers who lowered the tone of the district by bringing in uncouth, disorderly slaves so different from the neat and knowledgeable servitors of gentle folk established for a decade. But the porticoed facades and the romantic language covered over a ruthlessly driving system of production which increasingly set the norms for all Southern agriculture.

The well-regulated plantation was a modern, efficient, highly rationalized, productive unit, yielding its owner a respectable return upon his investment. These large enterprises stretched across hundreds of acres and employed hundreds of hands. The potentials for gain were high, but also the potentials for loss, so that good management was essential. Hit-or-miss methods were intolerable, for at this scale errors had disastrous consequences. Yet the vagaries of the elements complicated efforts at planning in this as in other branches of agriculture. Blight, pests, tornadoes and drought were standing dangers; and if the cholera did not sweep off the best hands, then a freshet during the harvest ruined the standing crops or a hurricane submerged good coastal lands in salt water. Nor could the planter control the marketing arrangements through which worldwide balance of supply and demand set the price he received; his task was to produce as much as possible while the factors in town took care of the rest.

Fortunately, the cotton planters were not far wrong in the assumption that the demand for their crops would rise steadily; they were relatively safe in pushing output as far as they could. But the more prudent among them realized that their only protection against price fluctuations, which they could not control, was scrupulous attention to production costs, of which the most important and the most flexible were those of labor.

The requirements of efficient operation put pressure upon the slaves. In the account books, each body represented a fixed investment of capital to be preserved and maintained in good working order, just as machines were in the North. The abuse of property was wasteful and foolish, for slaves like machines had to produce a return that would cover costs (food, clothing, shelter), interest, depreciation, and profit. In slack times, the factory could lay off its hands, the plantation could not. The system had to make the most of its resources—always.

Planters had to balance the need to increase production and to lower costs against the awareness that they could not overtax expensive hands. Southern slavery therefore never acquired the harshness of early-eighteenth-century West Indian gang labor. There were always variations from place to place, but everywhere the nature of the system created general constraints upon the conditions of life and work. To insure the total employment of the bondsmen, the plantation generally organized work in terms of tasks which could be evaluated to measure what each person or group did. The prudent manager sought to raise the levels of performance to prevent idleness and to get the utmost from his property; when not occupied with the cotton, rice and sugar, let them raise corn and hogs, mend fences and clear new fields. The same considerations of economy dictated minimum expenditures on provisions, shelter and clothing. The onerous toil, the lack of predictable rewards and the absence of prospects for improvement stirred in the laborers a simmering resentment which sometimes led to runaways, sometimes to outright resistance, and more often to muted gestures of defiance.

After 1830, Southern society learned to use violence systematically as a means of establishing order. Charleston had quivered with fear at the time of Denmark Vesey's "conspiracy" of 1822 and so had Virginia in 1831 during Nat Turner's rebellion. However unclear, then and later, were some features of those uprisings, the masters ever after understood the need for the total, unambiguous use of force. The widely read narratives of those events demonstrated that Negroes were a standing danger, particularly if they were free, literate and urban. Efforts to ameliorate their conditions were misguided. It was imperative to keep them strictly in subjection and the organization of the plantation was designed to maintain their servitude, to shut off opportunities for self-improvement, and to isolate them in a closed environment.

The terror worked, though at a price. The Deep South, even the counties where black slaves heavily outnumbered whites, felt no fear of uprisings even during the Civil War, when military service stripped it of manpower. A generation of compulsion had instilled habits of obedience. But vigilance and discipline forced masters and slaves into a totally impersonal relationship, so that the hard realities of plantation life departed ever more drastically from the idyllic images held of it. The chivalric figures who in the romances wielded the sword in defense of honor, in the fields wielded the lash in defense of profits.

Usually they acted through white overseers and black drivers, who were the keys to successful operations. Much depended upon their ability and their will to translate the master's wishes into practice, particularly when he was absent or possessed several plantations. Planters soon learned that plans, however carefully formulated in the study, came to nothing unless diligently applied in the field. Whoever disregarded the common maxim, "Never change an Overseer if you can help it," did so at his peril, for to find a new one was a time-consuming and uncertain process. Though there was a vast variety of types and many gradations of skill and skulduggery among the overseers, the objectives of maximized profits set the confines of their operations. They might achieve their goals by terror or by manipulation—by threats of whipping, solitary confinement and sale to a strange master or by promises of extra rations, time off and gifts. But in the end, they were accountable for security and for output. They had to maintain discipline and prevent runaways; they had to increase yield. No matter how!

In a sense, the overseer and driver performed on the plantation the same function that the superintendent and foremen did in the Northern factory; the intermediaries separated the master from the slave, the manufacturer from the proletarian, so that both relationships were abstract and impersonal. Only, in the one case, force controlled the relationship; in the other, a wage transaction.

At the middle of the nineteenth century, the plantation dominated the South as the factory did the North and the family farm the West. In a nation where the majority assumed that wealth was the product of free labor, one region had developed an alternative mechanism based upon slavery. In any assessment of total wealth produced, the one system may have been as efficient as the other; comparisons of the average per capita income, in the aggregate, did not display a marked superiority on either side. The significant differences were those in the social implications and in the economic consequences of the two modes of production.

Inequality of rewards was characteristic of both the North and the South. An immense distance lay between the styles of life of the master and the slave, as it did between those of the merchant and the unskilled laborer. Then and later, observers speculated about who did better, the hireling or the slave, an interesting question but one not as relevant as the question of why some slaves longed to be hirelings, but no hireling ever yearned to be a slave. The answer to the latter question lies not in the balance sheet of rewards reckoned in dollars, but in the difference between the uses of wealth in the two labor systems. Freedom opened and the lack of it narrowed the range of opportunities available to all. The distinction set the odds on everyone's chances of advancement. The North used its riches to stimulate growth, the South did not. Northern growth multipled goods and lowered costs by utilizing labor-saving machines and new production techniques; the South increased the output of cotton by expanding the area devoted to plantation slavery.

Merchants in the North treated their income as potential capital; underconsumption remained general down through the Civil War and left large surpluses for further investment. And the numerous middle classes, even artisans and craftsmen, swayed both by the ideals of saving and the temptations of speculation, also accumulated the little hordes which nestled in banks or went into the stocks of turnpikes, canals, and railroads or into the purchase of real estate.

The greatest share of Southern wealth went to planters, whose manners and attitudes encouraged high levels of expenditure. Except in the very largest holdings of absentees, the plantation was also the home of the master, and even the best-managed of these enterprises did not successfully separate the expenses of production from the privileges and perquisites of the household. Primitive bookkeeping, or none, obscured from the owner the margin of his profits and the scale of his expenses. Dependence upon factors who marketed the crop but also made purchases for the planter's family had the same effect. Since aristocratic aspirations encouraged extravagant outlays, often only the year's end, if then, informed him whether he enjoyed a surplus or suffered from a deficit.

The planters blessed with a surplus did not think of it in the abstract as a means toward further investment. Their thoughts ran usually to more lavish ways of consuming it. Joseph Davis of Mississippi had no patience for visionary railroad schemes. But he did not count the costs of his tremendous three-story house which easily accommodated twelve guests and their body servants; and he did not hesitate to bring mechanics down from Cincinnati to install an enormous tank in the attic, into which slaves every morning pumped enough water to supply all the bathrooms. Then too, in recurrent trips to spas and to the largest cities of the North and of Europe, living on "dainties & riding on railcars and steamboats," the planter forgot where his money came from and champagne seemed moderate, very, at two dollars a bottle.

If a surplus nevertheless remained, the planter usually lacked the habit of calculating the merits of alternative methods of disposing of it. Choices existed; the South, like other regions of the country, had its share of promoters and of schemes for launching banks, railroads and factories. There was also advice in abundance on how to improve agriculture. But the temptation was well-nigh irresistible to sink whatever funds were available into the additional land and slaves which brought with them a good immediate return and the additional esteem of a society that measured worth by the size of those holdings. Little capital was therefore available for diversification and development.

Perennial shortages of cash and a marketing system controlled by factors and bankers, whether close at hand or in Northern or European cities, drew into unproductive debt even those rich in land and in slaves. A. A. Lawrence, Yankee merchant, in 1849 noted that he sold fabrics to Southern buyers on six to ten months' credit, while the planters were in no condition to give the same terms for the staples shipped North and had to sell for cash or very short terms. Years of falling prices and gluts as in the early 1840s caught many short, without reserves or the means of meeting fixed charges for interest and for the upkeep of slaves. On the whole, before 1861, the periods of distress were of brief duration, so that the unlucky could usually ride out the storms. But the effort to do so without cutting back on familiar luxuries left them without a disposable surplus.

In bad times or good, planters struggled against distinctive obstacles to attain efficient management. Overseers and drivers, haphazardly selected, trained and promoted, were careless and dilatory unless strictly supervised by the owners. The slaves, like most yeomen, North and South, were largely unskilled and lacked the opportunity to learn. But unlike the free farmers, the bondsmen had few incentives

to improve their performance. Travelers and writers, like Frederick
L. Olmsted and others, often noted the corrosive effects of unfree
labor; and informed Southerners were also aware of it, especially when
it came to rice and sugar plantations in which thousands of dollars
in machinery and irrigation were invested. The *New Orleans Crescent*
thus deplored the humiliating exhibition on Louisiana sugar estates
of ignorant Negroes working partly by instinct, partly by instructions
from some half-made engineer, and partly by chance. Such operations
put expensive equipment at hazard; yet the surplus they yielded more
often went into more land and slaves or into consumption than into
improvement or diversification.

Plantation owners were only a small minority in the region's
population. But the other Southerners were no more likely than they
to generate development capital. Everywhere, thousands of yeomen
worked their own farms or exploited the labor of a few slaves. The
small units were at a disadvantage when competing with the large
ones in the production of cotton; apart from the few economies of
scale that came with size, the wealthy planters did better because they
remorselessly preempted the lands with the best soil and with the
most favorable access to shipping points. The more prudent cultivators
of farms of modest size, especially in the border states, therefore aimed
for self-sufficiency or stayed with tobacco, corn, hemp and hogs—not,
then or later, crops which enriched anyone.

The nineteenth-century Southern smallholders could not pull
themselves away from lives of continuing dreary toil by remaining
where they were. The ambitious consequently yielded to the pull of
migration, either to Indiana, Illinois and Missouri or, if they had
resources enough and slaves to take along, to the southwest, in the
hope of rising to possession of a great plantation. The less ambitious
drudged along, while the fertility of the soil oozed away, and while
old household crafts lost their markets to the factory-sustained Northern producers.

Many among these people slid into the ranks of the poor whites.
In the back country and the uplands, hundreds of families had long
eked out a subsistence by rudimentary tillage and by hunting and
fishing. Their numbers grew after 1820, when the focus of Southern
energy emphatically shifted toward the plantation. Strong kinship
ties kept them inert, immobilized; and pride of color prevented them
from taking on the manual labor associated with Negroes. Futile
dreams of the mastery few ever attained drained away the energy for
any alternative way of creating wealth.

Nor did the urban South produce the capital, labor or entrepreneurship for industrialization. Bustling seaports from Baltimore to New Orleans and promising inland towns like Richmond and Atlanta rivaled their Northern sisters in activity. Skilled artisans, canny shopkeepers and powerful merchants did business much as did their counterparts elsewhere. William Gregg, J. D. B. DeBow and other promoters wove ingenious schemes which they aired in the pages of the press and on the floors of commercial conventions.

Little came of them. Commitment to a peculiar institution shaped a peculiar society, ingrown, unreceptive to change. The governor of Mississippi bragged in 1857 that the state had two banks only, having rid itself of the system for fifteen years past. Gregg noted that the hostility to corporate charters prevented association of capital for worthy purposes. Others noted the fear that links to the North might be a curse instead of a blessing, encouraging the arrival of unprincipled newcomers, "enemies of our peculiar institutions" and "ever ready to form combinations against the interest of the slaveholder."

Proposals to improve communications or to stimulate trade therefore competed unsuccessfully for attention against the more attractive images of the plantation. The middle classes in the South were less numerous than in the North; and they operated in the shadow of planters who wielded greater political power, enjoyed more social esteem, and set the context for all thoughts of the future. Discussion here ran to slaves, not machines, and carried along ministers, physicians, and lawyers as well as factors and businessmen. As a result, surpluses, when they appeared, more often went into land and slaves than into securities. Harry Hill of New Orleans, Gazaway Lamar of Savannah and other merchants and bankers put their money into plantations when they could.

The vision the plantation cast across the ocean also affected the choices of Europeans. English investors were reluctant to send funds into the region, particularly when some Southern states repudiated their debts after the panic of 1837. Immigrants were unwilling to venture into places where they would compete with unfree labor and where opportunities seemed limited. The whole context of Southern life was uncongenial to enterprise—and, increasingly, consciously and boastfully so, as attacks from the North put the peculiar institution on the defensive. The evolving pro-slavery argument offended men who wished to be neither slaves nor masters and who therefore migrated and invested elsewhere.

Away from the plantation, slavery had few economic advantages, considered either as labor or as a capital investment. The experience of free Negroes and of bondsmen rented on contract showed that black people were capable of learning crafts and certainly of working in factories; and entrepreneurs were tempted to use them when white workers were recalcitrant or in short supply. But slave labor was costly both in terms of the substantial initial purchase price and in terms of the burden of support even in slack periods. The wage earner, by contrast, came to the job without charge and could be laid off when not needed. Northern entrepreneurs were therefore quit of the heavy costs for interest and maintenance borne by Southerners who used unfree labor.

Furthermore, away from the discipline of the plantation, the employment of slaves created disquieting problems of control. On the construction gang or in the city, the opportunities for escape and for malingering multiplied. Apart from those obvious risks, other nuisances caused expense and uncertainty. Slaves who did not work on a plantation still had to be lodged, fed and clothed. Or if, as happened in many Southern cities, they were allowed to fend for themselves, provided they made an annual payment to their owners, they got the heady feel of money and independence. In the absence of the prospect of improvement and of the fear of the lash, there was never the certainty that they could be cajoled into doing the job. Any taste of independence, given as an incentive, threatened the social structure designed to keep Negroes separate and inferior. Slavery could not supply the self-recruiting, self-supporting labor force that had eased industrialization in the North.

Increasingly, the necessity for defending its peculiar institution shifted emphasis in the South from arrangements which depended upon contract to those which depended upon force. Only part of the population was free to act in the open market; a large minority was subject to power wielded by others. As a result, the decisions of legislators, judges, sheriffs were more important than in other parts of the country; and those usually revolved about the preservation of the slave status.

More significant than the cash outlays for policing, reflected in tax rates and in the allocation of communal resources, was the subtle shift in social values. Down to 1820, the South had shared the open outlook of the rest of the country, willing to hazard development toward future forms not entirely foreseeable in the present. In the decades that followed, hardening social relations and the desire to create and preserve a hierarchical structure in which each sector of the population had a fixed place increasingly put the emphasis upon stability. The posture of the dominant groups gradually froze and the whole society displayed signs of rigidity. A defensive reflex converted intolerance of the anti-slavery argument into intolerance of any criticism and of any suggestion of change.

Southern intellectuals located the desirable models for the South in the antique past—classical Athens, or the romantic Middle Ages. But in actuality their region was tending toward the situation of Eastern despotisms, rich in wealth, lavish in the personal expenditures of a few, but stagnant and unreceptive to suggestions of development. Although bitter sectional and group conflicts continued to divide the people of the region, the defense of slavery was a unifying force which, by the 1850s, established the political and social leadership of the great planters.

Few industrial ventures took hold in the Southern states. The Tredegar Iron Works of Richmond, using the work of slaves, held on through the Civil War; but attempts to develop cotton manufacturing got nowhere despite the advantage of closeness to raw materials. In 1860, of the 5,236,000 spindles in the United States, only 290,000 were Southern. Some railroads did in time probe the interior but mileage and traffic remained far behind that in the North, by whatever indices the comparison was made. A society increasingly dominated by the ideals of the plantation pasha did not provide entrepreneurs with the environment for economic development. Cyrus Hall McCormick and William Kelly hit upon their great ideas of the reaper and the bessemer process while still in Virginia and Kentucky; but they went north to put them into practice. Southerners who stayed within the region bent every energy toward replication and multiplication of the plantation.

Like the Oriental despotisms also, the South sought to compensate for the lack of interior growth by external, territorial expansion. Some masters were by temperament militant, given to measuring their worth by the acres and souls they possessed; they spread themselves—in dreams at least—not through manipulation of bits of commercial paper, but through manly conquest that added to their land, their people. Even planters who were not so aggressive understood, as did others who shared their aspirations, that perpetuation of the system demanded expansion. Everyone involved in the cotton trade, everyone who owned or wished to own slaves doubted that the peculiar institution could endure as it was, cooped up within the limits set by anachronistic compromise lines. The South could resist the competition with the booming regions of the North and West only if it too had room to expand. Growth of the area open to slavery would strengthen the political forces that defended the institution and would raise the value of bondsmen everywhere. Planters in Virginia and Kentucky would profit from the sale of surplus hands; ambitious young men would have the opportunity to clear new plantations; and limitless crops would bring wealth to all—if only there were space enough.

Yet after 1850, ambitious Southerners suffered from a frightening sense of narrowing prospects. Enemies everywhere were on the attack; having manipulated emancipation in Mexico and the British West Indies, they were now corrupting the Northern press and pulpit with abolitionist poison. Opportunities were shrinking as the black belt of the Mississippi delta filled up and the edge of settlement moved into eastern Texas. Were the best lands gone? That would be a denial of every man's right to a chance to be a master.

The response, never reasoned through, was a demand for more—more slaves, more land. Suggestions, tentative and hesitant at first, gained strength in the repetition—repeal of the law prohibiting the import of new slaves would result in beneficent resumption of the transatlantic flow of Africans. Actually, there were indications that the law was being flouted—although in what frequency and in what volume was not clear. The higher the price, the more attractive was the trade in blacks.

The insistence upon expansion fed the insatiable desire for more territory. The acquisition of California and New Mexico after the war with Mexico touched off a prolonged controversy over whether those areas were to be slave or free. Neither the Compromise of 1850 nor the Kansas-Nebraska Act quieted the increasingly bitter sectional conflict. Northerners who hoped to avoid an outright break consoled themselves with the thought that the geography of the new area was hostile to cotton culture and therefore to slavery. But that was far from being the case, as later agricultural developments in Arizona and California would show. In any event, visions of Southern expansionists were far from parochial. They planned and talked of adding chunks of Cuba, Central America and Mexico to the territory of the United States; and talk sometimes led to filibustering action.

The expansive pressure of slavery generated the irrepressible conflict over the future of the territories in the 1850s and mercilessly exacerbated relations among the sections. The culmination was secession and war in 1861.

In little more than the single generation since 1820, the slave plantation had fastened upon the South a labor system increasingly out of accord with the dominant social and cultural trends in the rest of the nation. The eighteenth-century compromises remained credible as long as the citizens of the Republic could tell themselves that bondage was on the way to ultimate extirpation. When, however, the area given over to slavery expanded rather than contracted and the prospect of emancipation even in the distant future disappeared, then the conviction flickered out that the national destiny would in itself assure the victory of freedom. Then compromise was intolerable. The nation faced the agonizing decision—whether to accept the permanence of slavery and thus to surrender the hope of ultimate liberty for all inherited from the founders of the Republic.

Four years of bitter conflict provided the answer. Whatever the relative merits of the free and slave labor systems, the test of battle proved that the plantation had inhibited the development of the strength necessary in modern war. Without a free population large enough to man the ranks, without the industry to furnish the supplies and without an articulated transportation network, the Confederacy went down to defeat.

The Union victory emancipated the slaves; but it did not solve the economic problems of the region. The South continued to pay the costs of its peculiar institution long after 1865. The war itself had been expensive; the shift of manpower away from the farms and shops, the decline of output and the interruption of established patterns of trade caused heavy losses. In addition, the South had been the battlefield; and the repeated crossing of armies had wrecked its productive plant. It took a decade to repair the direct damage of war. Furthermore, the currency was in disorder; Confederate paper money and bonds had lost their value entirely and credit—public and private—was in disarray. Recovery under these circumstances presented a formidable challenge.

Emancipation, made permanent and universal by the Thirteenth Amendment, destroyed the whole familiar labor system so that the plantation could no longer function in the form developed before the war. Yet deep ideological and social divisions left the character of Reconstruction uncertain. With the old masters temporarily deprived of leadership and with the old political organizations shattered, control was fragmented among numerous competing elements in Washington and the state capitals. Government lacked the power to make decisions—either to impose a Northern pattern of yeoman farming or to support some large-scale equivalent of plantation agriculture.

The grandiose illusions of the ante-bellum Cotton Kingdom dissolved into a nostalgic vision of the lost cause, a vision within which the values of the plantation retained their integrity; hierarchical order, agrarian virtue, the martial spirit and a disdain of striving for material goods were among the sentimental and spiritual legacies of postwar Southerners. But nostalgia was not a firm basis on which to reconstruct the economy, especially since it nurtured attitudes hostile to enterprise.

The labor force was a drag upon, rather than a stimulus to, the economy. Emancipation did not endow the Negroes with equality. White Southerners, having lost the legal mechanism of slavery by which they formerly maintained the inferiority of the blacks, after 1865 developed social instruments for achieving the same goal. Racist ideas justified, and Jim Crow practices implemented, a pattern of segregation that divided the population along the color line. Racial considerations influenced every decision about the interrelated problems of education, occupational training and productive efficiency.

Only the fact that the worldwide demand for cotton and tobacco continued to rise offset the perils of the drift which followed the end of the war. Cotton never regained the preeminence as an export it had enjoyed in the 1850s, and its price in the nineteenth century did not return to its former advantageous level. But output had regained its 1860 level by 1875 and in the next fifteen years more than doubled. Income from use of the cotton seed for oil supplemented that from the sale of the fiber; the cigarette opened new markets for tobacco; and food processing took hold in some parts of the South.

A generation passed, memories faded, and another cast of characters occupied the prominent places of the scene. In the 1880s, the rhetoric subtly changed as politicians, editors and businessmen more frequently called for a New South, devoted to enterprise and integrated into the national economy. Transportation improved. Some manufacturing took root in North Carolina, Kentucky, Tennessee and Georgia. But in 1890, less than 3 per cent of the labor force was employed in industry, as compared with about 20 per cent in the country as a whole. The great bulk of the population lived by agriculture which remained essentially unchanged, locked into immobility by the encrusted social patterns of the rural South.

Without the compulsion of slavery, the ante-bellum plantation could not be restored. Although the great estates were not confiscated, they could not function as before. The freedmen resisted every effort, whether through the Black Codes or through informal pressure, to keep them in the old productive unit and refused to work in the old way, even for wages. They wanted plots of their own, because that was the setting in America of free family life. In a discouraging environment in which others were ever ready to cheat and exploit them, they learned to plant and pick without the direction of an overseer, to buy and sell, to make contracts and to perform all the other tasks of independent existence. By 1890, fully 120,000 of them were land-owners, a small proportion of the total, but a respectable one in terms of the obstacles surmounted.

Most former slaves, and many whites as well, remained poor. In the absence of an acceptable labor supply, the planters had no alternative but to divide their holdings into small plots which they rented either for a fixed sum in cash or cotton or for a portion of the yield—the amount owed depending on who supplied the tools and equipment. Whites were usually share tenants, considered by law to be owners of the crops, from which they paid one-third as rent to the landowners. Blacks, on the other hand, were generally held to be sharecroppers, whose produce by law belonged to the landlord, from whom they received their two-thirds as wages. The distinction was important mainly in defining the inferior status of the former slave, for under either condition, tenancy was unrewarding and inefficient. The laborers lacked incentive to improve holdings that were not their own; the owners lacked control over production.

Southern agriculture therefore remained backward, without the virtues of either the large-scale plantation or the yeoman farm, and shut off from the gains through mechanization and scientific techniques developed elsewhere. The factor disappeared along with the plantation he had once served. In his stead, the local merchant in the crossroads store or in the small town bought the cotton, sold the food, clothing and supplies. But debt remained. Tenants, white or black, lived from harvest to harvest on credit supplied by the owner or by the middlemen who marketed the crops. Debt became a bog from which the cropper never extricated himself. Bending every effort to increase the yield, he punished the land; yet though output rose, he could never get ahead of the game. At the year's end, the calculations—even when honest—showed that accumulated borrowings plus interest had eaten up all the earnings. Whatever rewards cotton brought rarely went to the men who tilled the soil; and the competition between the races inhibited every attempt to break out of the hopeless cycle.

The 1890s, a decade of falling cotton prices, a decade of desperation in the countryside, witnessed a social and political struggle to escape that cycle. The inspiration was Jeffersonian—the tradition, never totally extinguished in the South, which emphasized the virtue of the self-sufficient yeoman. Now the protesters, like their Northern counterparts, ascribed the failings of the existing order to the grasping selfishness of middlemen, speculators and the great landowners. Let the producers but join forces to break the hold of the monopolizers, then each could live in contentment from the fruits of his own labor. The farmers' unions spreading through the region dared to enlist blacks and whites in the same or parallel organizations, set up a variety of cooperatives and girded for political battle. The forces thus mobilized sustained the People's Party, which gained power in several states and for a time became a consequential force in national politics.

The failure of the Populists was partly due to the instability of leaders who themselves occasionally yielded to the temptations of power and wealth. At critical moments also the race issue divided whites and blacks despite their common economic interests.

But the failure was also due to the inadequacies in 1900 of the eighteenth-century vision of the yeoman farmer. The South had gone its own way after 1820 and had bypassed the process of industrialization which had transformed the rest of the country; its own wealth, drawn from the plantation, remained agricultural, extracted from its soil by the labor of slaves. When war destroyed the plantation, Southerners improvised, replacing the bondsmen by tenants, but committed still to agriculture; and even the Populists were not radical enough to conceive an alternative source of wealth. Yet at the very same time, in the North and the West, some Americans were learning that more was needed for the success of agriculture than simply to plant each cultivator on his own acres.

7

The Farm Business

*I*n the second half of the nineteenth century agriculture outside the South expanded dramatically. The spread of settlement across the Great Plains added immense new territories to those already under cultivation; and, at the same time, improved techniques everywhere raised the output of foodstuffs. The farm became a modern business enterprise linked to the world market economy and yielding larger and larger outpourings of commodities.

Yet the farm was also a household, home to millions of men and women. It was a source of wealth and also a setting for family life. The two functions were not always altogether compatible; and the tension of the effort to unite the two erupted in recurrent agrarian crises. The tillers of the soil could not escape the cruel choice between the values of the market and those of the home. On into the twentieth century many of them struggled in vain to prevent changes that increased their commercial role.

The line of settlement in 1850 had edged beyond the Mississippi and had dipped down from Minnesota all the way through eastern Texas to the Gulf of Mexico. But large areas of Michigan, Wisconsin, Minnesota, Kansas and Nebraska were not yet occupied; and westward through the plains and mountains to California were hundreds of miles of totally empty space, much of it blocked off by a forbidding reputation as the Great American Desert. Yet in the two decades after 1850, despite political controversy and war, a surge of population thrust its way across the plains; and after twenty years more, so many people had found places there and in the area beyond as to confirm the conclusion of the Director of the Census that Americans had at last conquered their final frontier. In 1890 almost 3,000,000 people lived in Kansas, Nebraska and the Dakotas, 2,500,000 in Texas and Oklahoma, 1,888,000 on the Pacific Coast and 1,213,000 in the mountain states—a total of more than eight million in the vast expanse almost uninhabited a generation earlier.

Although the remaining Indian tribes fought fiercely, they were unable to stop the advance of settlement. Military and economic pressure cleared the way. With the end of the Civil War, western defense became the main business of the Army; scattered garrisons maintained a protective presence in a chain of posts through the interior and, when roving bands of warriors became a danger, mounted expeditions to subdue the Redmen. Meanwhile, decimation of the buffalo herds destroyed the staple of Indian subsistence on the plains and further drained their ability to resist the oncoming farmers and miners. From time to time, the federal government tried to protect its wards in the Indian Territory and on reservations, occasionally ejecting white intruders by force. But those sporadic efforts were ineffective; without more consistent help, the tribes ceased to threaten the new arrivals who took possession of the soil.

The railroads hastened the process of settlement. Once the war was over, the dream of the transcontinentals approached fulfillment. Four bands of iron reached westward from the Mississippi to the Pacific by 1880; and in 1893 a fifth joined them, when James J. Hill combined a number of smaller roads to form the Great Northern. At the same time, numerous feeders reached out from the main lines; in 1881 farmers anywhere in Minnesota could get to a railroad station and back in a single day. Nationwide, the miles of track multiplied fivefold between 1850 and 1870 to a total of 59,922; then tripled between 1870 and 1890, to a total of 166,703; then doubled to 240,439 in 1910.

The immediate effects upon migration were phenomenal. The concern of the surveyors was with the termini; it did not matter to them that the routes laid out for the Northern Pacific, the Union Pacific and the Santa Fe passed through hundreds of miles of unpeopled territory in Minnesota, the Dakotas, Nebraska and Kansas. The objective was to reach the West Coast as quickly as possible.

But the empty space acquired significance of its own once the lines were open; passengers then arrived quickly and cheaply. The painful overland journeys of the past receded into the memories of garrulous old-timers; travel, if still not commodious, was at least expeditious, a matter of days rather than of weeks, on schedule rather than at the mercy of chance. The prospective settler could buy a through ticket in Chicago or New York, and even in Liverpool or Hamburg, thus eliminating the painful hazard of diversion from his destination.

The railroads also attracted settlers with their assurance of close links to markets. In earlier moves to older frontiers the farmer's tasks had included clearing the wilderness, building a home, and making a crop, but also hacking a way to a buyer at the river landing or cross-road store. Under the new circumstances, he found already in existence cars on tracks to carry his products in vast quantities swiftly and cheaply to elevators, yards and processors in distant cities. Reduced transportation costs made his grain and meat competitive with those of settled areas and integrated his holding into a worldwide market. A limitless demand for these goods seemed to underwrite the success of every new settlement.

Tempting bargains proffered by accommodating railroads pulled newcomers on to the frontier. The transcontinentals had a standing incentive to find purchasers for the huge slabs of federal land received by way of subsidy. In the short run, any cash was welcome to replenish empty treasuries; and, in the long run, income depended upon the volume of traffic generated by thriving farms which produced and consumed the commodities carried as freight. The railroads were willing to offer reasonable terms and credit to settlers and, in some cases, established colonization offices in the East and in Europe to induce people to come to the areas served.

Land was within every man's reach, whether through railroad sales, through the operations of speculators, or through direct government grants and aid.

Well before 1865, the hit-or-miss speculative dealing in farm properties had developed into an organized business that directed prospective purchasers to holdings in the West and that helped finance those without enough cash in hand. The warrants which entitled veterans of the Mexican War to government land thus passed into the control of middlemen who retailed the claims to settlers; one firm in Richmond, Virginia, alone handled some 400,000 acres between 1852 and 1861. A network of agents and brokers took form through which buyers and sellers accommodated one another. Land speculation, although rarely rewarded with smashing success, generally yielded a return as good as that in other types of investment and attracted a steady supply of capital that financed migration.

The Homestead Act of 1862 further stimulated settlement. It granted a tract of 160 acres free of charge to any citizen who spent five years residing on and improving a claim. Some farmers, although in most regions probably a minority, took advantage of the opportunity; and the existence of the homestead alternative was important even to those who continued to buy land from speculators, paying the premium for an immediate title and for presumed advantages in location or soil. The existence of the free and low-cost public tracts set a ceiling on the prices in private transactions and stimulated the inflow of new settlers. Speedy settlement was the overriding consideration—as many people as possible, no matter where. The Desert Land Act of 1877 and the Carey Act of 1894 aimed to stimulate irrigation in the haste to pull prospective yeomen onto even the least tractable soil.

Thousands of prospective farmers were poised for migration. In the older sections of the country, where the dreams of a former day had now grown stale, tales of the miraculous resources of the Great West fired imaginations and stirred the perpetual impulse to wander. First came the drifters; Herman Reinhart left his father's Illinois homestead in 1849 at the age of seventeen, moved through Iowa, Nebraska, Utah, Wyoming, Nevada, California and Oregon, sometimes farming, sometimes ranching, sometimes mining, running a bakery where he could, or a saloon or bowling alley, then ended up in a small Kansas town, keeper of the livery stable and restaurant. A thirty-five-year-old native of Maine, in 1870 shared his Oregon farm with the evidences of his transcontinental migration—a wife born in Indiana, a child born in Minnesota and another born in California.

After the restless ones came the weary. Mothers, fathers and children looking for homes. With the way cleared, a sober army of families resumed the quest for opportunity beyond yet another frontier.

Europeans added to the press of population into the areas now opened to settlement. The Civil War briefly interrupted the transatlantic flow; but peace brought a resumption of the movement out of Ireland, England and Germany. Almost 5 million people reached the United States from those countries between 1861 and 1890. In the same three decades, 850,000 Scandinavians and about a million Canadians joined the migration. Some newcomers proceeded directly to the virgin plains; others brought with them enough capital to buy operating farms east of the frontier and thus released the earlier proprietors for new ventures into the West. In either case, the new arrivals exerted a continuing expansive pressure on settlement.

Year by year, the number of men and women engaged in American agriculture rose. Although they often experienced frustration, and sometimes defeat, when it came to harvesting the fruits of their labor, the soil rewarded their country with abundance.

Nationwide, the number of farms grew—a million and a half in 1850, two and a half in 1870, four and a half in 1890 and not far short of six and a half in 1910. Acreage under cultivation and value of holdings climbed correspondingly. More—everything was more: hands at work, number of fields, size, everything. Above all, output. The count of bushels was in millions: of wheat, 100 in 1850, 254 in 1870, 449 in 1890 and 625 in 1910—dispatched to become bread throughout the nation and the world; and of corn, in the same years up from 600 million to 1,124 to 1,650, to 2,852—fed to pigs and poultry, distilled into whiskey, ground into meal. Also, in time, vast quantities of beef, butter, milk and fruits. Plenty.

American agriculture had long been developing the traits that made possible this lavish flow of commodities. A high element of risk offset the possibility of great gain; specialization was more usual than diversification; and relatively large units, unencumbered by tradition, were ready for modernization.

Since early colonial times, farmers in the New World had produced for the commercial market, had therefore been prone to borrowing and speculation. So much was familiar in 1850 and continued to be in 1910, only more so. Transactions on the floors of exchanges in Chicago, New York and Liverpool and a chain of remote intermediaries brought Western harvests to purchasers in distant cities. The farmer had no means of knowing, when he sowed, what the demand would be when he reaped, or how conditions in the Ukraine or New Zealand would affect supplies. He plunged, planted to the maximum, and, if he did well, expanded to reach for still higher stakes the next time. He was quick to borrow for he counted on rising land values, in the long run, to pay off his debt. They always had, or so it seemed. Credit made his world go round, in the mortgage acquired with the land, in the payments due on the new machine, in the account owed during the wait for proceeds of the year's work. Thus it had been; thus it remained while the output soared.

Changes in organization also contributed to the rising volumes of the second half of the nineteenth century. Farms in the United

States became specialized. The scale of operations increased. Mechanization took hold. System replaced habit and improvisation. These were signs of modernization, of the transition toward a rationally planned process of production. None of these trends was altogether new; but the hastening pace after 1850 quite transformed the character of American agriculture.

Specialization was a product both of the spread of settlement and of the development of communications. The scope of agriculture became truly continental; and the reduction of transportation costs ended the isolation that had formerly protected less favored areas from competition. The limited local markets for foodstuffs that survived from a previous period or that sprang up around new mining camps and trading posts dissolved when the railroad intruded. Thereafter, the peculiarities of topography and climate that gave one region an advantage over another were decisive. Thus the Midwestern Lake Plains, with their open prairies, good soil and abundant grass, enjoyed such superiority over the forest and hill country of the East that they accounted by 1860 for half the American output of wheat, corn and meat. A shift further west came with the settlement of the Great Plains in the next two decades.

Wheat, the most profitable of the grains, had once been grown everywhere. But Eastern farmers had long given up the effort to compete commercially; by the 1830s the center of production had shifted to Ohio and the contiguous areas of New York, Pennsylvania and Virginia. By the 1860s the center had moved to a band from Illinois northwest to Minnesota. Then the plowmen penetrated the semi-arid plains of Kansas, Nebraska and Dakota, learned, by reversing the traditional order, to plant in the fall and harvest in the spring or summer, quickly outdistancing the older areas of the country, which in turn shifted to other crops.

Ultimately the new West also dominated the cattle business. The Texans had long grazed great herds on the still unsettled public lands, and after the Civil War a few of them drove their stock to Northern markets, feeding them without cost on the open range along the way. The approach of the railroads stimulated these drives by shortening the distance the longhorns moved on foot; in the 1870s as many as 350,000 head thus found their way in annual roundups from open range to railroad shipping points, then to the stockyards and slaughterhouses. But the romantic cowboy interlude ended in the 1880s. Settlers arrived, fenced in their farms and closed off the best routes. The cattle industry became more stable, less rough, conducted on enclosed ranches and concentrated in areas like Texas, western Kansas and Wyoming, where plenty of space and enough water were available.

As the new regions preempted the markets for wheat and beef, the older ones shifted to other crops. Some Midwestern farmers then specialized in corn and hogs, others in sheep and wool, and dairying took hold in Wisconsin and in New York. The Pacific Coast states still produced wheat, barley and oats down into the twentieth century, but once the railroad with its refrigerated cars linked them to national markets, they also turned their energies to commodities in which they had a geographic advantage—fruits, grapes and vegetables.

An increase in the scale of operations was also an indication of modernization. Three wheat ranches in California's San Joaquin Valley, in the 1870s, stretched across 76,000 acres. At Casselton on the Red River, in Dakota Territory, a single mammoth bonanza farm occupied 115 square miles and, during the harvest, used 600 laborers. The topography of the Central Valley of California and of the Great Plains encouraged the deployment of vast numbers of men and machines in this extensive fashion; and a good deal of English and Eastern capital went into them. After 1890, their owners often found it more profitable to divide these vast units; but the family-sized holdings which took their place were still enormous by earlier standards.

These ample enterprises were receptive to innovation. They employed machines as a matter of course; and smaller farms were not far behind in the adoption of labor-saving gadgets—the silo, the centrifugal cream separator and the butterfat tester. The first primitive harvesters gave way to more complex devices, which performed more, faster; at the end of the century huge combines, some of them powered by steam, reaped and bound tremendous crops with relatively little manpower. The instruments contrived to increase yield varied from one region to another, as did the problems posed by nature. On the Great Plains, cheap barbed wire replaced scarce wood fences as protection against trespassing animals. The Oliver drilled-steel plow and a variety of listers cut through the hard-baked topsoil. In California and in the arid plateaus of the mountain states, irrigation ditches or deep wells powered by windmills compensated for the lack of water. The value, in millions of dollars, of the machines and implements on American farms rose from 152 in 1850 to 271 in 1870, to 494 in 1890 and to 1,265 in 1910. Increasingly, success on the farm, as in the factory, depended upon access to capital for investment in improvements and equipment.

The steps toward rationalizing production, also demanded by modernization, created difficult problems for both large and small landowners. The household of the past had operated by habit and by trial and error, working as much or as little as the temperament of its members dictated, absorbing itself the consequences of failure or gain, consuming less in bad years, more in good. But big enterprises by the 1880s could not function in this fashion; they had to calculate return upon investment, earn interest on capital, pay wages to managers and decide whether to hire many or few hands. Even the family farmer made choices, whether to buy a machine or make do with the old, whether to give over so many acres to which crop. Such judgments called for a plan, that is, a reasoned estimate of the relationship of present act to future outcome.

An imperfect understanding of the balance of forces which affected the demand, supply and price of commodities traded in global markets complicated the task of agricultural forecasting for everyone. Tricks of the weather at home or thousands of miles away often made a mockery of the most careful predictions. No single producer, among the millions, appreciably influenced the total supply; and since no one knew when his plow turned the soil what the yield would ultimately be, maximum output generally seemed the safest goal. The absentee investors in the bonanza farms could absorb occasional losses or take their capital elsewhere when profits became inadequate. Not so the husbandman whose farm was home; he struggled painfully to limit risks, offset losses and make the most of opportunities, seeking what guidance he could find in the reports of his weekly paper.

The tremendous leaps in output owed much, although the debt was not usually recognized, to development of a remarkable distributing structure that carried goods efficiently and speedily from farm to consumer.

Transportation was the most visible feature of a complex organization. The teams plodding along rutted roads to the railhead, the heavy cars pounding the tracks eastward, the sluggish barges on the lakes, canals and rivers and the great oceanic steamships, holds laden with grain, offered beholders a glimpse of the capillaries that carried nutrients through an intricate system. But the distributive system as a whole was beyond the vision of gazers.

The sheaves ripened, acre upon acre in county after county— at once. Felled by the advancing combines, they lay bound across the fields—inert. And became bread.

The fallen wheat was not ready for the table; intermediaries processed and prepared it.

In a matter of days, the crop came in. But the buyers of bread were not ready for the whole of it. Or the bakers or millers. Or the cars to bring it from the prairie station to which the farm wagons hauled it. The intermediaries held the goods, managing the flow so that in the end each loaf reached the eater fresh. They also provided the capital that moved the grain and flour along until the last sale.

In the 1840s Buffalo, at the head of the Lakes, built an elevator to store grain. Imitators soon appeared everywhere—along the railroad tracks, at the riverheads, on the lake shores. As they spread westward, the new structures increased in size, in number, and in their capacity to receive, grade, store and finally disgorge the grain for further shipment. In 1890 twenty-six elevators in Chicago could hold 28,675,000 bushels. Speed was one of their virtues. The lines disappeared of porter after porter, back bent by bundle after bundle; now conveyers swiftly and cheaply carried the grain to the appropriate bins. Along the way shellers separated the cob from the corn, and fans blew out the chaff and ventilated the wheat. Sorting was another service, so that sales were of a general grade rather than of a specific lot, again a saving of time and money.

Transactions became abstract and impersonal, executed on the commodity exchange by commission merchants and brokers who bought and sold warehouse receipts and rarely saw the property traded or had occasions to breathe the dust of the cavernous storage spaces. It was not even necessary to deal in corn or wheat actually in existence. Speculators were ready to purchase and sell contracts for future delivery, thus providing the more cautious a hedge against abrupt price fluctuations.

Changes in flour manufacture expanded the ability to consume the increased output of the farms. Adoption of the Hungarian technique of roller milling in 1871, and improvements upon it by Charles A. Pillsbury and others, equipped American plants to handle the hard spring wheat of the Northwest efficiently. From Pillsbury's, advertised as the largest mill in the world, and from its rivals, the sacks of flour hastened to thousands of bakers and grocers in all parts of the world. Most bread still came from the ovens at home; but Americans were adapting the factory methods long since in use for the less-perishable biscuits and crackers. In 1901, fully one-third of the bread consumed in the cities was commercially prepared; and new kneading and mixing machines, which lowered costs and increased volume, steadily raised the percentage thereafter.

A similar transformation improved the delivery of meat to consumers. Gustavus Swift, droving cattle every week from Cape Cod to Boston, where he peddled the butchered cuts, reckoned that it would be cheaper to slaughter the animals close to the source and ship only the meat. To prove it, he moved West, finally locating in Chicago, where in 1875 he began to send carloads of dressed beef to Boston under refrigeration. It worked. Great stockyards as close as possible to the ranches and farms received vast herds of cattle and hogs, sorted them, processed them and dispatched the product expeditiously to every corner of the United States as well as to England and Europe, to Japan, China, the Philippines and Singapore. Vastly improved canning techniques also facilitated the wide distribution of meat products and, in time, milk, fruit and vegetables.

The immense quantities of food flowing to purchasers in every part of the country developed new marketing channels. A network of brokers, wholesalers and retailers reached out from central distribution points in the big cities to the smallest hamlets. At the same time vigorous entrepreneurs experimented with methods of simplifying and speeding the process of distribution. George F. Gilman's Great Atlantic & Pacific Tea Company had concentrated on the high-volume sale of a few items through the mails, through itinerant peddlers and through a scattering of shops until 1878. Then, with his partner, George Huntington Hartford, he added a full range of groceries, expanded the number of retail stores and systematized the enterprise so that it operated as a chain, bypassing intermediaries and lowering costs.

The welfare of the farms thus hinged upon the towns which processed and marketed their crops. New urban communities developed to handle the transactions that carried food from the fields to consumers, not only Chicago and St. Louis, but also Omaha, Kansas City, Spokane, Minneapolis, Duluth and hundreds of lesser station stops, fewer in the South than in the North and West, but some everywhere. Within the cities of all sizes an elaborate array of wholesalers and retailers weighed out into purchasable packets the commodities which had arrived in bulk. The farm, by the end of the nineteenth century, as surely as the factory, depended for expansion and even for survival upon links to an intricate business network which distributed its products.

But the farm could not function as factories did. The farm was a productive enterprise, but also a home. Modernized, mechanized, rationalized, it was nonetheless also the setting of family life, so that in all decisions emotion was as important as calculation.

The yeoman ideal, each man on his own holding, still fascinated Americans. The farmer, said William Jennings Bryan, reared his children near to Nature's heart, where they mingled their voices with those of the birds. His soil and barn were one with the schoolhouse erected for the education of the young, with the church where he praised his Creator and with the cemetery where rested the ashes of his dead. Inevitably family and field fused in thought and feeling, and the passion roused by one extended to the other. However recent the arrival, however tenuous the stake, a desperate determination to hold on and to make it gripped the farmers—and the more so as they became aware that there were no farther wests to which to retreat.

The unremitting tensions of the defense of home prevented farmers from responding to market fluctuations or to mistakes of judgment as manufacturers did. For thirty years after the end of the Civil War, agricultural prices sloped downward; corn from an average of 54 cents a bushel, 1866–1875, fell to 28 cents, 1896–1900; wheat from $1.24 to 65 cents. Prolonged price weakness on this scale was not unique to farm commodities, but the consequences differed from those in manufacturing. In industry, declines of such severity eliminated marginal producers, reduced supplies and left the field clear to the ablest competitors. But the farmer, no matter how marginal, hung on; drops in price set him working all the harder. Fighting to save not a business but a family, he considered heartbreaking sacrifices justified.

When the toil lavishly plowed into the soil nevertheless failed to bear fruit, the farmer, unwilling to surrender, lashed about against the unseen enemies who stole his reward. The distributing system, he thought, took a staggering toll; the immense difference between the price of bread in the shop and the pittance he received for the wheat in it went to middlemen. The elevators, railroads, mills, bakeries and stores battened on the suffering of the husbandmen. It did not help to explain that rates by the ton-mile had fallen sharply and steadily for carriage by rail and by lake or ocean steamer. Costs should have been lower, low enough to leave the farmer a margin.

There was some merit to this complaint. The farmer was never in a position to bargain when he disposed of his crop; he took what he could get in sales and paid what he had to in fees because he could not let the produce rot on his hands. The impersonal corporations with which he dealt charged what the traffic would bear and made up by squeezing out of little customers what they lost on rebates to big ones. On the other hand, the farmer could not understand the extent to which the intermediaries added value to the products he harvested, so that his dependence was the result of service rendered, not of conspiracy.

Nor did farmers understand the shortage of money. During the Civil War the government had issued large sums in paper; prices had risen. Later the decision to retire the greenbacks and to cease coining silver dollars had contracted the currency supply; prices had fallen. Aggrieved farmers demanded more money in circulation to get prices up again. Inflation was the favorite rural remedy, particularly attractive to people always short of cash.

Taxes and interest were fixed costs, first charges upon farm income; whether markets were high or low, whether harvests were good or bad, foreclosure was the penalty for failure to pay. The volume of farm debt climbed steadily. By 1890, fully 28 per cent of all farms were mortgaged, by 1900 fully 30 per cent; and in many places—in Kansas, for instance—the percentages were far higher than the national average. Borrowings from local merchants and payments on machines were an additional cause of concern, for interest rates were high, often with hidden charges coming to 20 per cent a year. The farmer did not think of these costs as businessmen did; these were not abstract elements in a balance sheet but insidious enemies undermining the foundations of his home.

In earlier times, the dependable rise in land values had helped dissolve debt; the farmer who was not doing well sold out for enough to pay off what he owed and still retain a stake for a try further west. But the vast areas thrown open to settlement after the Civil War kept values stationary down to the 1890s; and the close of the old mode of escape contributed to the spread of tenancy throughout the United States in the same period. In 1880 tenants operated almost one-quarter of the farm acreage in the nation; in 1900, almost one-third. The peculiarities of post-plantation agriculture in the South accounted for part of the development; but there were almost as many tenants outside that region as within it, some on large tracts held by absentee owners for speculation, some on foreclosed farms tilled by their former proprietors until sold. Tenantry in any form made a mockery of the yeoman ideal, of the faith that possession of the soil guaranteed the freedom of those who worked it. Americans, deprived of the chance for ownership which, they had assumed, empty space would always assure them, now understood that homelessness might be the ironic outcome of success in multiplying the fruits of their fields.

The hard-pressed farmers, accustomed to voluntary association, organized in self-defense. Leaders were available to direct their efforts—small-town lawyers, ambitious politicians and businessmen without capital. In the 1870s the old Northwest, from Ohio to Minnesota, was the chief seat of protest, and the National Grange of the Patrons of Husbandry was the outstanding agency for it. Founded as a fraternal mutual aid society in 1867, the Grange spread rapidly; in 1875, its 20,000 branches had enrolled some 800,000 members. It then possessed the clout to launch a political campaign that persuaded several states to create regulatory commissions to control the operations and rates of railroads and grain elevators. The Granges also experimented with producers' and consumers' cooperatives, founded in the simple faith that middlemen were unnecessary and parasitic. These enterprises taught their participants, the hard way, that the distributive function in the economy called for large amounts of capital, for considerable skill, and for the ability to take risks and absorb the consequences of error. Distribution proved to be a necessary and costly service, not merely an extortionary device of rapacious intermediaries.

Disillusionment set in as the cooperatives failed and as regulation had only limited effect. After 1880, the Granges lost membership and those which survived confined themselves to social activities.

The faith in cooperatives and in political action revived in the 1880s in regions where social frustration added to economic discontent. In the South, racial tensions and a running conflict between poor whites and former planters deepened the problems of debt and tenancy. In the Great Plains, nature was oppressive; periodic droughts, plagues of grasshoppers and sudden tornadoes laid waste the results of years of labor. The visual bleakness of the landscape and sheer loneliness added to the burdens of men and women worn down by hard work. Various farmers' alliances and unions sprouted in these areas, offering participants the opportunity to visit with one another if nothing else. These organizations stretched, in the West, in a broad band from Kansas northward into Minnesota and South Dakota, and in the South from Texas and Arkansas eastward to Georgia and South Carolina.

The Alliance members perceived two causes for the plight of the farmer—low prices due to the scarcity of money and excessive railroad charges. An increase in the currency supply through the free coinage of silver and through elimination of the bankers' control of paper would rectify the former; government owership of the means of transportation would take care of the latter. Public warehouses and low-interest loans would also help farmers hold their crops until prices were right and thus resist unfavorable market fluctuations.

In 1890, the Alliances launched a sustained campaign for political power. "Man plows and sows, but the dominant political party watereth and giveth the increase." With that message, they elected some fifty congressmen that year and gained strategic positions in eight states. Now the farmers picked up allies among socialists and reformers; and two years later formed a national People's Party, just in time to gain momentum from the widespread distress caused by the panic and depression of 1893. Foreclosures and unemployment soared; General Coxey led a tattered army of malcontents upon Washington; the day of ultimate reckoning was at hand.

In fiery orations, insistent tracts and vivid novels the Populist spokesmen delivered a simple message. The greed of the wicked was the source of all evil; the new party would show the way to redemption. The bloated plutocracy had enslaved the many through an insidious conspiracy of British and Jewish international bankers and Wall Street dealers who manipulated the currency to control the whole economy. Free and unlimited coinage of silver, nationalization of railroads, telegraph and telephone lines, an income tax and a galaxy of political reforms would restore the people's control of government. The movement gained steadily in strength, only to go down in disastrous defeat in the presidential election of 1896.

The Populist failure was due partly to the tactical error of fusion with the Democrats in 1896. The gains since 1890 had opened the possibility that union with a major party might unlock the White House gates. Yielding to the temptation, the Populists lost both the election and their identity, for the campaign destroyed the integrity of their organization and dissolved the loyalty of their voters. But other, deeper factors prevented recovery and made the tactical error fatal. The Populists offered little to the steadily increasing urban population, and they failed to hold the allegiance even of the farmers who had sought them out in distress but turned elsewhere as soon as relief came.

Away from the blare of rhetoric and the shrill cries of the office seekers, Americans slowly and spasmodically adjusted to their roles in the farm business. The full process would extend for fifty years into the twentieth century; but its character was evident in the very first decade.

Shortly after the climactic election of 1896, the issues heatedly debated during the campaign lost relevance. New discoveries in Alaska and elsewhere lowered the price of gold and abruptly eased the currency shortage. Credit also expanded as banks began to be somewhat more responsive than formerly to the needs of agriculture. In the boom that followed recovery from the depression of 1893, the demand for commodities soared; in 1909 James J. Hill, the railroad builder, expressed the somber view that the nation would soon face a famine. Prices then were already into a steady two-decade-long ascent. Farm values moved in the same gratifying direction, doubling under renewed speculative pressure in the twenty years after 1890. These trends dissolved a good deal of rural bitterness—particularly as the hasty, provisional, frontier features of life receded, as the railroad and the Ford motor car began to penetrate the former isolation of country homes.

Sustaining all these developments were structural changes which in time altered the position of agriculture in the national economy. It would be decades yet before the nation felt the full effects; but in 1910 the tremors were already at work. Competitive pressure forced out some marginal producers. The number of farm units ceased to increase after 1900. The victims displaced by the hard times of the 1890s could not simply move on to another new start; they had to find other occupations. The gain in output therefore was the result not of a multiplication in the number of producers but rather of an increase in efficiency. However difficult for individuals to surrender their dreams of being yeomen, the outcome was the survival of more specialized, stronger, more mechanized units.

New scientific methods also had a profound impact on the quality of American agriculture. Investments in education and research made many years earlier paid dividends after 1890. The Morrill Act of 1862 had given each state the means of creating a land-grant university in the hope of rearing a new generation of husbandmen equipped with the most advanced knowledge and techniques and therefore better able than their parents to manage the soil. A chain of agricultural experiment stations and numerous independent investigators provided alternatives to the trial-and-error methods of the past, diffusing practical information on how to improve yields. Farmers, receptive to new ideas, hastened to stay ahead of competitors. Ranchers brought in Durham and Hereford bulls to develop a breed with more beef than the nondescript Texas longhorns. Dairymen replaced the multi-purpose cow with Holsteins and raised the yield of milk. New types of cotton from Egypt, of wheat from eastern Europe and of oranges from Brazil improved the domestic plants. Ingenious experimenters and scientists developed new crossbred strains particularly appropriate to urban markets—the navel orange, the loganberry, the youngberry, and the grapefruit, for example. Insecticides and the use of natural enemies countered the destructiveness of pests and disease; and artificial fertilizers maintained the productivity of the soil.

The full consequences of these changes were yet to emerge. They would transform American farms from households to business enterprises. But enough had already happened by 1910 to show the character of the later development. Prosperity had restored confidence to agriculture. There had been 23 million bodies to feed and clothe in 1850, 50 million in 1890 and now, in 1910, 92 million. All the indices of national wealth soared, decade by decade proof that more and more people would consume more and more goods, drawing nourishment from and yielding ample profits to the possessors of the soil.

But in 1910, for the first time in history, the farm population of the United States was smaller than the nonfarm population, and industry vastly overshadowed agriculture. That, too, was an omen of what was yet to come.

8

The Iron Age

*J*ohnny, having just a few years back come marching home from war, in 1870 looked to the oceans of wheat waving across the prairies for assurance of American economic strength. Four decades later the young men, who would soon go off to another war, associated productive power with the blasts of smoke that mounted from a blaze of furnaces up the looming chimneys of Pittsburgh, Gary or Birmingham. The contrast measured the extent of the transformation in the nation's economy.

Between 1870 and 1910, the United States ceased to be a rural country in which manufacturing had made interesting beginnings. It became an industrial society, in which agriculture still played an important role, but was no longer pivotal. The change in emphasis influenced every element in the population and subjected existing political and social forms to acute strain.

The most important indices of economic well-being moved upward at impressive rates. The increase in the output of the whole productive system more than matched the growth of population. The average annual gross national product for the years 1903–1912 was more than three times as high as for 1869–1878. Those numbers were evidence of a capacity to turn out goods equal to that of the most advanced economies of Europe.

Manufacturing gained as much as agriculture from the unifying effects of developments in transportation and communications. The nation became a single, coherent market of continental dimensions, insatiably consuming the flood of products from the expanding factories.

Dramatic improvements in railroad service were as important as the sheer increase in mileage. The scattered lines of 1850 fell into place in a national network, bound together by connections which provided speedy through traffic among distant points. The gauge of tracks, the time zones and schedules became standard and therefore precise and interchangeable; in the 1880s dispatchers could hook up the wagons into any system, send them anywhere and know in advance the moment of arrival. Rebuilding and double-tracking, improved signal systems, new bridges capable of bearing heavy loads, bigger trains and more powerful locomotives raised dependability and lowered charges. Marshaling yards and depots eased the problem of transferring passengers and freight; and the expanded telegraph network established instant communication along the line and enabled the roads to operate safely and effectively. New pipelines to carry oil, and canal, lake and coastal vessels for bulk products played an important role, supplementary to that of the railroads. With increasing foreign trade, the tonnage engaged in oceanic shipping soared, although a declining percentage of it bore American registry. Factories raised output in the secure expectation that a dependable transportation system would bring in their raw materials and carry away their finished products to multitudes of willing consumers.

At the same time, buyers, sellers, managers and dealers got word to one another by speedy dependable communication instruments. The telegraph carried a heavy volume of private as well as of railroad messages, and the transatlantic cable came into widespread use in the 1870s, the telephone in the 1880s.

The rails and wires, along which people, things and messages moved, smoothed efficient distribution within the national market. Sample products of distant factories emerged from the drummers' cases in thousands of little corner shops in the tiniest villages and the most obscure urban districts. Each traveling salesman sent his orders back to the wholesaler or jobber for whom he worked; and they in turn divided their stocks into small lots for the retailers' shelves. The middlemen also supplied their customers with three to six months' credit, thus reducing the capital requirements of trade.

The shopkeeper linked the wholesalers and manufacturers to the consumers. Knowing his customers, he offered them as much as a year's credit and thus increased their ability to buy. Knowing their tastes, he made a first selection for them among the numerous products of the factories. The wholesale and retail distributors also began to organize inventory to even out somewhat the seasonal fluctuations in demand. The sale of coats zoomed in the fall, declined after Christmas. The factory could neither sew on demand, as the hand tailor had, nor cram its storerooms with enough to outfit everyone who might, or might not, buy. Nor could the mill which supplied the cloth. The middlemen provided the slack; the stocks they received and held made the garment available when the purchaser appeared, so that the manufacturer could spread his work out and so too could the mill. Although the elaborate distributing system required the services of thousands of men and boys and thus added to the final costs, it made the credit available which permitted sales without cash and spread the goods around.

Entrepreneurs in the thousands, each scheming to outdistance his rivals, felt the relentless pressure to offer the better deal. In the effort to gain a competitive advantage, they devised ingenious arrangements of all sorts to lower costs, to widen variety and to fix prices so as to eliminate haggling. Thus, in the 1880s F. W. Woolworth, who ran a five-and-ten-cent shop in Lancaster, Pennsylvania, developed a chain of similar outlets which together bought cheaply and sold cheaply large quantities of merchandise. In the large cities, aggressive dry goods dealers added new lines—crockery, kitchen utensils and ready-made clothing—and transformed themselves into resplendent department stores where tempting displays of buyables instilled unexpected desire in the passerby. At the same time, the members of thousands of farm households learned from the bargains offered in the mail-order catalogues of Aaron Montgomery Ward and of Sears, Roebuck & Company to need what they might otherwise not even have known existed.

Some manufacturers developed sales organizations of their own to escape the dependence on wholesalers and retailers who used their positions at the selling junctions to play one producer off against another. The Singer Company opened its own shops, the better to service its sewing machines; and Swift and Standard Oil developed outlets to assure direct access to consumers.

Changes in advertising techniques stimulated efforts to control the market. Manufacturers wished to make their trademarks known, shops, their names; and both addressed the public through the press. Earlier newspaper notices of goods for sale by local dealers had rarely run a full column long. But after the Civil War, department stores introduced display ads that gradually preempted the best space. Manufacturers, not to be outdone, used agencies to insert an appeal to buyers in hundreds of newspapers simultaneously, as well as in magazines with national circulations. By the end of the century, strident billboards lined the roads and streets with the same messages. Over and over, the consumer heard the same calls—on the one hand, to turn to Wanamaker's or Macy's for dependability; on the other, to ask not for soap or cocoa or woolens but for Pears' or Baker's or Forstmann's. The summons to buy was loud in the land, directing and stimulating the expenditures of numerous Americans.

A subtle transformation altered the consciousness of factory managers. They now looked out at a nation prepared for persuasion. Millions of consumers with an aggregate purchasing power of hundreds of millions of dollars were ready to gobble up the products of the machines. The vision of the waiting dollars accelerated the industrialization long since under way in textiles, extended the process to other products consumers might desire and provided the base for the expansion of iron and steel manufacturing.

In 1908 the American Woolen Company opened its giant Wood Mill in Lawrence, Massachusetts. One of the corporation's twenty-six plants, the six-story building stretched over twenty-nine acres and housed 225,000 spindles. Across the road, the same company was completing its Ayer Mill, almost as large.

The structures bore the names of two men, Frederick Ayer and William M. Wood. Frederick was the brother and business partner of James C. Ayer, the druggist and pill manufacturer prominent in the early history of Lowell. From the 1850s on, their patent-medicine company had invested some of its surplus cash in textiles (as well as in railroad, lumber, canal and smelting enterprises). In 1886 Frederick, by then in sole command of the family holdings, picked up the ailing Washington Mills of Lawrence, hiring away from the Wamsutta Mills in Rhode Island assistant treasurer William M. Wood, son of an immigrant seaman from the Azores. Two years later, the lines joined; Wood married Frederick Ayer's eldest daughter, took control of the corporation, and in 1899 merged it into the American Woolen Company. The two new mills in Lawrence were a monument to his achievement.

They were not typical of the textile industry as a whole, within which older, smaller plants continued to operate. But American Woolen expressed the confidence, shared by many, that expansion would continue, although punctuated by occasional poor years to eliminate marginal producers. A good part of the manufacture of cottons had moved away from its earlier base in northern New England, taking advantage of access to raw materials and to cheap labor in the South. But though the fortunes of specific firms might rise and fall, the process of growth in spinning and weaving that had begun in the Lowell of 1820 had continued without serious interruption. The demand for cloth, cotton or wool, kept machines everywhere busy.

The industries directed at consumers, already well established in 1870, all followed the same expansive course. The bolts of cotton became shirts and camisoles as well as sheets and drapery. Worsteds from the Wood Mill went into ready-made clothing, cut in massive quantities in large factories and stitched up either there or, even more economically, by thousands of pieceworkers in their homes. The value of the garments fabricated leaped from $214 to $1,367 million between 1870 and 1910. The transition from handicraft to large-scale methods of production which had already occurred in the manufacture of furniture, pianos, soap and carpets now extended to other articles. Thus, the inventions of Gordon McKay and Charles Goodyear opened the way to mechanization of the shoe industry and final liquidation of the old hand workers. As earlier, too, the new production methods generated their own demand. Vast modern enterprises turned out a multitude of tools and of textile, sewing and agricultural machines. Secondary effects then spread outward as increased requirements pressed expansion upon the spinners of thread, the tanners of leather, the vulcanizers of rubber for boots and shoes, and the cordage and paper makers.

Since manufacturing after 1870 was either located in or administered from the cities, every increase in industrial activity added to the urban population. In 1890, almost 30 per cent of all Americans lived in places with 5,000 or more inhabitants, 12 million of them in the fifty-eight cities with populations of 50,000 or more. In 1910, the respective numbers had become 40 per cent, with more than 24 million in 109 cities. Life in the new environment created massive demands, some entirely novel, some which the individual household had been able to meet for itself in a country setting. New large-scale enterprises supplied the needs of the city dwellers for places in which to work and reside, for food, water, light and the means of getting about. Construction boomed in the haste to bridge the rivers and fill in the shorelines, to extend and pave streets, to erect homes and public buildings and to lay conduits for water and sewerage.

Building methods did not change substantially in these decades.

Thousands of laborers wielding picks and shovels, driving nails, and laying bricks did the basic work; and draymen brought materials to the site. But the extra volume of the goods used and the secondary requirements of residence in the city opened profitable markets for manufacturers able to provide great quantities of asphalt, plate and window glass, carpets, paint, wallpaper and pipes. Everyone now paid for the means of illumination—gas, kerosene refined from petroleum and, later, electricity—thus opening opportunities for suppliers.

Many articles packaged in the first instance for urban buyers, before long attracted rural ones as well. The purchasers of food carried home not only fresh bread and meat, but also canned fruits and vegetables and salt, baking powder, starch and borax. Great breweries competed with the makers of soft drinks and candy. Paper poured in for print, for messages and for packaging, then was carted away as waste. The national markets for each of the products were large enough to sustain substantial industries.

All the people in the city moved around—vertically on elevators up the high buildings, horizontally on bicycles and horseless carriages, after 1888 on cars which drew electricity from overhead trolley wires and, by the end of the century, on underground and elevated railways. Meanwhile, interurban trolleys linked up hundreds of neighboring towns.

The nickels and dimes, in the spending, piled up into dollars— hundreds and thousands, millions of them. The prospect kindled the imaginations of thousands of promoters and inventors; the air thickened with schemes, some fraudulent, some harebrained, some sensible, some creative. O'Sullivan's heel—any little gimmick might make it, an idea, an angle, a tool, a machine—a watch to wear on the wrist, a razor with a changeable ever-sharp blade, a torch that cast light from electricity stored in a battery, a keyboard to set lines of type for a printer or to replace elegance of penmanship with legibility and speed in business correspondence. Scores of mechanics working away in 1900 produced a grand total of 6,000 motor vehicles; in 1910 the industry put 225,000 on the road.

The contrivers and dreamers, the big talk-and-plan men ran on; the size of the prize justified the odds. In the end, no doubt, success depended more on organizational skill, attention to detail and command of capital than on nimbleness. But the palpable magnitude of the market, nationwide, the fivefold rise in the flow of goods to consumers, kept everyone in motion—inventors and investors, salesmen and dealers. The objects the multitudes desired did not dribble out in cupfuls from scattered local sources but surged forth in torrents from mighty factories flooding the whole country by the force of their resources for innovation, efficiency and mass output.

The iron and steel industry felt the effects at once. It did not sell directly to the consumer but it was sensitive to rising demand from every branch of the economy.

All the needs soared, of railroads for locomotives, cars, rails and bridges; of factories for engines, machines, tools and castings; of high buildings for structural steel; of farms for wire; and of towns for pipes and tubes. The ironmasters and steel fabricators rushed to make the most of the situation.

The market drew them on. Persuaded that only expansion assured survival, that whoever failed to advance would be advanced upon, they reached out to meet the limitless demand of a country bound to boom and became entangled in operations of extraordinary complexity. Andrew Carnegie, for instance, while still a division superintendent for the Pennsylvania Railroad figured out where opportunities lay—iron bridges to replace the flimsy old wooden structures. Time proved him right; his Keystone Bridge Company thrived. But since a sure source of materials was essential if he were to profit from contracts which stretched over long periods, he moved into steel, where he met novel problems of fabrication and engineering. With the best technical advice available, risky decisions early supplemented bessemer with open-hearth operations, introduced alloys and reorganized the production flow in the interests of economy. It was not enough. Alert to developments in Europe, he integrated plants, aligning converters, blast furnaces and rolling mills to move the product along at low cost. With the stakes so high, he sought still more security. An alliance with Henry C. Frick brought assurance of adequate coke; and a deal with John D. Rockefeller set up a supply of high-grade, low-cost ore from the newly discovered Mesabi Range. Lest transportation fail him or cost too much, Carnegie built his own Pittsburgh and Lake Erie Railroad.

Yet even with all these elements under control, Carnegie could not rest. Hungry rivals snapped at his flanks, ready to tear away at any sign of his slackening, while his own weary partners begged for a halt so that they could enjoy the gains in hand. At the end of the century Carnegie agonized over the decision whether to stop expanding and thus risk new attacks, whether to draw in fresh forces at the cost of diluting his power, or whether to struggle on as in the past, reaching out for still more territory. The old man cashed in his chips, consoled by the stupendous sum he raked in for the heartache of leaving the game.

In 1901 the United States Steel Corporation, capitalized at a billion dollars, drew together all his and a clutch of ten other enterprises in a single fully integrated company operating 785 mills, mines, railroads and quarries. But there still was no limit. The new plant it opened in 1906 spread seventy coke ovens, fifty blast and open-hearth furnaces and related mills and shops across 1,250 acres in Gary, Indiana.

Undergirding this elaborate structure and others like it was the vast population of consumers. The five-cent piece dropped into the subway coin box, multiplied a million-fold, paid for the rails and cars built of steel. The kitchen stove and the pot upon it, the fire escape by the window and the fence around the farm also made their contributions. So too did the boot and coat, fashioned of leather and cloth, fabricated by machines built of the sovereign metal. Mounting output of steel ingots and castings was the evidence—up from 68,000 long tons in 1870 to more than 4 million in 1890, when the United States outdistanced Britain, and to 26 million in 1910. And in 1910 the metal cost all the producers who used it less than half what it had in 1870. The whole world now turned on the iron hinges industry fabricated.

Steel as well as glass, aluminum and other products of large-scale enterprise depended upon access to a great national market. The vertical integration and technological innovation characteristic of these industries demanded both specialization and also linkages to consumers.

Links to the market were reassuring—much of the time. Often, however, they chilled the entrepreneur with evidence of how dependent he was. The proud structure, built by his effort and his money, and all the ingenuity invested in it, rested upon the fragile foundation of the willingness and ability of remote consumers to buy. Were the flow of nickles, dimes and quarters to slacken, then all would come tumbling down.

Any undue strain might snap a link and put an entire enterprise at hazard. At long intervals—1873, 1893, 1907—depression settled across the land, purses emptied and buyers vanished; failure then dragged down the unprepared, great and small. At short intervals seasonal stoppages halted the construction and garment industries, idling workers and drying up orders to suppliers of glass and steel. Then again, every position in the market was only temporary; often, a new product, fashion, method or location cut the ground out from under established producers.

Each was therefore always on his toes to keep from going under, everyone selling to keep from being sold.

The best way to sell was to bring the price down. The traveling salesman's jaunty talk, the confident display of ads softened up the prospective buyer. But in the end the shopkeeper's eye went to the bottom line—price. No fool he; a competitor, too, he could afford to take account of no other consideration.

The sellers therefore kept the prices low. In the early years, big shippers grabbed an advantage by extorting rebates or preferential transportation rates; but the gains from that bloody game were only temporary and ultimately damaging to everyone because it kept markets unsettled. The railroad that gave one customer a secret special deal, might, behind his back, very well give another an even better arrangement. Sooner or later, the players decided to sheath their knives and to develop a dependable set of uniform charges, even if it took government regulation to do so.

The preferred way to get selling prices down was to keep manufacturing costs low—of raw materials and labor and capital. That was the essence of management in the iron age.

Industrial expansion drew upon abundant resources. In good times and bad, American farms produced plenty of cotton and wool for the spinners, plenty of grain and meat to feed the workers, most of the time at falling prices, but at not too painful a cost when rising.

There was also no shortage of timber; generations of use had depleted the Eastern forests, but the Southern uplands, Wisconsin and the Pacific Northwest yielded enough to supply all calls for lumber and for pulp. Anthracite from Pennsylvania still provided a good share of the nation's fuel; and after 1870 Americans dug into a vast bituminous field stretching from Lake Erie to northern Alabama for plentiful, cheap energy. Amply stoked, the furnaces in homes, on locomotives, in steel mills and generating plants never ceased to glow when needed. The uses of petroleum steadily broadened. The output of the wells in Pennsylvania, West Virginia, Ohio and Indiana had served as kerosene for illumination and as lubricants. But at the turn of the century, when the Texas fields came in, the internal combustion engine was already drinking up impressive quantities of gasoline. By then, too, the flow of electricity for light and power had increased substantially.

A plenitude of minerals from beneath the earth added to the

nation's wealth. The stocks of iron ore grew more swiftly than the steelmakers depleted them. The older sources in Pennsylvania remained productive while new deposits opened up in the Lake Superior region and in the area between Chattanooga, Tennessee, and Birmingham, Alabama. Periodic discoveries of gold and silver, in Nevada, in the Dakotas and in Alaska sent quivers of excitement among the adventurous. But the baser metals out of Michigan, Montana and Missouri served industry more directly, galvanizing, lining, conducting scores of products. The thousands of short tons of copper, lead and zinc piled up from 14, 17 and less than ten in 1870 to 129, 157 and 63 in 1890 and to 540, 393 and 269 in 1910. Somber scientific predictions that finite supplies would run out in the foreseeable future now and then roused the interest of conservationists. But providential new finds dispelled the gloom the forecasters spread. Texas oil flowed just as Pennsylvania's gave out. Daniel C. Jackling's strip-mining method permitted the extraction of low-grade copper deposits just when the high-grade ore was exhausted. A bounteous nature in the nick of time provided enough of everything, and pushed costs down.

Ample man- and woman-power kept labor costs low. Although the expanding factories required thousands of new hands at just the same time as did the construction of the railroads and of the cities, entrepreneurs rarely worried about shortages. The number of wage earners in industry tripled, from 2 million in 1870 to 6 million in 1910; and the amounts they took home remained, in the judgment of employers, gratifyingly small. The bosses paid as little as the market would bear yet drove their workers at a pace which helped raise the average output of each by 60 per cent between 1890 and 1910.

The labor supply remained plentiful. Fears during the Civil War that industry might suffer from the drain of manpower into the Army had proven unfounded. The contract labor law then enacted to permit the recruitment of immigrants turned out to be superfluous and languished unused on the statute books until repealed in 1885. An abundant pool of willing hands accumulated of itself, fluid in the sense that it flowed in the direction of any demand, and economical in its effects upon company budgets. The available reserve was largely a product of immigration, which reached unprecedented heights as the steamship and railroad shortened the time in transit and lowered the cost.

The 8 million newcomers who entered the United States in the two decades after 1870 still originated mostly in northern Europe; and a considerable number of them moved into the expansive agricultural regions of the country. Another experience awaited the 12½ million or so who arrived between 1890 and 1910, among them numerous peasants from eastern and southern Europe, from the Near East and from Asia, regions now shaken by the economic changes which had transformed Britain and Germany earlier. All immigrants, whatever their place of origin, after 1890 stepped ashore in a country quite different from that which had greeted their predecessors. The soil of the West, in the decades that followed, did not sustain the cultivators already native to it; foreigners, without resources and unfamiliar with life on the plains, could not strike roots there. The ideal of farm life remained alluring; reality warned newcomers away.

After 1890 the greater pull was to the factories, the mines and the railroads. Cornish tinworkers, English loomfixers, Belgian glassmakers, German brewers and other fortunate possessors of valuable skills readily found commanding places. But the mass of immigrants brought only muscles and need with them. They formed the pool, available for any labor, at any price, under any conditions, flowing into the construction gangs, lining up at the factory gates, thronging to the mining towns.

Some employers drew upon the pool through contractors. These intermediaries, often countrymen who spoke the same language as the hands they took on, managed the group, assumed responsibility for recruitment and payment and, outside the city, provided food and shelter. Laying the rails along the right of way or maintaining them later, bridging, tunneling, building dams and reservoirs, the padrone was absolute, his service efficient, paid for in large part by exploitation of those who toiled at his command. Control by such a boss was scarcely less effective in urban building, although the diggers and carriers retained some freedom of choice among jobs. Where homework was common, as in the clothing or cigar industries, a variant of the contracting system organized labor in which whole families participated seven days a week.

These arrangements did not fit the factory. The very size of the new plants and the complexity of the methods of large-scale production required other means of recruiting and managing the bewildered, unskilled laborers. Workers of many different origins had to get along in interdependent tasks—had to reach the job, and leave, at the same time; had to follow a prescribed routine, and had to avoid accidents to persons and damage to machines. Only military officers and the masters of plantations had previously dealt with numbers in the hundreds; and their management experience, grounded on the threat of coercion, did not fit the circumstances of a labor force which was not servile. Entirely apart from the provisions of the law, the industrial workers had some degree of choice, so that there were limits beyond which employers could not go without diverting the supply elsewhere. The reluctance of immigrants to go to the South, out of fear for their freedom, showed employers the limits to their power over wage earners.

Alternative forms of compulsion that held the laborers to their jobs varied with place. Thousands of employees retained their liberty, qualified however by circumstances which limited their options, so that they had to wish to work in order to survive.

From the pithead, the miners' homes straggled off down the uneven road punctuated along the way by store, church, saloon—all within reach of the siren's sound. This was Connellsville, Pennsylvania, or Virden, Illionis, or Houghton, Michigan—mining towns.

From the great factories and the piercing whistles, the workers' homes spread away down streets which fanned out from the iron entrance gates. This was Pullman, Illinois, or Homestead, Pennsylvania, or Gary, Indiana—mill towns. In each of these communities, a single industry, often a single plant, employed the entire labor force and therefore controlled the economic destiny of the whole population. The mill town generally was close enough to some large city—Chicago or Pittsburgh—to afford managers good communications and both raw materials and finished goods cheap transportation. Yet it was also far enough away so that the workers could not readily move back and forth, and were therefore immobilized by the need to live where they worked, to work where they lived.

In the virtual isolation of these enclosed towns, the worker depended totally upon the employer. There were no alternatives, save the few places on the lowest rungs of the middle class for those elected to public office or able to open little shops. For most, the job at the mine or mill was the only job there was. The gates closed upon blacklisted troublemakers, however skilled they might be. Here the reality of power was such that even benevolence turned into a mode of discipline. Company housing reduced to dependence the workers whose families resided in them; and the employer only increased his authority when he helped employees purchase homes, for then they were bound not only to their property but also to him. Self-generated discipline took the place of external coercion. Credit in the company store, a godsend when the worker was out of cash, had the same effect; debt tied the borrower to the lender.

The system of subordination and restraint sometimes broke down. Cutbacks squeezed the workers. There was nothing to do. No earnings. Meager savings ran out. Yet the company demanded its

rent, its mortgage payments, settlement of accounts in its store. Or,
simmering grievances over hours, conditions of work and rates finally
boiled over.

These towns were small enough so that the laborers knew one
another, were able to form communities and to take steps in their own
defense. Strikes, sometimes violence, ruptured the usual pattern of
control.

In the cities, too, discipline was a product of need. As far as
possible, the company organized jobs so that anyone could do them,
so that everyone was a replaceable part. The introduction of gas, and
later of electric lights, lengthened the working day; and the pace of
production quickened so that the velocity of motion, the deftness, the
quickness, the constant strain dazed European visitors. The high turnover rate did not matter to managers. Men and women eager for
places were always waiting at the gate.

But in the cities, no peal of bells or shriek of siren reached all the
distant homes of the laborers who, outside the plant, led their own
lives. They therefore had more resources than the mill town workers.
The urban family often drew upon multiple incomes; if one member
lost a post, another still brought in a pay packet, if one factory was
tight, another had openings. There was not, as in small communities,
the single adherence to a single employer that limited the possibility
of choice.

In town or in city, the annals of labor were brief, simple and un-
glorious. Wages, close to subsistence; work, insecure—subject to long
layoffs in seasonal industries and to periodic unemployment during
depressions. No protection against the hazards of the job. Each man
for himself. Only the consistently falling prices of food down to 1900
mitigated the hardship somewhat.

Craftsmen and others with scarce skills still had bargaining
power. Carpenters, bricklayers, printers, typographers and locomotive
engineers, among others, possessed the leverage to push their earnings
upward. They supported their families in moderate comfort and put
aside savings for emergencies or to purchase homes. They lived at a
great remove from the mass of other workers. In one Illinois town in
1882, when common laborers averaged $9 a week, blacksmiths aver-
aged $15 and plasterers $24. Nationally, in 1890, weekly wages averaged $8.71 for the unskilled, $11.94 for all manufacturing, and $17.49
for the building trades.

The unskilled laborers were unable to help themselves. Briefly
the Knights of Labor had attempted to bring all Americans who
worked with their hands within a single association, excluding only

lawyers, bankers, liquor dealers and gamblers. At one point in the 1880s it enrolled almost 700,000 persons. But the illusion of identity of interest of all wage earners died quickly; in 1890, only 100,000 remained in the organization. By then the skilled craftsmen had decided to go it alone. After great strikes in 1877 and again in 1885, the railroad men entrenched themselves in occupational brotherhoods; and many other trade unions of artisans drew together in the American Federation of Labor, which decided in 1886 to bargain, pure and simple, in the interests of its own members. Let the others fend for themselves. In 1890, 550,000 workers had joined A.F. of L. affiliates, and the number rose in the next two decades to 2 million. But the unorganized majority lacked all bargaining power so long as numerous applicants waited to take their jobs.

Sporadic violence was the only recourse of the unskilled. They drifted into hopeless strikes out of desperation or under the influence of radical anarchists or socialists ready to lead them in blows against the system. Enthused by the touch of each other's shoulders, intoxicated with the sense of possible power, the laborers then demanded the right to be heard. They were free men. But the prospect of success was slim and scabs abundant; petty incidents resulted in exchanges of blows or shots, and then the intervention of police or troops revealed with each thrust and counterthrust the stark reality of where power lay. From the Molly Maguires to the Wobblies ran a consistent record of defeat. The war was most bitter in the mining and mill towns, where the middle classes and local officials often sympathized with the workers, who were the majority of the residents while the owners were distant corporations. The conflict also reached the migrant workers of farm and forest and spread into the cities.

Neither victors nor vanquished wanted war, however. Carnegie, the greatest industrialist of them all, recoiled at the bitter taste of his success in breaking the Homestead strike. The prospect of a permanent rift in society was not in accord with his vision of America or that of others in his class. As much as the factories needed cheap labor, they needed also not a cowed proletariat but consumers able to buy the products poured out at the end of the line. After 1900, the National Association of Manufacturers and the National Civic Federation puzzled over the contradiction between low wages and mass purchasing power and, while they more often whistled in the dark than grappled seriously with the problem, their concern was symptomatic of a desire to avoid a showdown, if possible.

Nor did the workers wish to go to the extreme. They caught most of the bullets and even peaceful strikes demanded costly sacrifices, were therefore measures of last resort. In the cities, frequent hops from job to job and plant to plant deprived them of any sense of identity with fellow workers and inhibited the development of class consciousness. Many immigrants considered themselves birds of passage, destined to return to their native villages after a few years. The foreign-born, whether they remained in America or left, had a standard of comparison; the meager American wages were bountiful by comparison with those of Europe. Now they lived in the golden land and, if the withered rewards of the moment left them unfed, there remained hope in the promise yet to be fulfilled, that they or their children would attain a status out of reach in the places of their origin. In fact, there was enough mobility upward to make the present tolerable despite low wages and periods of unemployment.

The manufacturer understood afresh the urgency of holding costs down whenever he considered replacing an old machine with a new one. Whoever did not keep up with it, fell behind. Carnegie was willing to junk a plant only a few years old if a new one using a better process raised productivity. The readiness in the United States to discard still-usable tools, machines, buildings and factories shocked visiting Europeans. Americans had a quite different conception of waste. Waste for them was the expenditure of energy to patch up the obsolete; or even the failure to get rid of any device, however intact, when an improved model appeared. Furthermore, expansion was the rule—another wing to the plant, another branch to the line, another territory to invade. Every such commitment reminded the planner of the crucial role of capital. The total invested in industry climbed more than sixfold between 1870 and 1910 in a process which absorbed an average of 7 per cent of the national product each year.

Manufacturers shied away from borrowing as a means of raising capital. The railroads had not; and though their business was more dependable than that of the factory owner, still they could not readily meet the heavy fixed charges for interest and debt retirement. As a result their shares ceased to attract investors, so that for new capital they turned increasingly to bond issues, which further depressed their situation. Industrialists, who enjoyed even less security, wished to avoid the burdens of indebtedness and the remorseless, regular costs borrowing entailed.

Lucky he who knew the mechanism of credit and could keep a check floating in the air until there were funds to meet it. Lucky he whose friends, countrymen, co-religionists or relatives provided backing when needed. But luckier he who never allowed sentiment to draw him into providing hazardous backing for others. And luckiest of all, he who always had a surplus in hand. He could afford to make judicious investments, even take moderate risks, perhaps now and then be game for a flyer. He might rake in the whole pot; and, however painful the loss if he did not, still a stake would remain. The squeeze came when the absence of a balance forced him either to miss all those juicy deals or else to stay in the game by taking in partners or selling shares to outsiders, thus diluting his own future gains.

In the end, therefore, the moral was plain: have a surplus. Get it by underconsumption, by spending less than was earned, by taking less out of the business than it yielded. That is, by plowing back the profits. Which meant making sure there were profits to plow back—as Carnegie did, or Ford later, by keeping costs low, of labor, of materials, of everything else. The iron necessity of economizing obsessed the manufacturers.

Efficiency, which was the other word for it, was the secret of good management. The old men who had come out on top later talked freely about the qualities of the successful entrepreneur—keen observation, rapid reasoning, trained imagination, all aspects of mental efficiency, so that the mind was always ready for every decision business required. The manager so equipped made the profits that kept him in capital; he held the costs of labor and of supplies down; and he outsold competitors.

Increasingly, however, the demands of efficiency required of the manager specialized training and information. The old-timers had learned from experience and had maintained control by close attention to detail. But as the nineteenth century drew to a close, enterprises were too complex and too large—the risks too great—for trial and error. The entrepreneur then utilized the services of educated experts.

Technology became the realm of the engineer. Carnegie himself had depended on the counsel of Alexander H. Holley; for no amateur tinkerer could keep abreast of new patents and new processes, in chemistry, metallurgy and geology, in France, England, and Germany as well as in the United States. Technical schools expanded rapidly; the graduates of Stevens and Cooper Union, of R.P.I. and M.I.T. and V.P.I. organized societies of mining, mechnical and civil engineers, began to publish journals and acquired professional status.

A few managers, at the end of the century, began to listen with interest to the argument advanced by some engineers that the position of the human beings in the plants might be arranged more efficiently than in the past, just as the machine had been. The workers handled expensive machinery, labored in large groups, and performed tasks that were but parts of a whole. Yet the owner or superintendent could not keep the thousands of employees in his factory under his constant oversight. Only a rational system of organization could control their performance, bring them to their appointed places at the appointed times, calculate the cost and value of their labor and pass commands along to them through a hierarchy of foremen, department overseers, and first hands. From 1895 onward, Frederick W. Taylor occupied himself with devising such systems and persuading industrialists of the utility of adopting them.

The larger the enterprise and the more remote the entrepreneur from its actual operations, the greater was the dependence upon intermediaries and the greater also the risk of that dependence. Alert and imaginative managers struggled to cope with the problems of organization.

On the other hand, ruin awaited the business which failed to meet the challenge. The appearance of prosperity might hide the inner rot for a while, but not indefinitely. The mills of the American Woolen Company, scattered in a dozen towns, and its central selling office in New York operated under the direction of William Wood in Boston, who rewarded himself with a fabulous salary. Even had he willed it, he could not be everywhere. Nor could he himself check the activities of all those to whom he delegated power. The opportunities for pilferage, for kickbacks, for private deals at company expense, for error and for miscalculation were horrendous. His factories wove for inventory; each produced whatever quantity of cloth its superintendent guessed would find purchasers, then hoped that the selling office would dispose of it. Not until the end of the year, if then, did Wood know whether he had made a profit or suffered a loss; and it was later still before he could add up the figures to know why. By then it was far too late to learn where the credit or the blame lay, or even whether the numbers were accurate. Besides, he could only go by the totals for each mill; and conditions and costs varied so from one to another that comparisons were never precise.

The railroads had made a first effort to devise accurate accounting and control systems. In their far-flung operations, cash dribbled in and out through numerous hands, from fares and freight, for supplies and services. The companies required some means of verifying receipts and governing expenditures if they were not to be robbed blind. In addition, state regulatory agencies and, later, the Interstate Commerce Commission, intent on snooping, demanded accurate records.

Carnegie's experience while he worked for the Pennsylvania Railroad had taught him the utility of organizing the enterprise so that a flow of data from it informed management of what went on; and he rigorously applied the lesson at every stage of his subsequent business career—a fact which contributed considerably to his success. Merciless to partners and employees who deviated from the rule, he demanded universal accountability; and others learned from him.

Gusts of paper fluttered through the business world. The old clerk on his stool gave way to a battery of shorthand secretaries; the letter press yielded to the typewriter; and piles of ruled blanks and books, printed forms and memoranda accumulated in the files. Additional employees handled these documents under the supervision of an array of new officers. A spreading bureaucracy interposed itself between the entrepreneur and his enterprise, assisting him in control in some ways, but creating formidable problems of its own. The talent now required for leadership was that of the administrator. Elbert H. Gary, for instance, commanded the far-flung empire of United States Steel with precision. But his role was far different from Carnegie's. Gary operated by rules set by a board of directors rather than by personal judgment based on personal ownership.

Most industrialists before 1910 had begun their careers without formal preparation, one-time grocers, clerks, drummers, telegraph boys, mechanics, learning across the counter to buy and sell, becoming familiar with business methods by copying letters or delivering messages, knowing the machine from the feel of grease on their hands, dealing with laborers as foremen on the job. Savings and scheming got them ahead. Few took the time out for college, or even to wait for a high school diploma. But young Henry Ford, while still in the machine shop, spent his nights at study in a business college because the accounting skills taught by books and lectures would help him ahead. Private proprietary schools of this sort sprang up in cities around the country; and various types of commercial instruction intruded into more traditional academic institutions.

The new administrators did not come up the old way. The boards which entrusted great enterprises to them sought convincing credentials of reliability and training. Furthermore, the unwillingness of some heirs of wealth to carry on made room for the professionals. Ernest L. Thayer, for instance, could have stepped into his father's place in command of several Massachusetts woolen mills. But a Harvard education spoiled the young man for the dreary life in trade; he toured Europe, wrote a column for a San Francisco newspaper and finally settled into leisurely gentility in Santa Barbara.

To hold the interest of people like Thayer as well as to develop and transmit ever more complex commercial skills, the nation's oldest university in 1908 opened a graduate school of business administration, an indication that business was coming to be regarded as a profession to which a formal course of education offered entry. Knowledge, here organized as science, would bestow on business the increased efficiency to solve all the problems of the iron age.

Professional business administration, however, was an aspiration, not an actuality, one aspect of an extended quest for more orderly forms of production to offset the tremendous hazards of private enterprise. The quest had begun long before, when the government had ceased its attempt to direct the economy. Industrialization increased the urgency for developing a systematic alternative to state action.

9

Corporate Enterprise

*T*he executives regarded the little empires they ruled and found them not altogether good.

The venturers who had aggressively made the firms what they were—Carnegie, Mellon, Ford—regarded their enterprises as extensions of themselves. The plants and all within them were their property, possessed in their own names or in partnerships or in closely held corporations controlled by their own friends or by members of their own families. The businesses were theirs, projections of their personalities. What they created, they jealously guarded and frantically sought to expand. Competitors were enemies, ruthlessly fought, eliminated when possible, as a chieftain would the strays of another clan.

In 1910—and in 1930 and 1970—as in 1870, new men who had yet to establish themselves continued to battle for places at the top. But those who had succeeded between 1870 and 1910 often tired of endless competition and looked for means to institutionalize their achievements. Then they found hitherto unperceived values in order and predictability and began to look about for surrogates who would keep things going, leave the owner time for other interests. Carnegie's thoughts turned to the castle in Scotland and the cause of peace; Frick collected art, as did Mellon, who also wished to play the statesman; and even Ford, in time, dabbled in politics and antiques.

Age also took its toll, so that the old zip was no longer there every morning and, remembering how he had pushed out the falterers in his way, many a tycoon wondered what obscure young buck down in the organization would someday brashly seize command. If there was no son to whom to pass the power, then better arrange the transfer so that it would at least memorialize its creator.

Even in the process of pushing out or swallowing up rivals, the venturers had recognized the utility of figurers and arrangers, of experts whose minds ran to statutes and blueprints, who found the ways to get done what they were asked to do. Sometimes soon and sometimes late, the decisions came, to let the lawyer or engineer or salesman take charge as executive.

The administrators approached positions of control, not by fighting their way up through the plant, but laterally, by invitation, often from the outside. A good many were lawyers. Calvin S. Brice, for instance, practiced in Cincinnati until some of his clients got him involved in the management of a group of regional railroads. He ran the Lake Erie and Western and promoted, planned and helped build the Nickel Plate. So too, Elbert H. Gary had been attorney for Midwestern railroads and industries before becoming a director of the Illinois Steel Company, then president of Federal Steel and ultimately head of United States Steel.

Certainly, such people wished to succeed as executives and hoped to make their enterprises grow. But the competitive spirit that moved them differed from that of the man on the make. They were not owners of property taking pleasure in aggrandizement but salaried officials finding satisfaction and financial rewards in a job well done for others. They valued the order, regularity and predictability that were essential ingredients of planning. They took command of great firms, often held dominant positions in the market; but whether the existing pattern required that they attack or defend themselves against attack, unlimited rivalry seemed to them chaotic, wasteful, and uncertain. Like the engineers, the administrators prized efficiency and hoped to attain it by emerging from the jungle where each clawed the others. More civilized, mutually advantageous relationships might follow from a process of integration that drew the savagely individualistic entrepreneurs into large units, controlled for the benefit of all by competent, disinterested managers. In an age of steam, electricity and machinery, such aggregations, they thought, were a necessity, yielding the greatest good to the greatest number.

Order, however, was difficult to attain. Where grab hold of a productive system ever in flux? Nowhere. Who possessed the power to establish binding rules and to provide sanctions for their enforcement? No one. Since early in the nineteenth century, the state had abstained from all efforts to direct the growth of the economy; and government, subject to popular control, was unpredictable and sometimes capricious in its attitude toward concentration and regulation.

In Europe voluntary associations portioned out the market and ruled many branches of industry with the benevolent approval of the state. But in the United States the ease with which anyone aggrieved could mobilize voters, legislators and judges by the cry of "monopoly" prevented the formation of such cartels. Instead American industrialists fumbled along for years, experimenting with schemes for consolidation on the margin of the law, usually evoking angry popular reactions in the process. Every effort at understanding or accommodation was vulnerable to the accusation of conspiracy, if not under a statute, then under some vague provision of the common law. Even investment bankers who managed to control some of the flow of capital soon discovered the limits of their power to induce integration; and the government, unable to clarify its own attitude, when pressed to act did so in a negative fashion. Wealth grew in the four decades to 1910 luxuriantly but in accord with no deliberate plan.

All the issues of order, control and law emerged in the process of exploiting the great untapped resource that supplied the nation's light and power after 1870. The development of petroleum dramatically illustrated the forces that also shaped the organization of other industries and means of communication.

Oil! The excitement of discovery in Pennsylvania in the 1860s and 1870s matched that of the gold rush. The wells blew in; the wealth gushed out. Then glut; and the price a barrel brought dropped. Demand raised the price. Then new supplies lowered it, while producers fought for shares of the market. The refiners, middlemen, also did battle among themselves; and one of them, John D. Rockefeller, warily maneuvered for advantage from his strategic location in Cleveland, a city linked by rail and lake to the fields and to markets. He gave no quarter and expected none. He built up his defenses by vertical integration; he manufactured the barrels and acid used in his plants and he owned a fleet of lighters and tankers and a drayage service. He also bought out competitors, as when he formed the Standard Oil Company of Ohio in 1870 to unite a cluster of neighboring refineries. Carnegie operated in the same way, as did the Edison General Electric Company a decade later.

Acquisitions were often awkward however; they either diluted control or called for substantial capital outlays. Once they had gobbled up the little fish, therefore, expansive entrepreneurs preferred amicable coexistence, live and let live—in the abstract at least. Railroads which ruinously reduced rates to take traffic from each other already understood that they would all prosper by sharing the business, reducing the total number of trains and increasing the charges. Thus in 1870 three roads serving the area between Chicago and the Missouri River agreed informally to pool their earnings and divide the proceeds equally. In the decade that followed various groups of Southern and Eastern roads set up similar private associations. So too, Rockefeller and some of his rivals in 1871 formed the South Improvement Company, allotting each other oil production quotas and deciding what percentage of their business all would assign the railroads that served them. The carriers, grateful for the ability to plan their traffic, rewarded the allies with a rebate on every barrel of oil shipped not only by members but also by non-members. Refiners who refused to cooperate therefore indirectly subsidized those who did.

Pools like South Improvement aimed to stabilize prices by limiting output and removing the incentive for competition. But such arrangements, although common in other branches of industry also, rarely remained harmonious for very long. They held while markets expanded and while each plant operated at close to capacity. When demand slackened, however, entrepreneurs forgot gentlemen's agreements and no sanctions restrained them in the pursuit of their own interests. Any resort to law would expose everyone to the charge of conspiracy.

In 1882, Rockefeller's attorney, S. T. C. Dodd, suggested a way to keep the errant brethren in line. The stockholders of Standard Oil of Ohio, in return for trust certificates, assigned all the corporation property to a board of nine trustees, which managed the enterprise, free from any public scrutiny. In the next few years, the same nine men by the same process acquired control of almost all the important oil refineries in the country, each of which continued its own operations under the general direction of the trustees. No pronouncement in law had yet declared whether this arrangement lay within the definition of conspiracy. Ingenious promoters in other branches of industry experimented with similar devices to achieve surreptitiously control unattainable through open competition.

The effort to rationalize industry through trusts boomeranged, for it drew fierce retaliation. No matter how clever the lawyers, how secret the documents, how mum the collaborators, no matter what persuasive bribes or political pressures passed to prosecutors and legislators, high prices and restrictive terms gave the game away. Effective controls made themselves felt; that was their purpose. Small, excluded competitors and consumers ran screaming to the state for redress, reviving the old battlecries of the tea party and of Jackson's war on the monster Bank. Monopoly! Popular opinion frowned upon the bullying Goliaths, particularly when the visible result was the concentration in a few hands of great fortunes lavishly thrown away in orgiastic living, while the virtuous little man lost his all.

Before the Civil War $100,000 had been a substantial fortune; only twenty-five New Yorkers and nine Philadelphians had possessed a million dollars each. In 1890 the scale had changed radically. A great fortune then was one of a hundred million dollars; and the ordinary millionaires were 3,000 strong. Americans were glad to have the convenient transportation and the cheap goods the railroad and the factory made possible but they wished to be sure that the masters of wealth did not become masters of the Republic. A hint of conspiracy touched off a wave of mistrust. In this atmosphere pools and trusts were vulnerable to prosecution, in so far as the common law forbade combinations in restraint of trade. The demand that government do something mounted through the 1880s.

Here and there, writers and politicians suggested radical solutions—nationalization of the means of transportation, appropriation of unearned gains on land, and public ownership of industry. A popular book by Henry George (1879) explained that the tendency to the unequal distribution of wealth, which had destroyed every previous civilization, was now evident in the United States. Edward Bellamy (1888) criticized the desperate strainings, the agonized leapings and plungings and the pitiless lashings of a competitive society, then went on to describe the utopian alternative in which the state owned the instruments of production and used them for the benefit of all. On into the twentieth century little groups of socialists, some Marxist in inspiration, stressed the need for a change to put the economy at the service of the masses.

Many Americans responded favorably to abstract appeals to communal solidarity, but few accepted government ownership as a solution. Democracy bred familiarity with the uses of power; and familiarity dispelled illusion. The cop on the beat, the legislator in the lobby, the mayor in his office, palms crossed one and all, were none evil by nature but pliable, as anyone might be, when violation of an ordinance, or award of a franchise or contract, or revision of a tax assessment gave them the chance. The remedy was, reduce the chances to a minimum. Any citizen who read the daily press grasped the validity of William Graham Sumner's prediction that "when the politician and the master of industry were joined in one," the country would "have the vices of both unchecked by the restraints of either."

No significant group clamored for a takeover by the state. People, with few exceptions, considered competition the preferable means of assuring equity to consumers and users, of furthering efficiency and of lowering costs. The proper function of government, they believed, was to prevent interference with free competition. The railroads most required oversight, for their charges influenced all others and their policies were crucial to the success of every pool or trust. Transportation rates and preferential shipping advantages determined the competitive position of everyone in the economy. Operated by managers who governed their little principalities much as petty German despots did a century earlier, the carriers had made more enemies than friends. Yet their very existence depended upon grants of charters and privileges. Demands mounted for their regulation by law.

New Hampshire had created a commission to supervise the railroads within its borders before the Civil War. Other states followed. Massachusetts in 1869 established one pattern; its board was primarily advisory and used publicity for sanctions. But Illinois a year later set up an agency that actually fixed rates; and the Supreme Court in Munn v. Illinois (1877) upheld the constitutionality of the practice.

However, since traffic increasingly passed across state lines much of it escaped supervision. The Wabash Case of 1886, in which the Supreme Court ruled that only federal law could control the interstate movement of passengers and goods, made national action imperative; and by then both shippers and railroad men favored a solution that would spare them the burdens of dealing with numerous, sometimes conflicting, state commissions. The Interstate Commerce Act of 1887, enacted in response to these pressures, fostered competition by forbidding rebates, discrimination between long and short hauls, and pooling arrangements. It also ordered a commission to investigate abuses and to seek in the courts redress for violations.

The Interstate Commerce Commission in practice did not give positive direction to the transportation system, especially after judicial rulings limited further the meager powers Congress gave it. But the legislation which forbade rebates and similar devices significantly reduced the leverage that differential transportation costs gave favored belligerents in industrial warfare.

In 1890 the Sherman Anti-Trust Act explicitly declared illegal any monopoly or contract, any combination in the form of trust or otherwise or any conspiracy in restraint of trade, whether by individuals or by corporations. It thus outlawed the pools and trusts of the preceding two decades. Separate firms could no longer ally themselves to organize the market.

The statute left the status of individual companies unclear however. Control of the market might expose anyone to accusations of monopoly; but a single firm could not be guilty of conspiring with itself. The law which outlawed trusts thus seemed to tolerate the merger as an arrangement for imposing order on the competitive industrial battleground. The rivals who, before 1890, reached understandings to control the production and distribution of goods, after that date consolidated in order to escape the penalties of the Sherman Act.

The purchase of one corporation by another involved millions, sometimes hundreds of millions, of dollars; and few businessmen possessed ready cash in those amounts. But some had access to mammoth financial resources, drawn from the vast store of capital heaped together by the American productive system after 1870.

The continued willingness of Europeans to invest in the New World, some support from the federal and state governments, repeated windfalls, and the widespread habit of individual saving mobilized substantial amounts of capital. Those accumulations not only met the exigencies of a massive, expanding industrial enterprise, but also provided the means of maneuver in establishing some order in it.

Foreign sources of capital remained important in 1910 as in 1870, sustained by faith in the free movement of funds across national boundaries. Investors in Britain, France, Germany and the Netherlands possessed mounting surpluses as a result of the early industrialization of those countries; and low yields at home made overseas securities attractive. The United States enjoyed substantial advantages in competing against other relatively underdeveloped areas for the financial patronage of Europeans. The Civil War had consolidated the national government, generating confidence in the stability of the society and in the value of shares in its growth. The United States still exported agricultural goods in return for manufactured products, an exchange which created balances available for the purchase of securities in the accounts of Europeans; and well-developed mercantile and banking channels facilitated the transactions. The amounts sent to America accelerated until the 1890s and remained sizable thereafter, although the rate of increase declined as imperial interests shifted attention to alternative opportunities in South America, Asia and Africa. By then, however, domestic sources had gained immensely in importance, so that Americans hardly noticed the abstention of foreigners.

The United States generated large amounts of capital internally, some as manna fallen from heaven, some as earnings diverted from immediate consumption.

Windfalls, when they occurred, seemed far more significant than they were. Fortunate discoveries dotted the passing decades—gold and silver in the West and later in Alaska, iron in the Lake Superior region, oil in Texas. It was true that finders were rarely keepers, that the prospectors usually failed to make anything of their luck. The types who located and worked the lodes were usually unable to transmute the minerals they dug out into productive capital. Their riches remained inert until dissipated in idle expenditures. More often than not the proceeds they carried back to town vanished into the pockets of dealers, big and little, more familiar with the bank balance than with the pick and shovel. The facilities needed systematically to develop and exploit a find entangled every discoverer in hazardous financial dealings from which few emerged intact. Attempts to outsmart the city sharpers rarely succeeded. Leonidas Merritt, who took his Mesabi iron mines into a deal with Rockefeller in 1893, complained that the bargain left him only the prospect of walking back on the ties from New York to Duluth. In the end Rockefeller, not Merritt, invested the proceeds of Mesabi; the gifts of fortune entered the economy through the same channels as did surpluses left from earnings.

Savings were individual and voluntary, the outcome of millions of individual decisions rather than of any communal judgment. Taxation no longer subsidized enterprise, as it had just after the Revolution, except when some states and municipalities had to pay the defaulted railroad debts guaranteed in moments of excessive optimism. Congress did hand over some 130 million acres of Western land to help railroad construction; now and then, too, a town provided the site for a factory. These grants put inert resources to use but did not directly drain away the earnings of the citizens. The general lack of confidence in the ability of government to manage money, confirmed from time to time by dramatic instances of waste and corruption, limited its income.

In a period free of war and of heavy military expenses, one also in which expenditures for public services rose little, taxes stayed low. Whatever surplus people acquired remained in their own hands, available for personal use; and strong incentives persuaded many to abstain from consuming everything they made. Various attractive opportunities induced Americans to put their money to work.

Businessmen believed that profits plowed back into the enterprise provided the funds for expansion. The firm generated the surplus for further investment through efficiency in holding down costs. It gained in the ability to do so by operating in a society that absolved it of many social charges—of the obligation to support the laborers it laid off or to clean the water and air it fouled, for instance. Furthermore, since development proceeded by trial and error, the successful did not pay the price for the miscalculations of the failures. Adversity isolated! Fools who indulged in acts of excessive scrupulosity or generosity could not survive. When his friend and benefactor, Tom Scott, approached bankruptcy, Carnegie turned his back, lest the ruin engulf him too. Each individual pursued his own welfare; that was the law of economics and of life.

The process of saving and investing spread beyond the ranks of the entrepreneurs to all levels of society, including the low-income laborers. Necessity and opportunity conspired to produce the same result, a consistent propensity to underconsumption. The sum tucked away to provide for the ever-threatening rainy day was also the nest egg with which to purchase a house, to open a shop, to become a contractor, proprietor or employer.

A general prejudice associated luxurious living with foreign, undemocratic, influences and established the moral superiority of the men and women who saved. The Vanderbilts and their ilk splashed fortunes about on great houses, liveried servants and Italian dukes for their daughters. But the thrift of the virtuous created wealth. The absence of an authentic aristocracy which set lavish standards and the general condemnation of nouveau-riche hankerings in that direction reflected a widespread desire not to waste earnings but to set them aside for future productive use.

Money allowed to lie idle was also wasted. Dollars had to work just as people did, and the miserly hoarder was as foolish as the wastrel. Tucked away under the floor boards, the coins did nothing; sent out into the market, they multiplied. "Here is the goose that lays the golden egg," cried Carnegie, upon receipt of his first dividend check. The man who never before had a hundred dollars began to feel poor when he laid hands on his first fifty thousand and spurred himself on to get more. Americans disapproved of gambling, outlawed lotteries, even for worthy purposes, because games of chance only transferred wealth among the players and did not add to the total as investment did. Almost two centuries of practice had legitimated speculation in land and in commodities. Criticized as a form of gambling, defended as a form of investment, it gained steadily in importance, justified by the pools of capital it assembled for further growth. Increasingly speculation also extended to securities and thus influenced the investment process.

Monetary policy and the development of corporation law created channels through which savings and speculative capital flowed to favored enterprises; and by the 1890s enough men had learned how to control the locks and gates to manipulate the passage of funds.

Controversy about the currency reached a peak of intensity in the 1890s, then subsided but echoed on through the new century. Speculators and debtors, as well as farmers, had long believed that an easier money supply, unshackled by arbitrary limits set by the quantity of gold or silver available, encouraged investment and raised prices. However, efforts to persuade the government to use paper could not quiet the prevailing mistrust of any tampering with the metallic mechanism which automatically adjusted the supply of money to the demand.

Actually, the circulating medium, of whatever kind, after 1870 expanded, although not as fast as some people wished it to. The stock of all currency held by the public went up from an average of between $500 and $550 million in the 1870s to $900 million in 1890, an increase not far from that of industrial production.

The supply of gold and silver coins, after declining until 1875, recovered as a result of the activities of Western mines, silver more so than gold. In addition, some paper served as legal tender, although not in amounts as great as inflationists desired. Gold and silver certificates simply replaced metal; but during the Civil War, the Union had also issued about $450 million in greenbacks, notes not redeemable for specie and backed only by the government's willingness to receive them for all obligations except customs dues. A law of 1875 directed the Treasury to redeem some; in the 1880s about $350 million worth remained outstanding and those approached parity with gold.

A limited supply of bank notes augmented the currency supply. But federal law in 1863 and 1864 had taxed paper issued by state institutions out of existence and had allowed the national banks it then created to print no more than an amount equal to 90 per cent of their holdings of United States bonds. The sum authorized diminished steadily as the national debt declined from just under $3 billion in 1865 to well under $2 billion in 1890.

By then, however, business no longer depended upon the transfer of coins or bits of paper from buyer to seller. Other means of effecting such exchanges had developed. Although banks lost their former note-issuing function, they became the instruments for managing credit. New trust companies, as well as the banks chartered under federal and state law, received and safeguarded demand deposits which they employed in short-term interest-bearing loans. Most transactions then took the form of additions and subtractions in the ledgers and most savings rested in account books rather than in cash boxes. The number of commercial banks doubled between 1860 and 1880 and then doubled again in the next decade. Their assets tripled in the first interval and nearly doubled in the second. The amounts deposited there—available on demand and transferable by check—rose from between $700 and $800 million in 1870 to $3 billion in 1890.

Other financial institutions also gained strength. Savings banks, first established before the Civil War to encourage thrift among workingmen, acquired a more general clientele and deposits in them climbed from under $400 million in 1870 to $1,300 million in 1890. The reserves in life insurance companies also increased, from $2 billion to $3.5 billion. All these sums would be even greater in 1910, and all were available for investment.

Commercial and savings banks, trust and insurance companies, often held their funds in traditional forms—land and government bonds. But they were also eager for more fluid as well as more profitable investments. Increasingly they turned for assistance to investment bankers, who knew how to employ money advantageously.

The investment banks of the late nineteenth century took the places of the great international merchants of an earlier day. Like their predecessors, these private firms traded in money and made loans to governments. Sometimes they still handled commodities, but more often they focused their attention on a few major investment decisions rather than on day-to-day commercial transactions. Personal judgment, family connections, and intimate ties with foreign houses shaped their operations. John Pierpont Morgan began his career with George Peabody and Company of London; August Belmont was an agent of the Rothschilds.

The investment bankers and their clients discovered new opportunities in the capital requirements of the massive industrial and transportation enterprises. For instance, when William H. Vanderbilt decided to sell his 250,000 shares of New York Central stock he had to find a purchaser able to pay out $30 million for them; not many such were around—but J. P. Morgan was ready to make the necessary arrangements. So too, Carnegie turned to Morgan at crucial points in expansion; and the Northern Pacific floated its securities through Jay Cooke.

The investment bankers assumed such obligations not only because they had vast resources of their own, as well as connections in Europe, but also because financial institutions with surpluses to put to work turned to them for advice. Corporate bonds had formed less than 1 per cent of the assets of a sample of life insurance companies in 1860; in 1890, the amount had risen to 22 per cent. The financial institutions of all sorts which made the same shift turned to men like Morgan for guidance in seeking the best return on their funds. The savings in millions of little accounts thus began to move in an orderly direction.

In 1890, however, when the Sherman Act became law the structure of control over industrial development was still feeble. The same changes in the character of the corporation which provided securities for the dealings of bankers also opened the field to thousands of small operators making their own investment decisions, stirring up unpredictable currents, perpetuating disorder.

The corporation in 1890 had shed the characteristics which had once linked it to the state. Its charter came through simple registration under provisions of general laws. Its participants were not members identified with the association, responsible for its actions and liable for its debts, but rather transient holders of the right to share potential profits. The stock certificate was evidence of an abstract relationship, readily transferred and therefore serviceable as a subject for speculation. For more than a century some Americans had gambled on future changes in the value of government bonds and bank notes. Now they put their money down also on shares in numerous industrial corporations; and the number of players multiplied phenomenally.

The Civil War spread the habit. A network of 2,500 agents, originally formed to sell Union bonds through Jay Cooke and Company, after the peace went on to market stocks. The patriotic connotations of the war had made the buying and selling of paper familiar in every part of the nation; and the practice survived, indeed became an addiction for some.

In the 1860s New York City was fast becoming the center where the whole country exchanged securities. In the 1870s and 1880s it far outdistanced its former rivals, Boston and Philadelphia. The close connection of the port on the Hudson with Europe, great mercantile and financial resources supported by a growing trade, a strategic location in the communications system, and attractions as a place of residence for wealthy or ambitious outlanders combined to create a truly national market within which the hardware dealers, lawyers, wholesale grocers and physicians of Omaha, Atlanta, Portland and Elmira could all buy and sell their chances for fortune—by telegraph.

Their transactions passed through the hands of brokers in the New York exchanges, who matched up purchase and sale orders. Speedy turnover most concerned the eager traders. The brokers took commissions on each deal; the more deals the better. The average yield of corporate securities was low and declining but investors paid little attention to interest or dividends. The lure they could not resist was a rapid and dramatic appreciation of capital values. Since purchasers were speculating on a fast rise, cash was not necessary; one could pay down as little as 10 per cent, borrowing the rest until the price rose enough to liquidate the debt. A decline, alas, liquidated the 10 per cent. Speculation in stocks offered respectable citizens an opportunity to win by taking a risk without the odium of breaking the law, indeed with the virtual assurance that they were helping develop the country's transportation, mining and industrial system.

The marriage of avarice and thrift produced unsavory offspring. There were bucket shops which never executed the orders of their customers. If the price went down, they simply pocketed the sum invested; if the price rose, they cheerfully credited the victim's balance until his fortune turned. When obligations became too heavy, the slickers absconded. The law rarely caught up with them. Daring operators, more careful not to pass beyond the letter of the law, manipulated supply and demand. The exchanges dealt not only in present but also in future deliveries. The bears sold short securities they did not yet own and tried to depress the price; the bulls bought the promise of later delivery and tried to raise the level. Groups on one side or the other pooled their resources to change the price by throwing large blocks on the market or by making concerted heavy purchases. The speculator who cornered or controlled the whole supply set the price he wished for the stocks due him.

Judgment of the value of any share was elusive and particularly if it was watered, as the old-time drovers had built up the appearance of weight in their cattle, or salted, as the old-time miners had built up the appearance of yield in a lode. Daniel Drew, Diamond Jim Brady, Jay Gould and other hard-bitten characters circled their prey ready to snap up those whose guards were down. The howls of protest

CORPORATE ENTERPRISE *171*

from the losers did not keep the throngs of new players away from the game. The number of investors grew, although not the number who succeeded.

Occasional panics did not extinguish hope. On the Black Friday in September, 1869, when Jim Fisk failed to corner the gold market, hundreds of unwary speculators plunged to their ruin. Four years later, the bankruptcy of Jay Cooke dragged the whole nation into depression. Depositors withdrew their funds from banks, which then called in their short-term loans. Confidence dwindled. Prices fell. Factories laid off hands. Consumption slackened. The economy ground to a halt. Panic struck again in 1893 and yet again in 1907. But between those setbacks, the speculative force spiraled upward, as much beyond control as when it plunged downward.

Capital composed of small sums responded sensitively and speedily to opportunity. Surplus funds in free and fluid movement coursed unpredictably through the economy, often with constructive, but often also with disruptive consequences.

The turbulance did not please some industrialists; it bothered administrators; and it infuriated the investment bankers. Risky investment (theirs), yes; rampant speculation (others'), no. The heavings and plungings of the stock market betrayed the presence of streaks of irrationality perilous to the economy.

Other symptoms of danger showed up in government. In February, 1895, J. P. Morgan came to the rescue of the United States; he bought a large issue of federal bonds for gold, bringing in half the specie from Europe. President Grover Cleveland had appealed for his help because the country's net gold reserve had dropped from more than $190 million to less than $65 million. Why? Because anyone for 84¢ could buy silver worth a full dollar at the Treasury; and many did. Other nations were abandoning the coinage of that metal, but the Silver Purchase Act of 1890 obliged the United States to take 4,500,000 ounces monthly at the artificially high price. Moreover, the alliance of Populists and miners was asking for more.

The Sherman Anti-Trust law also seemed disruptive. Its verbiage about conspiracy, competition and restraint of trade simply exposed the economy to unsettling raids by speculating freebooters, to disorderly pricing and marketing practices and to the costly cycles of panic and boom. The only defense left by the statute was merger, for one company buying the assets of another was not conspiring with itself.

The number of recorded mergers in manufacturing and mining

mounted rapidly to a peak in 1899. Some combinations were simple. In 1891, for instance, the American Tobacco Company, which had theretofore manufactured cigarettes, acquired the smoking-tobacco factories of Marburg Brothers and the Gail & Ax Company in return for cash and some of its own common stock. Such relatively small deals required no large outlays and no significant dilution of control.

But the availability of substantial amounts of capital in the security markets enabled promoters of larger combinations to use the procedures of the New Jersey Corporation Act of 1889. The holding companies chartered under the terms of that law operated no plants of their own but simply held the stock of other corporations doing business anywhere. Extensive multi-layered pyramids took shape with each stratum of subsidiaries owning or controlling scores of smaller firms. The device offered some of the advantages of the old type of trust yet was not, on the face of it, illegal.

The American Sugar Refining Company organized in 1891 was one of the first to use the technique. Itself a successor to a trust that had held twenty refineries, it took over its five leading competitors and for a time accounted for almost 90 per cent of the national output of sugar. A year later Standard Oil, under attack in the state courts, abandoned the trust form and secured a New Jersey charter, which survived the fierce onslaughts of critics and rivals until dissolved by the Supreme Court. In the decade after 1891 the holding company spread; and some combinations, once formed, were themselves assimilated in larger groupings. Between 1899 and 1901 American Copper, American Smelting and Refining, Consolidated Tobacco and United States Steel all sprang into being. By 1904, 318 important holding companies, capitalized at well over $7 billion, controlled 5,288 plants in the United States. A ruling by the Supreme Court (1895) that manufacturing was not subject to regulation under the commerce clause stimulated the process.

The resources for these combinations came from the stock of savings by individuals and by financial institutions. The assets of commercial banks soared from less than $5 billion in 1890 to $18 billion in 1910. Deposits in savings banks almost doubled in the period, while the assets of life insurance companies rose in the same twenty years from $771 million to $4,400 million.

Usually the investment bankers, eager both for the orderly arrangement of the economy and for the business of floating new issues, managed the flow of capital. Familiar with the securities of competing companies and able to provide the necessary funds, the bankers often took places on the boards of firms they created or consolidated. They served partly out of responsibilty to the investors who followed their advice, partly out of the desire for power. As directors of railroads, commercial banks, life insurance firms and manufacturing companies, they influenced policy, planned further mergers, and gave financial counsel. Since they often sat on the boards of several corporations, interlocking the directorates, they provided a means of coordination. The rewards were tremendous. J. P. Morgan and Company, the prime architects of the United States Steel Company, directly or indirectly received some $150 million in return for promoting and underwriting the union.

Such payments added water to the stock of the holding company. The capitalization usually included an amount large enough to cover the estimated value of the component companies and also the expenses of floating and managing the consolidation. The market value of the shares was therefore often far higher than the value of the assets. The constituents joined in United States Shipbuilding in 1902 were capitalized at about $20 million and owned plants valued at $12 million, with a working capital of only about $5 million. Yet the company issued stocks and bonds of the amount of almost $68 million—a substantial overestimation, magnified still further when a receivership later revealed that even the original stated values were inflated. This was an extreme case, but more moderate promoters also left themselves ample margins.

The holding companies put those who controlled them in strategic economic positions. The enormous stakes engendered intense rivalry, as competing capitalists carved out empires and established alliances in order to mobilize maximum strength. Although the boundary lines were not distinct, several complex groupings took form at the opening of the twentieth century.

John D. Rockefeller and his Standard Oil associates had the longest experience in manipulating great enterprises; and their control of 80 to 90 per cent of the nation's oil business put vast sums at their disposal. Connections with the National City Bank and the Equitable and Mutual Life Insurance Companies added to their power. An understanding with the Widener and Elkins interests involved them in United Gas Improvement of Philadelphia and other public utilities. An association with Jay Gould gave them a voice in the affairs of the Missouri Pacific, the Wabash, and the Chicago, Milwaukee and St. Paul railroad systems, and in American Telephone and Western Union. The Standard Oil crowd also dominated the great copper, smelting, mining and tobacco corporations, and they had a share in United States Steel.

Their only peer was J. P. Morgan and Company, with its tight connections with the First National and Chase National banks, the

Guaranty Trust and the New York Life Insurance Company. Morgan interests were preeminent in steel, shipping, and rubber and were solidly entrenched in the New Haven, Chicago, Burlington and Quincy, Northern Pacific, Southern and Atlantic Coast Line railroads.

Smaller groups held lesser positions of influence; and scores of capitalists in Boston, Philadelphia, Chicago, and San Francisco as well as in New York orbited as satellites around the great financial stars, contributing local resources to the force of one element or another, deriving some share of profits as a reward.

There were, nevertheless, limits to the process of concentration. Political force to some extent offset economic power. Mutual mistrust always troubled the uneasy relationships between government and business. In the rough-and-tumble decades after the Civil War, the bagmen trotted between legislative halls and corporate offices; in those days, a critic said, Standard Oil could do anything it wished with the Pennsylvania legislature except refine it. In time, the glare of publicity, the fear of exposure and the sense of each party to the transaction that it was the victim of the greed of the other, diminished the open trade in influence. But enough buyers and sellers of votes still turned up in the twentieth century to ruffle the order bankers desired.

Trust busting, the popular term for any attack on big business, was more irritating because it clouded every operation with uncertainty. The accusation that the holding company was a conspiracy in restraint of trade drew an audience for any politician, sold magazines for any scribbler. On this issue, the law was resolutely ambiguous. Theodore Roosevelt moved beyond rhetoric; a Bureau of Corporations (1903) threatened to pry into board-room proceedings and prosecutions began to hamper convenient arrangements in beef, oil and tobacco. Morgan's cherished scheme for uniting the railroads of the Northwest fell afoul of an adverse Supreme Court decision in 1904. Nevertheless, the President acquiesced in the same banker's plan to add the Tennessee Coal and Iron Company to United States Steel. The trusts, T. R. seemed to say, were hideous monsters created by the enlightened enterprise of men who advanced progress. On the one hand, he would stamp them under foot; on the other, not so fast. Nothing there for a rational businessman who wanted to know how far he could go.

In any case, internal forces were slowing consolidation. Sometimes integrated enterprises toppled because they lacked a firm base to support their topheavy capitalization. There simply were not enough orders, for instance, to generate profits from shipbuilding. Not every activity supported a holding company pyramid. At times, too, errors of judgment were expensive. Morgan, in 1902, established the International Mercantile Marine with the expectation of uniting all the North Atlantic shipping companies. However, the Cunard Line refused to join and fought for its independence with the aid of a British government subsidy. As a result, the International controlled only about 40 per cent of the traffic, lost out in the competition and paid no dividends.

Furthermore, the efficient management of very large enterprises sometimes called for complex arrangements beyond available techniques and skills. The great life insurance companies, for instance, wrote policies in all the states and in many foreign countries. They dealt with many governments and operated through thousands of agents. They invested hundreds of millions of dollars in reserves and maintained connections with dozens of banks and trust companies. Lacking computers or even calculators, they did everything by hand, depended upon primitive controls over subordinates and sometimes suffered from the want of qualified personnel. The magnitude of the task set a brake on inclinations to consolidate.

Above all, unforeseen changes disordered the best-laid plans. In the 1890s the American Sugar Refining Company expanded until it commanded almost 90 per cent of the national output. Then the development of beet sugar reduced its share to less than half. In the same way, the discoveries of western oil after 1900 undermined the Standard Oil monopoly; and William Wrigley, Jr.'s promotional maneuvers shook the chicle trust. Industries like automobiles and aluminum, which grew in importance in the twentieth century, escaped the control of the old barons, whose empires did not widen to encompass the new areas of production. The Morgans and the Rockefellers lacked the power or the will to push concentration any further. A balance began to develop between the tendencies toward integration and the forces for dispersal.

From up close, however, the prospect pleased few observers. In the absence of assurance that the developing equilibrium would hold, bigness was more of a threat to democracy after the Sherman Act than before. Widely read books and magazines tirelessly exposed the danger of wealth to commonwealth; Populist zealots apart, an army of muckrakers fell upon big business, alerting the citizens to the immediate need for defense. Yet the legal system obstructed any effective action against the masters of capital.

Since the middle of the nineteenth century, interpretations of the right of contract had shifted from emphasis on the relationship among individuals to emphasis on their relationship to government. The federal Constitution as ratified and the Fourteenth Amendment had forbidden the states to pass any statute impairing the obligations of contract or depriving any person of his property without due process of law; and the courts had held that corporations were persons protected by the same provisions. A line of judicial decisions beginning with the Dred Scott Case (1857) went farther, asserting that the guarantees were substantive, prohibiting not only arbitrary procedures, but any action that diminished the ability to make agreements or use property, in effect, any economic meddling by the government. The inviolability of property and contract created a climate congenial to enterprise and thus stimulated expansion; but it also shackled the polity. The feeble efforts during Reconstruction to exert some directional or promotional influence faded, along with the possibility of using politics to establish goals for the economy or the society as a whole. Federal, state and municipal governments thereafter confined themselves to policing and regulatory functions.

The distinction between "public" and "private" sharpened. The former word denoted those affairs, very few in number, directly subject to government; the latter referred to the much wider range legally free from interference. Only those matters were public which involved no private property—the maintenance of certain roads, streets and bridges, for instance. Railroads, however, were private, built by investment and sustained by profits from fares. The distinction was historical not logical, shaped by the circumstances of origin rather than by any abstract principle. The postal system was public, indeed national. But the telegraph and, later, the telephone were private. The line did not define clear-cut spheres; it resulted from accommodation to pressures exerted in response to specific issues at specific moments.

The government acted positively toward communal goals only on the public side of the line, wherever drawn. In all other matters the economy was presumably self-regulating, developing by its own rules, finding its own equilibrium through forces generated internally which cured its occasional imperfections. Nature knew best and functioned most effectively to yield maximum benefits for the whole population when free of interference. So ran the widely shared axioms. The phrase "natural selection," reminiscent of Darwin, was the equivalent of the older references to a providential guiding force. The state stood by—neutral, a passive policeman—acting only to forestall any meddling with the finely balanced mechanism.

The rules of the market mechanism after 1870 were the subjects of study by scientific economists, usually situated in the universities. Formerly, the operations of the productive system had been the province of the political economist, a term which recognized the relationship to government. Now academic scholars analyzed the economy in abstract detachment; the state was extraneous.

No doubt, the world of making, buying, using often bore contradictory appearances. The consumer-oriented economy depended upon growing markets; yet investment required underconsumption to accumulate savings that became capital—the sums put in the bank were beyond the reach of the sellers of coats and Kodaks. Labor was a factor in the cost of production, its price held as low as possible; but wage earners were also potential purchasers of the goods industry produced—low pay, or none, meant low spending, or none. Each entrepreneur sought orderly planning in his plant, yet fiercely fought as monopolies the like efforts of others—what was free enterprise to some was restraint of trade to others.

A common formula resolved all such apparent contradictions to the satisfaction of the economists. The rational choices of men pursuing their own interests through the free operation of market forces would establish an equilibrium at the optimal point between saving and spending, between earnings and purchasing power, between concentration and fragmentation. So ran the academic theories.

The economists were not persuasive enough. The ingenious projections, sound in the abstract, did not work out in practice, not so much because of defects in abstract reasoning but because they never fitted precisely the circumstances of concrete cases and because they took no account of political and social factors, which perversely continued to intrude, however insistently exorcised in theory.

Persistently, therefore, injured Americans called upon the state to be less passive as policeman than prevailing economic theory dictated. Perhaps the coming and going of industrial crises followed rules as regular as those of the planets; but the worker knew that he was out of a job and hungry. Perhaps nature intended the master of great volume to swallow his marginal rival, as the shark the minnow; but the small businessman, customers vanished, debts soon due, investments dead, new ventures hazardous, still refused to be digested. Perhaps some tamper-proof universal calculator of itself set the charges for elevators and railroads; but the farmers wanted to pay less, get more. Perhaps the waste of competition was a small price to pay for expansion; but corporation executives wished to plan with confidence. Everyone aggrieved yelled for help; and their notion of democracy required the state to respond.

True enough, the Constitution and the law protected private enterprise from political interference. But some private enterprises, in 1910 as in 1870, depended upon rights or franchises granted by government on account of their utility to the public; there were grounds therefore for regulation of railroads, transit lines, and gas and electric services. Nevertheless, the tortuous history of the Interstate Commerce Commission demonstrated the difficulty of the process. The solution was to extend its powers by legislation; the Elkins (1903), the Hepburn (1906), and the Mann-Elkins (1910) acts gave it extensive rate-fixing authority. The same grounds justified laws compensating the victims of accidents on common carriers and fixing the hours of trainmen. The concept of police power after 1900 stretched to include pure food and drug and meat inspection acts, however intrusive upon the property rights of the packers.

Furthermore, the free competitive market always needed defense against the trust, a term which by 1900 had lost its precise meaning and now expressed a vague general fear of concentrated economic power used by a few for undemocratic and immoral purposes. The self-regulation of the New York Stock Exchange and the Chicago Board of Trade or the informational services of the American Iron and Steel Institute might involve no more than the simple relationships of voluntary associations to their members. Then again, an unknown something more might be there. Any activity might have a sinister, shadowy aspect.

The courts became battlegrounds across which lawyers sallied to establish the boundary between licit combinations and conspiracies in restraint of trade, between regulation which satisfied the requirements of due process and respected the rights of contract and of property, and that which did not. Precedent, to which American attorneys habitually appealed, proved no guide at all. Swiveling their way from decision to decision, the judges left a trail no one could follow with assurance on the way to definition of what was reasonable. While litigation was a wholesome alternative to the overt violence and chicanery that had enlivened entrepreneurial contests in the 1870s, it still was deficient in the neatness dear to the hearts of administrators. As in any trial by battle, chance or whim played an uncomfortably large part in adversary proceedings before courts and regulatory agencies. In the end, nothing offset the inconveniences, hazards and unpredictable qualities of the free market. The argument over trusts and their place in American life was thick with slogans, thin when it came to solutions. The ambiguity of the law encouraged expansion, but at the price of waste and of the inability to plan.

In 1910, George W. Perkins gave up a lucrative partnership in J. P. Morgan and Company. He was not yet fifty; and he had held only two jobs in his life. At age fifteen he had started as office boy for the New York Life Insurance Company and had worked his way up to become president of the firm. Then in 1901 he had come to Morgan, where he had helped organize International Harvester and Northern Securities. He could have continued to form great corporations, attempting thus to eliminate the outmoded and wasteful competition inherited from the past. But he understood the limits of a banker's power and knew that there was no divorcing politics from economics if Americans were to effect the changes he considered desirable. He intended to devote his full efforts to the presidential election two years away.

Perkins questioned the desirability of a totally free market and espoused a more positive role for the state. He had exchanged views with Theodore Roosevelt, who by now had decided that it was unwise to split into small units great business aggregations that strengthened the economy. Roosevelt, Perkins, Frank A. Munsey, the newspaper publisher, and T. C. DuPont, the powder manufacturer, talked vaguely about some type of national planning; and they read with interest Herbert Croly's *Promise of American Life* (1909), which explained that the corporation could serve as a means for attaining goals set by the public.

In 1910, Roosevelt issued the call for a new nationalism which would increase efficiency, conserve resources which reckless exploitation would otherwise soon deplete, and add to the country's power in international affairs. A strong directing government would neither smash nor yield to the trusts, but would safely encourage their development, by harnessing them to socially useful purposes.

The capacity to produce had put the United States in the company of the great powers; but the country had as yet failed to develop the appropriate institutional forms to make the most of its strength; and the failure exposed it to the double dangers of incessant instability at home and weakness in taking its proper place in the world.

10

The Failure of the Global Economy

*I*n 1910, the United States approached a crisis. Few Americans then perceived the looming difficulties in their relations with the world, which in four years would be at war. Nor did any understand the seriousness of the impending impact of Sarajevo upon their welfare.

Not at Jamestown or at any time thereafter had the economy functioned in isolation. International trade had been vital to the United States throughout its history. A simple set of assumptions, so widely shared as to be commonplace, described and justified the free movement of goods within and across the country's borders.

In the nineteenth century, these assumptions had steadily gained ground on both sides of the Atlantic. Adam Smith had long since applied the metaphor of the division of labor to the ways of work; everyone gained when all specialized in the tasks appropriate to their talents. Wherever enlightened states had removed internal barriers to trade, the whole nation had benefited. The same principle applied on the global scale. Just as the regions of a single country all profited by concentrating on the products favored by culture, climate and soil, so the various areas of the earth would thrive if each devoted itself to the pursuits for which history and nature had best prepared it. The result would be rising efficiency for the greatest good of all.

The symbol of the increasing intimacy of the world economy was the appearance of a single standard for currency transactions. In Adam Smith's day, trade had involved cumbersome transfers of coins from scores of mints and of paper from hundreds of mercantile and governmental sources, all of which fluctuated from moment to moment so that merchants kept their records in an abstract money of account.

Such were the blessings of nineteenth-century progress that the number of currencies shrank—one to a nation, with values stable enough to make possible a dependable rate of exchange among them. In time, most countries ceased to coin silver, except for small fractional units; then, since all used the same metal, worth in gold became the common international unit. The dollar, mark, franc and pound served for internal purposes; but a common measure stated the value of one against another. The gold standard linked each national economy with the larger world system of which it was a part. Informed Americans frequently recited the meticulous proofs by which David Ricardo and other British economists demonstrated that the gold standard equalized prices everywhere, preserved stability and prevented the excesses of inflation or deflation.

In the 1890s, the need for increasing quantities of currency to serve the expanding global economy revived the idea of restoring the coinage of silver. But an international monetary conference in Brussels in 1893 failed to reach agreement, and soon thereafter fortuitous discoveries in Alaska and South Africa increased the supply of gold, thus preserving its viability as a standard of value and demonstrating that an apolitical economic order was more natural and more responsive to the needs of the people than one shaped by governments.

Differences in rates of development seemed to maintain the symmetry of the order and sustained the willingness to lower barriers to international trade. Industrialization had come first to Britain, then to western Europe and the United States, and only later, if at all, to other areas. National economies therefore complemented rather than competed with one another, so that the free movement of trade, populations and capital was to the advantage of all. Cutlery from Sheffield appeared on Moscow tables and cotton goods from Lancashire clothed the field workers of Assam; in return, abundant timber supplied English carpenters and cheap tea filled their pots. European investment funds made the exchange possible and also earned lucrative rewards.

Ideally, in an apolitical economic order, individuals decided for themselves—merchants, where to buy or sell; laborers, where to work;

savers, where to seek returns. Such judgments were most likely to serve the interests of those who made them, and also in sum most likely best to serve everyone's interests. Mercantilism, which had justified centralized control of priorities by the state, was in retreat in the nineteenth century—in Europe as in the United States. Trade barriers crumbled, old privileges fell into disuse, and government-granted monopolies dissolved. The trend was far from complete in 1880; and some nations had moved more speedily than others, but those regarded at the time as most advanced had gone farthest in freeing their economies.

The desire to divorce international economic relations from political considerations had exponents in every European country and influenced the United States also, although there it competed against alternative perspectives on the outer world. The historic assumption was that Americans were a pilgrim people, morally superior to others by virtue of their mission to build a city upon a hill, a model which all nations would in time follow. Recurrent efforts to convert, redeem, improve the less fortunate subjects of foreign despots reflected the certainty that archaic political systems in Asia and Europe would soon evolve according to the American pattern. The censorious attitude toward other regimes was not altogether compatible with the view that one could advantageously do business with anyone. But the ambiguities and contradictions that resulted from the wish simultaneously to hold ideal and profitable positions rarely disturbed practical people. The conviction persisted that the earth's contraction as distance shrank would sooner or later integrate all national economies into a single global order.

Economic policy in the United States, although subject to qualification and exceptions by political exigencies and the pressure of interested groups, nevertheless largely conformed to this expectation. The fact that efforts to reduce the levels of the protective tariff ended in raising them did not shake the abstract faith in free trade. Down to 1917 the gates were entirely open to European and American immigrants. There were no restraints whatever on the movement of capital into or out of the country.

After 1880 subtle changes everywhere signaled a reversal. As other countries caught up with Britain, the differences in rate of development evened out so that their productive systems were no longer neatly complementary. Everywhere, demands for protective tariffs challenged the free-trade premise; and cartels which allocated shares of the market limited competition among great industrial enterprises.

Meanwhile, an excess of capital in Europe sought overseas outlets as domestic interest rates declined. Money sent abroad increased not only earnings but also power, for the desire to safeguard investments induced the exporting nations to expand their political influence or simply to make colonies of the places in which they had stakes. The British, who had been in process of dismantling an old empire, now began to strengthen the hold on their possessions and indeed cast about for ways of adding to them. France did the same; and Germany, Italy and Japan, which had not expanded overseas in the eighteenth century, looked for areas in which to establish their own spheres of influence. The ensuing conflicts among the rival nations often evoked bitter jingoistic responses and sometimes led to the clash of arms before good sense suggested compromise.

As practice changed, so did opinion. Each country developed doctrines that justified its unique role in the world. The white man's burden, the obligation to establish a civilizing presence, and the cultural mission of the nation summarized in slogans the ideas which explained the activity of Europeans in other continents. Racist concepts accounted for the inferiority of subject peoples. Some theorists also argued that the very survival of the state required the extension of its overseas economic power. A steady erosion in the belief in an apolitical economic order followed the change in attitudes in the quarter-century after 1880.

The situation of the United States was anomalous. The soaring output of agriculture and industry through the second half of the nineteenth century had made it a great power. The products of its fields found markets in every part of the earth; and foreign industrialists envied and feared the performance of its factories. America had indeed become the golden land. Yet it had neither the military force nor the political and administrative apparatus, nor even the formulated ideology and will for acting beyond its borders as other great powers did.

Shrinking distances painfully exposed the country's diplomatic immobility. The New World was no longer months away from every other part of the earth; the cable and fast steamships narrowed the oceans, drew America close to Europe and Asia and complicated the pretense that unfavorable developments elsewhere would in time rectify themselves and therefore need not affect the Republic.

But time also closed in. Earlier, there had been no limits to the future which had beguiled the citizens. They were the vanguard whom all others would follow. What lay beyond their grasp at the moment would surely fall within reach as history unfolded; the progress would somehow uncover solutions to seemingly insoluble problems. After 1880, these optimistic certainties flickered out. Europe had not entered upon a period of decay but was in fact expanding. Its cartels, spheres of influence and colonies revealed that there was vigor yet in the Old World. The empty spaces on the map of the earth were being filled not by republics modeled upon the United States but by aggressive Britishers and Frenchmen who did not at all accept the American judgment that their governments were relics of a past stage of human development. Monarchy, for a century considered a decadent institution, showed unexpected vitality as ever-larger areas owed allegiance to the Queen, the Kaiser, the Czar and the Mikado. The old assumption that the world would inevitably follow the American way now seemed dubious indeed.

The United States was in danger of falling behind. Whoever did not expand would be pushed back. In Hawaii, for instance, the choice was not between annexing the islands and allowing the idyllic native kingdom to lead its own life; the choice was annexation by the United States or by Japan or Britain or Germany. In Samoa, too, the issue was dependence on whom. Commercial options also narrowed as the scope of free trade contracted. Yet anti-imperialism shackled the country in the race for colonies; and anti-trust sentiment hampered American firms in competing with, or joining, the great international cartels. Year by year these dilemmas became more oppressive.

Writers and orators were quickest to propose solutions, for words were more readily at hand than deeds. Some people appealed to internationalism. The shrinkage of space had thrust men and women together and had revealed the problems all shared. As awareness spread of their common humanity, a global government would eliminate unnatural political boundaries, war would vanish, armies would lose importance, and economic conflicts would subside. Socialists had inherited this faith from the early nineteenth century and clung to it, as did many humanitarians and participants in the labor movement.

But the international vision commanded only a slight following. Many more could imagine the happy but distant goal than could see the practical steps leading to it. The pleas for peace were calls for the conversion of the human spirit, not programs that elicited any sense of relevance or informed Americans what to do while the Czar, the Kaiser and the Mikado gained strength. Few summoned up the will to believe that the lion and the lamb would here and now respond to the exhortation that they rest together. Furthermore, reformers bemused by the silver panacea emphasized a national solution for all economic problems, thus diluting the support for universalistic programs.

A more vocal though not more numerous group urged the frank adoption of the ideology and techniques of imperialism. A. T. Mahan had demonstrated the national interest in seapower and in the bases to support a fleet in being. Brooks Adams took a large historic view of the moral need for expansion. Empires were up for grabs. The logic of power demanded that the United States shed its distinctiveness and compete with other countries for the acquisition and possession of colonies.

These ideas also drew support from religious impulses. American missionary enterprise was almost a century old. The members of numerous congregations and parishes in many denominations throughout the country sustained the missionaries, who labored to convert the natives and to advance their material welfare by setting up schools and hospitals and by providing training in crafts and agriculture. These institutions created an American presence in almost every part of the world, and strengthened the sentiment in favor of expansion.

The imperialists vociferously urged the laggard nation on. The other countries were doing it; it was the wave of the future; and the United States had no alternative but to follow if it were to attain a global position commensurate with its size, wealth, and potential power. The wreckage of civilizations too flabby to defend themselves littered the record of the past, as imperialists read it. Besides, it was a duty to spread the advantages of Americanism to inferior people. Besides too, it would be profitable—to commerce, to industry, to agriculture. In Africa, Asia and the Caribbean weak indigenous governments and docile natives invited conquest. Colonies there would furnish the United States abundant raw materials, cheap labor and markets for manufactured goods free from competition. It was time, therefore, to shed anti-colonial scruples inherited from the eighteenth century and to compete with others for the spaces on the map that would determine the future of the world.

The imperialists gained in political strength down to 1900. Strategically situated in the administration elected in 1896, they thrust the country into acquisitions in the Caribbean and in the Philippines after the Spanish-American War. The presidental election of 1900, while by no means a referendum on imperialism, kept in office the government responsible for those territorial gains. And shortly thereafter, the assassination of President McKinley advanced to the White House Theodore Roosevelt, a leading exponent of imperialism. The way seemed then open to further gains.

Nevertheless, for all the Rough Rider's thrashing about in Panama and the Caribbean, American territorial expansion ceased, replaced by an uncomfortable, embarrassed process of withdrawal from the unrewarding possessions seized in the splendid little war. From time to time, the desire to prevent disorder, to protect American lives and property and to forestall European intervention led to the temporary occupation of neighboring territory. But in 1914, on the map of the world, the United States was not only behind England, France and Germany but also behind Japan, Italy, Belgium, Portugal, and the Netherlands in colonial possessions. And it blithely passed by the opportunities for territorial gain that the First World War soon presented.

The paradoxical alteration of course reflected a judgment that the colonies were not worth the cost. The distant island possessions did not attract investors; and politicians shied away from the legal, constitutional and social problems of governing alien races. The imperialists addressed an unresponsive nation.

Brooks Adams, Alfred T. Mahan, Theodore Roosevelt, John Hay, Albert J. Beveridge and Josiah Strong were men of ideas who thought of power as an instrument with which to give reality to their words. They understood the need to find allies among large segments of the population; and they couched their arguments in terms they hoped would mobilize such support. In vain. They watched the withdrawal after 1900 with a dismay matched only by the impatience with which they had earlier observed their country's hesitation in joining the competition for empire. Their polemics mingled passionate appeals to the interests of businessmen, farmers, Christians, with furious contempt for all those who remained deaf to their calls.

But rhetoric, from whatever camp, was no guide to practice. The injunctions of the ideologues were not decisive or even important to the decisions of individuals about how best to do business; and the broad economic trends of the period were the sum of numerous such decisions.

In practice, the range of contacts between the United States and the outer world continued to broaden. Exports mounted steadily. As always, agricultural products formed a large part of the cargoes shipped from the United States, although in the 1890s tariffs and discriminatory inspection laws began to protect foreign producers in their own markets. But by then new commodities added significantly to the value of the nation's sales abroad. Petroleum, particularly in the form of kerosene, formed an increasing share of the total exports. Shipments of refined kerosene mounted from 80 million gallons in 1868 to more than 400 million in 1879; and the climb upward continued despite the opening of competing sources as the century drew to a close.

The freight carried to other parts of the world included also substantial amounts of manufactured goods. European manufacturers then were, in general, still technically more advanced; yet sophisticated products made in the United States were already prominent in Old World showrooms. The tendency had gone so far in 1901 that a book published in London warned against the American industrial invasion. At home and abroad the Yankees were supreme in many new industries of the 1890s—the telephone, the portable camera, the phonograph, the electric streetcar, the typewriter, passenger lifts in houses and machine tools. Managerial skill and advanced technology accounted in part for their success. Railroad men like George Whistler who worked for the Russians, mining engineers like Herbert Hoover, employed by British firms in China and Australia, and the suppliers of oil-drilling equipment to Rumania, Poland, and Russia were evidence also of the same industrial leadership. A parallel development for a time transferred American life insurance techniques to the Old World. The Equitable began to work in England in 1869, in France in 1871. Until restrictive foreign legislation narrowed opportunities, other insurance firms followed its lead.

But advanced technology did not fully explain the strenuous American overseas efforts. It might account for the Colt branch factory in England in the 1850s or, later, for the sale of McCormick reapers and Singer sewing machines in Europe; but not for the decision of Tiffany and Company, the New York jewelers, to establish a store in Paris. Nor did salesmen rush abroad because the domestic market was satiated. Foreign sales were only marginally profitable, rarely more so than within the United States, and sometimes even subject to very sizable losses. Entrepreneurs attached a non-monetary value to the European markets, as they did to the display of goods in world expositions. Having succeeded at home, they felt challenged to compete against the best of the Old World with the prizes prestige and self-esteem as much as profit.

The effort to sell abroad sucked Americans into permanent foreign investment. Remote local distributors, agents and jobbers did business in their own ways and often ran into difficulty precisely because profit margins were narrow or nonexistent. The Americans then responded by setting up their own marketing organizations. To do so, they accumulated stocks of goods abroad and invested in warehousing and other facilities. They thus began to accumulate capital overseas. Occasionally, in the process, they uncovered opportunities for exploiting local resources. Americans thus put funds into railroads, ranching and mining in Mexico and into sugar plantations in Cuba. More important in the long run than such extractive enterprises were the branch manufacturing plants established in other countries. The Pullman Company, R. Hoe, the printing machinery fabricators, and the McCormick Harvester Company, for instance, proceeded from the initial stages of selling their products abroad to manufacturing them in Europe. After 1880, the number who took the same path increased, and with it the volume of exported capital. By 1900 Eastman-Kodak, American Radiator, Western Electric, National Cash Register, Singer, General Electric and the great meat packers and oil refiners operated twenty-eight very large plants in the Old World, as did a few smaller firms; and some of them were gobbling up local competitors. After the turn of the century, European protectionism made itself felt; and, to compensate, fifty more American establishments of substantial size appeared abroad in the next decade, 1900–1910.

Out of these experiences developed a new kind of corporation. Its creators did not fully understand its character; nor did they think through or clearly articulate a theory to describe it. The peculiar qualities of doing business as these entities did, emerged rather in a variety of specific circumstances, discontinuous, abrupt, and without any effort to pursue the implications. To an agent of Western Electric in Bangkok, for instance, who complained in 1907 that the anti-American government of Siam would not give him an order, the vice president of the corporation rejoined, "We have offices and factories making our standard apparatus in Great Britain, Germany, France, Russia, Austria, Italy, and Japan, so that so far as this matter goes we are international rather than American." The company "could arrange to have the order go to any one of those countries that might be preferred." This was an *ad hoc* response to a specific problem; but it was also the seed of a concept that would flower later—one that regarded the enterprise as somehow, somewhat detached from the governments of the areas in which it operated.

In 1914 the direct foreign investment of the United States amounted to some $2.5 billion, the equivalent of about 7 per cent of the gross national product at that date. That percentage was about the same as it would be in 1960—a significant indication of the importance foreign investment had already attained.

Investment, however, did not follow the lines advocated by the imperialists. Backward countries, blessed with impoverished populations, with low costs, and with feeble governments did not attract American entrepreneurs. Africa, Asia, and the Caribbean were areas to which the dollars did not flow. In all of Africa, with which the

United States had had some contact since the establishment of Liberia and, in a certain sense, since the seventeenth century, American investment amounted to only $13.5 million—a minuscule sum. In all of Asia, from Turkey in the west to the Philippines and Australia in the east, the total amounted to some $20 million, less than 5 per cent of the whole—and this fifteen years after the battle of Manila Bay, five decades after Perry's opening of Japan, a century after the first dealings with China. Moreover, the capital sent to both Africa and Asia was preponderantly mercantile—stock-in-trade and facilities for distributing American products—that is, an outgrowth of activities which had existed in the same areas virtually since independence.

Even in the Caribbean, expansion did not take the form fancied by the imperialists. There the United States held important possessions —Puerto Rico and the Canal Zone—and was also deeply involved in the affairs of nominally independent countries like Cuba, Haiti, and Nicaragua. In the whole Caribbean region and in all of South America, the total American investment amounted to about $700 million, held primarily in commercial distribution facilities, with only secondary attention to the exploitation of natural resources. Taken together, the four continents which imperialists defined as backward and fit for colonial development thus absorbed only about a third of American overseas holdings, and not in the form the expansionists considered appropriate.

Since capital moved in a flow incidental to the effort to sell goods and services, its owners valued stable social and political environments, populations advanced enough to acquire new consumption habits and markets prosperous enough to pay for rather expensive products not previously regarded as essential.

Investments in the northern and southern neighbors of the United States were therefore heavy. Canada and Mexico absorbed more than one billion American dollars. The old nineteenth-century manifest-destiny visions of annexing all of Canada and all of Mexico had disappeared, and in fact the independence of both countries was more secure than ever before. Nevertheless, Americans regarded both as extensions of their own market. Emphasis in investment remained chiefly on distribution, although the Canadian protective tariff persuaded some manufacturers in the United States to establish branches north of the border; and mining and ranching attracted some speculative capital to the south.

A sum almost as large moved to a region where involvement made no sense whatever from an imperialist point of view. In 1914 Americans had invested more than $600 million—about a quarter of their total overseas holdings—in Europe. In sending their dollars eastward across the Atlantic, Americans were rejecting a basic premise of the imperialists, that which affirmed that capital was to flow from the more developed to the less developed places of the earth and thus to extend with it political power. Furthermore, they were investing in an area which was itself exporting capital elsewhere. Yet the trend grew steadily, and continued well after 1914.

The entrepreneurs who embarked upon these hazardous foreign adventures justified their decisions—to partners, stockholders, and to themselves; and their elaborate calculations appeared in company reports and in the internal correspondence of their firms. In the last analysis, the goal the investors discerned was always described in the same terms—profit. Their arguments were appropriate to the image hardheaded businessmen held of themselves. There was indeed a case for going abroad to protect patents which foreign pirates might otherwise infringe. There was a case for safeguarding the value of a trade name by providing service for complex machines in widely scattered factories. And there was a case for subsidiaries that could join European pools or cartels and that could manufacture abroad when American tariffs on raw materials made that advantageous. Then again, anti-trust laws which prevented expansion within the United States sometimes made it necessary to expand elsewhere.

Still, many a businessman protested his hardheadedness too much. With investment as with sales, there was rarely such evidence of surfeit at home as would have made recourse to overseas outlets imperative. That there were alternative domestic uses for capital was evident from the fact that the United States still attracted the investments of Europeans in sizable amounts; in 1914 twice as much had come westward as had gone eastward.

Calvin Brice, who planned a railroad from Canton to Hankow with the same aplomb as from Buffalo to Chicago, was one hardheaded businessman. Another, Edward H. Harriman, would indignantly have rejected the epithet "romantic"; he thought his vision of a transportation system to girdle the globe was utterly practical. His ships would connect his rails which traversed the American continent with those he proposed to lay across China and Russia. Add a few lines in western Europe and some Atlantic steamers and the job would be done. As simple as that. With the same fanaticism, Willard Straight advanced his harebrained schemes for developing China. These were men pursuing hidden dreams. Some investors, having attained kingly dignity in their own country, sought larger realms in which to become emperors. Others strove with the determination of provincials to prove themselves not only against local competitors but against everyone in an ever-widening planetary metropolis. They acted as if committed to the faith that nothing—not even national boundaries—would circumscribe their endeavors.

The new conditions made for new ways of doing business. None, taken alone, was important; but taken together and in context they were significant. The proliferation of handbooks, manuals, and directories for international trade showed the importance of detailed, precise, current information from every corner of the earth; publishers assembled the rapidly changing data in increasingly sophisticated and elaborate form. The desirability of academic training to handle this knowledge evoked calls for systematic instruction in international trade in the business schools and universities. Finally, the quest for some means of association and cooperation to enlighten entrepreneurs about overseas opportunities culminated in the formation in 1914 of the National Foreign Trade Convention.

Americans with overseas involvements consistently pressed global considerations upon their government. The inadequacy of the banking system, for instance, concerned everyone who operated beyond the country's border. Anachronistic laws permitted the national banks to do business only over the counter at the places named in their charters. They could establish no branches, effect no foreign transactions. Those restraints remained serious until the Federal Reserve Act (1913) freed the banks to engage in some foreign activity.

Cautiously, the government entered upon agreements with other nations to facilitate business. It opened negotiations, which reached fruition later, for the reciprocal lowering of barriers to trade. In 1891 the International Copyright Act for the first time recognized the validity of those literary property rights. In 1906 the United States subscribed to the Universal Postal Convention. A series of heroic efforts aimed to establish the uniformity of consular invoices; the ideal—a slip of paper which bore an identical meaning in every part of the world.

The International Chamber of Commerce, which held its first session in Liège in 1905, became an instrument for attaining these improvements. Seven years before Americans felt the need to form their own United States Chamber of Commerce, they participated enthusiastically in the international body. The fifth congress of the Chamber in Boston (1912) stressed the mutuality of commercial interests which transcended national lines. Charles Nagel, United States Secretary of Commerce and Labor, pointed out that improved communications brought everyone together so that there was no such thing as ultimate advantage at the expense of a neighbor. The need for rules of the game to govern all transactions equitably called for uniform standards of weights and measures, of quality, of labels, and of declarations. Agreement on those matters, in his judgment, was more important than on those which were the usual subjects of diplomatic negotiations. The businessmen of the world had to establish "a relation so intimate commercially, and ultimately socially" that no country could afford controversy. After the rhetoric came earnest discussion by the delegates of topics not usually deemed diplomatic— the variability of the Easter season, for instance, which fluctuated from year to year by as many as thirty-five days, damaging some industries. Or the desirability of general calendar reform. Or the need for an international court of arbitral justice to hear suits among individuals and foreign states.

Business people desired some universal equivalent of the courts which adjudicated conflicts within the United States. They edged toward a concept of international law which dealt not only with relations among sovereign states but also with private disputes among individuals in different countries; and increasingly a clearly defined group of lawyers specialized in that practice. Entrepreneurs were also for peace, not so much out of ideological conviction as because war was expensive and disruptive of their affairs. Impatient with high-blown expressions of the martial spirit, they believed that their own prosperity depended on stable relations among all states.

Entrepreneurs in every part of the globe to some extent shared the same aspirations. But Americans lacked the government support that sustained their counterparts elsewhere. There was no equivalent in the United States, for instance, of the direct participation by Britain in the Anglo-Persian Oil Company (1914). In the absence of such assistance, Americans embraced the idea of unrestrained commerce with particular intensity. They were arriving at an image of one world, which they called free, an image in which political forms and cultural norms receded to the dim background while the economic connections stood forth boldly. Their world was free in the sense that it encouraged the uninhibited decisions of investors, buyers, sellers, employers, and employees. Perhaps because it was not framed in a coherent theoretical system, that image suffered from ambiguities and contradictory qualifications; but it evoked support or at least assent from farmers for whom it meant freedom to ship their products to expanding markets; from laborers for whom it meant freedom to migrate to where jobs were; and from thousands of petty entrepreneurs who drew parallels with the freedom they sought for their own enterprises. The concept, thus understood, offered Americans worried by an abrupt

technological foreshortening of distance and disturbed by the unexpected expansion of Europe a means of restating and preserving the
patriotic connotations of earlier beliefs in the freedom of the seas, in
the mercantile virtues, and in the manifest mission to redeem the
world.

Theodore Roosevelt launched the New Nationalism, the better
to compete in that world. Internal order and prosperity would
strengthen the United States for its role among the great powers. Since
there was no realistic prospect that Americans would conquer a
colonial empire, their best hope was to preserve opportunity against
encroachments by the empires of others. Support for the territorial
integrity of China and of the open door for trade and investment there
had been basic to the country's Asian policy; and resistance to external political control had been its attitude toward Latin America
since the Monroe Doctrine. To strengthen the economy so that it
could hold its own in international markets without special privileges
or concessions, Roosevelt urged Americans to outgrow their anti-trust
prejudice. The effort to restore old-fashioned competition was as foolish as reliance upon the flintlocks of Washington's Continentals in
place of modern weapons. Properly regulated, the great corporations
would safeguard the interests of the people. In dissolving the Standard
Oil Company, the Supreme Court in 1911 had established a Rule of
Reason: combinations which aimed to monopolize the market were
illegal, those which increased efficiency were not. A strong bureau in
the executive branch, Roosevelt believed, could best distinguish one
type from the other.

The election of 1912, however, brought to the White House the
champion not of the New Nationalism but of the New Freedom.
Woodrow Wilson, too, was an intellectual; but Jeffersonian agrarian
ideals and aversion to bigness glued him to nineteenth-century economic ideas. Wilson believed that the country needed above everything else laws to look after men on the make, for industry was
not as free as it had once been and the owner of only a little capital
found it hard to compete with the big fellow. The government was
to prevent restraints upon the free market and thus foster competition.

During the electoral campaign, Wilson had called for lower tariffs
and vigorous anti-trust action; and in 1913 and 1914 he set about
attaining those goals. The Underwood Act sharply cut back the in-
ordinately high protective rates set under the previous administration;
and the income tax, permitted by the Sixteenth Amendment, made up
the deficiency in revenue. The Clayton Anti-Trust Act reaffirmed the

ban on monopolistic practices and set up the Federal Trade Commission to enforce it. However, few prosecutions followed, and Wilson's reforms had little immediate effect.

Wilson's effort to resolve the currency issue had more constructive results. The panic of 1907 had once again revealed the drawbacks of the conditions under which American banks operated. But Congress, fearful lest the financiers seize control, had refused to adopt the National Monetary Commission's recommendation in 1912 of a central bank to give elasticity to the currency. Ultimately a compromise quieted legislative suspicions of the money trust. The Federal Reserve Act in December, 1913, divided power between the politically appointed Board in Washington and the twelve district banks responsible to their members. While marred by many imperfections, this was the initial step toward establishing a fiscal mechanism to regulate the economy.

The inconsistencies of Wilson's policies were not at once apparent. Little more than a year after he took office war swept across Europe, and shortly after the beginning of his second term the United States entered the conflict which overshadowed all domestic issues, shattered the economy of Europe and reduced to dust the fragile conception of one world.

In 1914 the great European powers had settled the outstanding economic problems that divided them. Give a little, take a little—when it came to Asian ports or African swampland or concessions in Turkey, reasonable men reached arrangements without drawing swords. After a quarter-century of negotiation with arms at the scabbard, the danger seemed over—territorial lines fixed, grants portioned out, business in order.

In that year, nevertheless, war came. The fighting started not in a dispute over trade or colonies but as a result of the injection of irrational, nationalistic elements which the system of alliances and balance of power proved incapable of absorbing. The immense social and economic damage caused by the conflict left ineradicable traces on the next half-century of world history.

The American economy felt the consequences of the fighting long before the United States became a formal participant. Almost at once the Allies began to purchase munitions and other supplies; and before long they also requested and received commercial loans. Sales of manufactured and agricultural goods boomed; but the resultant prosperity hung upon an Anglo-French victory.

Pressure upon the productive system increased with American

entry into the war. Europe in 1917 had suffered almost three years of destruction; the United States supplied much of its food as well as weapons to continue the battle, while at the same time mobilizing, equipping and transporting an army of almost 5 million men. The response was gratifying. Between 1913 and 1918 American steel production increased from about 3 million to more than 4 million long tons. Although Americans learned to live through breadless days because the supply of grain was sometimes inadequate to feed the troops and civilians in Europe and at home, agricultural output grew by 24 per cent. The ton miles of freight carried by railroads rose by a third; and the value of all exports leaped from $2 billion to $6 billion.

Shocked by shortages of all sorts and by the sudden disappearance of such humble imported commodities as potash, Washington whipped the loose and decentralized farms, mines and factories into line. The existing government departments were hopelessly inadequate; specially created agencies, staffed by dollar-a-year businessmen, frantically set to work adapting industry, food, trade, railroads, and shipping to the urgencies of the war economy. But the hastily improvised boards, appointed by a Council for National Defense, had little power. They depended on voluntary collaboration, that is, on the willingness of entrepreneurs to forego profits. In effect, the war effort penalized the patriotic and rewarded the greedy.

A dearth of shipping antedated American belligerency, for the country had consistently neglected its merchant marine since the Civil War. Suddenly aware of the seriousness of the problem, Congress in September, 1916, created the United States Shipping Board with the authorization to buy or build $50 million worth of merchant vessels. The Board in turn formed the Emergency Fleet Corporation, which acquired some 9 billion tons of shipping by the time of the Armistice.

In the summer of 1917 the internal transportation system was also in a tangle. Traffic rose, shippers clamored for space, and freight cars were unavailable; yet the roads lost money. On December 26, 1917, President Wilson by proclamation took over the railroads, which the United States operated throughout the war. Federal control sliced through many persistent problems. Twelve uniform types replaced the 2,000 different kinds of freight cars earlier used. Standardized equipment and consolidated schedules improved efficiency and raised the volume of goods carried, while permits assigned priorities for essential commodities. Meanwhile, the post office department assumed responsibility for telephone and telegraph service.

The emergency did not, however, override the American faith in private ownership or dissipate the deep-rooted mistrust of the bureaucracy. The rest of the economy remained under the control of the old entrepreneurs, although now under general government supervision. The Fuel Administration organized in August, 1917, allocated coal, while other bureaus tried to assure the equitable distribution of scarce foods. Ultimately the War Industries Board, set up in March, 1918, assumed the power to plan the whole productive system. The Armistice ended the war before these efforts produced conclusive results.

The price of the war had been substantial—$22 billion spent by the United States and, in addition, 10 billion more loaned to the Allies. Total federal expenditures in the three years from 1917 to 1919 amounted to about $33 billion, with receipts of only 10 billion and a resulting deficit of about 23 billion, a charge which hung over the future.

Victory on the battlefield obscured some serious failures in the productive system at home. Until the coming of war the United States had paid little attention to the new weapons of the twentieth century and, despite its economic might, was unable to build its share of ships, aircraft, artillery and tanks. Furthermore, there were heavy hidden costs to mobilizing a decentralized economy in a period of crisis. The dollar-a-year men who came down to Washington to run the agencies did not forget the companies that still paid their salaries. The general abandonment of competitive bidding in favor of cost-plus contracts and the absence of prior planning produced inequities in rewards, especially since there was no effective restraint upon profiteering. Heavy government spending, the deficit and feeble controls all contributed to inflation. The index of consumer prices rose from 100 in 1914 to 149 in 1918. For the time being, increased earnings kept pace with the rise, but a disagreeable postwar situation was in the making.

The uneasy interlude of peace lasted only two decades. Restoration of the world destroyed in 1914 was impossible. The conflict had inflicted heavy physical damage on immense areas; it had also complicated international finance; and it had shattered beyond repair the earlier patterns of trade and investment.

Yet the postwar concern with reparations and debt reflected a willful disbelief that the old order had really changed. The Germans had been guilty (by the declaration of the treaty) of causing the war's damage; they had to pay for it. The Allies had borrowed large sums from the government of the United States and its citizens. Those debts would have to be repaid. Business would then revert to its prewar character. Hardly a glimmer of awareness that a common fate bound victors and vanquished intruded upon these blithe estimates.

Instead, nationalistic emotions, whipped to a fury by war, shaped economic policy after 1918. Out of patriotism and self-interest, people demanded that their governments act to preserve a vigilant posture against the outside world. The great powers now totally discarded the free-trade doctrines of the nineteenth century and protected domestic producers by excluding foreign goods through import quotas and tariffs. Rigid commercial restraints and monetary controls deepened the dependence of colonies on their masters. Everywhere nationalism magnified the role of the state in generating production and in directing the flow of goods and funds to improve its strategic position.

The desire spread for a self-contained, protected, national economic order. Agriculture in advanced countries sought shelter against competition as industry already had; and labor, which had formerly leaned toward free trade because of its international orientation, turned to tariffs and quotas as the means of saving jobs. Autarchy, national self-sufficiency, was an increasingly attractive goal.

These policies further drained the strength of economies reeling from the shocks of prolonged war. The effort under duress to transfer $33 billion in reparations from Germany to the Allies and $10 billion in debt from them to the United States blocked the return to mutually beneficial economic relationships. These heavy burdens complicated by boundary changes, repudiation of obligations by revolutionary regimes and disorderly currencies set inflation loose. As governments manipulated their monetary systems for their own ends, confidence faltered in the durability of the gold standard and of all the relationships based on it.

The postwar trends common to other industrial societies extended also to the United States. Few Americans were aware in the carefree 1920s that they had lost the shelter of their favorable historic situation. Free immigration and relatively free trade had formerly given them unlimited access to Old World pools of goods, markets, manpower and capital. Sellers on one side of the ocean had found buyers on the other; and men and money from Europe had poured across when the needs of expansion had called for them, had stayed home when not required. Now capital ceased to flow westward, new laws shut out immigrants, and prohibitive tariff rates excluded imports so that foreigners could neither purchase American products nor make payments on the debts due Uncle Shylock.

The boom-era euphoria dulled perception of the problem and left unchallenged the assumption that a return to normalcy permitted business as usual. Real per capita income moved upward through the decade. For the moment, mechanization reduced the demand for unskilled hands, and internal migration channeled people to the factories which needed them. Credit was plentiful. The Federal Reserve Board, far from damming the tide, in 1927 lowered the discount rate to increase available funds. Substantial tax cuts in 1921, 1925 and 1926, along with reductions in the national debt, had the same effect. Easy money set off manic speculation—in California and Florida land, in urban real estate and above all in securities. Brokers' loans for margin accounts climbed from $2.8 billion at the beginning of 1927 to 3.5 billion at the end of that year and rocketed to 6 billion by the summer of 1929. Values spiraled upward and heady performances encouraged suddenly prosperous consumers to spend freely on the products of the fields and the factories. How all these elements would respond to fluctuations in the business cycle would meet the test after 1929.

Continued growth made the United States the world's most advanced industrial power. The Webb-Pomerene Act of 1918 exempted from the provisions of the anti-trust laws combinations to engage in export trade. America's position as an international creditor furnished additional muscle. In 1914 it had owed foreigners some $3.5 billion; in 1919 foreigners owed it 12.5 billion, and the balance of payments continued in its favor through the 1920s. Americans used their strategic financial situation to establish more branch plants overseas, to invest in distant areas and to stake out claims to oil and minerals in South America, the Near East and Africa. The total capital thus dispersed doubled between 1919 and 1929. The stringencies in payments seemed temporary, to be eased by loans to Europeans, as under the Dawes and Young plans.

American businessmen wished to restore some of the conditions of the pre-1914 free one-world. They approved the reaffirmation in the Nine-Power Pact of the open door policy which bound the signers not to create in China spheres of influence or exclusive opportunities or any monopoly or diminution of equal opportunity. Mutual understanding, when possible, paid off better than violent intervention. In 1927 Dwight W. Morrow, a Morgan man, went down to Mexico, which was expropriating the property of American oil companies and landowners, not to threaten but to persuade. Reasonable adjustments, to everyone's advantage, would permit business as usual. Then the sales techniques of industry, aided and guided by the Department of Commerce, would steadily widen markets. Few considered seriously how foreigners would pay as long as the United States maintained its own protective walls.

Panic struck in September, 1929. The New York stock market, having gleefully climbed to extravagant heights, then fell into a precipitous decline. On September 3, General Electric sold for 396 ¼ and Radio Corporation for 101; on November 13, they went for 168 ½ and 28. Month after month brought no relief. The Dow Jones industrial index which stood at 364 in September, 1929, slid to 62 in January, 1933. Enterprises with a speculative base, like the utilities empire of Samuel Insull, tumbled into ruin, depriving thousands of investors of the last glimmer of hope.

Panic touched off depression, which dragged on for a decade. As the value of securities fell, banks contracted their credit and the squeeze affected the funds for other forms of investment. Manufacturers cut back production. Funds for private loans to customers abroad were no longer available, and there was a consequent curtailment of the export of such key commodities as cotton, wheat, and tobacco. Instead of unfreezing the supply of credit, the Federal Reserve Board allowed interest rates to rise. Thereupon money became still more difficult to get; bank failures increased; and the whole economy slowed down.

The collapse had domestic as well as international causes. But the delay in recovery was due in part at least to the rupture of old economic links. President Herbert Hoover vainly attempted to invigorate international trade and investment. But his countrymen, in no mood to take risks, raised rather than lowered barriers. Other nations did the same. A moratorium in the summer of 1930 which halted payments on international debts—public and private—did no good. In 1931, the failure of the Vienna Credit Anstalt dragged down the Austrian banking system; and the chain reaction spread across western Europe to the United States. As confidence melted away, disaster struck one financial institution after another.

Franklin D. Roosevelt restored enough confidence to permit the banks to reopen; but he found no relief from the depression and did little to solve international economic problems. Although Roosevelt had been a Wilsonian in 1920, in the next twelve years he had become sensitive to the desire for self-sufficiency among his constituents and brought to office a bias toward isolation. He made no effort to revive the question of membership in the League of Nations or the World Court. He also dragged his heels at the London Economic Conference of 1933, originally called while Hoover was still President. Roosevelt rejected every scheme for stabilizing world currencies that limited his own freedom of action, and the meeting dissolved without results. Soon the United States abandoned the gold standard and devalued the dollar.

The end of the gold standard for the time being killed any remaining hope for international cooperation. An act of 1934 authorizing tariff reductions of up to 50 per cent in reciprocal trade agreements was a lonely gesture toward the outer world, passed at the behest of Secretary of State Cordell Hull.

Through his first administration the President focused upon domestic problems. Many New Dealers, intent on planned production, thought in terms of a self-contained system. Secretary of Agriculture Henry A. Wallace's influential *America Must Choose* (1934) thus argued that the preferences of individuals or corporations could no longer determine trading decisions; future exchanges would come through bilateral barter arrangements in accord with a national economic plan. Adequate controls required autarchy. That position was congruent with the attitudes which prevailed in the rest of the world. The appearance of totalitarian regimes in Japan, Germany, Italy and the Soviet Union and of closed trading systems in France and Britain extinguished for the decade the prospect of one world, set formidable barriers in the way of recovery from the depression, and complicated all the tasks of economic reconstruction.

11

The Tensions of
Reorganization

*E*conomic nationalism and the collapse of the global economy were evidence that the vaunted self-governing mechanism, in which millions had once believed, now failed to adjust the productive system to changing conditions. Through the 1920s some businessmen, politicians and economists continued to grope for means of putting the economy in order. Those feeble efforts came to an abrupt end in 1929. In the decade that followed, attention focused on recovery from depression and reform of the abuses which had led to it. But every stab at tinkering in the attempt to get the engine turning over raised anew the unresolved question of whether a new model was needed. In 1939, the New Deal efforts had not brought back prosperity; nor had they introduced a new economic order. But fumbling on in the determination to get something done, the Roosevelt administration had begun to create the guidance mechanism for later use.

Many observers fully anticipated that the postwar boom would lead to a financial panic and then to a depression. Prosperity in the 1920s had not by any means reached everyone in the United States; and feverish expansion which, for the moment, brought a glow of apparent vigor to important sectors of agriculture and industry, actually enfeebled them.

Furthermore, the alternation of good times and bad made sense in terms of conventional economic theory. Business always revolved through cycles of boom and depression, so that the exuberant economic activity of the 1920s was a certain portent of the decline about to come, just as in the past; and just as in the past, the dip would lead into a greater rise. The conventional faith also held that such alternations increased efficiency by eliminating marginal producers and thus strengthened the whole system. Ingenuous theorists linked the pattern to sun spots and to other natural sources of regularity so that the appearance of danger signs—a rise in the rate of commercial failures after 1923, a sag in the price level after 1925—pointed to no more than a temporary interruption in the inevitable climb.

The downturn after 1929, however, did not arrive at a trough and then become an ascent. For a decade the economy held to the same depressing course; neither the methods of the Hoover administration nor the New Deal reforms reversed the trends. Farm incomes remained low; unemployment remained high. Those indices registered the misery of the most numerous elements in the population.

Roosevelt's soothing assurance that the nation had nothing to fear but fear itself did not get at the source of disorder. The depression was grave because it was worldwide and because it struck at a moment when changes in the social environment and in the structure of agriculture and industry exposed problems of economic organization unresolved since early in the twentieth century. All the while Americans wrestled with the need for recovery, they jabbed away also at the need—not always recognized—for realignment of the whole system of production.

For almost a half-century, scholars, publicists and politicians had noted the approach of the end of the historic expansion of the United States. First, the territorial frontier had disappeared; then the country had turned its back upon acquisitions outside the continent; then immigration had come to an end; and by the 1920s the rate of population growth slackened. The unique combination of dynamic forces which had impelled economic development in the past no longer existed. During the depression no flow of new settlers appeared to buy mortgaged farms so that debtors could start anew further West. The hands laid off at the factories and construction sites were American citizens who did not go back where they came from but festered on the spot. And producers no longer relied upon a steady increase in the number of consumers. Adjustment was unavoidable.

Less visible but equally drastic changes profoundly influenced the course of the economy. Times were tough on the farms for almost a decade before the crash of 1929. In the great days of the war and even after the Armistice, when famine had stalked Europe, American farms had fed the world, acreage had expanded and profits had soared. But by 1921 foreign demand had fallen off and surpluses depressed prices and incomes. The farmers were in for a long, hard season, even the best of them.

Not until another war restored demand did the pressure really ease. In the interim, modernization crowded marginal operators to the wall. The continuing shift of cotton culture to the Southwest, into areas free of the encumbrances left by slavery, exposed the anachronism of Old South tenantry patterns. Falling prices squeezed out the croppers, for whom there was nevertheless no alternative mode of earning a livelihood. In 1930, an absolute majority of Mississippi's population had no gainful employment whatever.

The situation outside the South was only slightly less harsh. Americans ate less wheat and corn, more dairy products, fresh vegetables and fruit; and these changes in taste further upset established patterns of agriculture. Mechanization was not new; but the accelerated pace and the replacement of the horse by the tractor increased the advantages of the more efficient producers and bore harshly upon the little family holdings. The weight of debt rose even in the 1920s and became intolerable during the depression, despite government efforts to ease credit. In 1932, more than half the total farm debt was in default. Foreclosures and evictions then imposed the additional penalty—there was no place to go. To top off the misery, dust storms and drought blew away the topsoil of large areas in the Great Plains.

Prices fell and also land values; yet, though many small farmers abandoned their plots, monstrous efficiency kept production uncontrollably high. The index of output for each man measured 39 in 1909, 78 in 1929 and 100 in 1939. Too much of a good thing! American agriculture choked on its own abundance. Frantic political action brought momentary relief, but no cure.

Soft spots appeared in industry also, even during the prosperity decade of the 1920s. Aging plants weakened New England textiles; and the merchant marine collapsed after the expansion of the war years. Railroads no longer presented attractive investment opportunities. Electrification and the use of diesel locomotives did not restore confidence in the profitability of these enterprises. Mileage in operation and passenger revenues declined while income from the haulage of freight remained constant.

Bustling urban terminals and hurtling express trains still displayed the railroads' power; but while the nation's population rose by more than 13 per cent between 1920 and 1930, the number of passenger miles traveled fell by 43 per cent—an ominous indication of troubles to come. Textiles, the leather trade and coal mining were lethargic in the face of shifts in consumer tastes and the appearance of attractive substitutes. Pockets of technological unemployment bothered a few observers.

The depression also revealed the costly features of industrial developments which had seemed entirely beneficial before 1929. The new products and the new modes of production, at first evidence of progress, then proved encumbrances which threatened to drag down the whole economy.

The war had stimulated the growth of industries which had only been in their infancy in 1917. The manufacture of dyes, drugs and other chemicals had until then concentrated in Europe, which possessed the skilled labor and the research facilities unavailable in America. The seizure of the rights to German patents and processes and the demand for munitions during the First World War touched off a boom in the United States that carried through the next decade, when synthetic materials like rayon entered the market. In the same years, the expansion of electric power lowered the costs and increased the output of aluminum. A variety of electrical products passed to the consumers. The 100,000 radios produced in 1922 increased to 3,250,000 in 1929, by which time 10,000,000 families owned sets; and thousands of homes also boasted refrigerators, toasters, clocks and oil burners. Like the growing sums expended on education, movies, sports and other forms of entertainment, like the rising levels of total output and income per man and of the power and machines each used, the new products were signs of progress.

Above all, there was the automobile. In 1910, the United States was still behind France, Germany and Britain in technology and output of motor cars. Then the American volume rose—not so much of the finely crafted machines upon which European manufacturers depended, but of cheap models which sold in the hundreds of thousands. In 1910, a good year, American factories turned out just over 180,000 automobiles, in 1930, 4.5 million. Vehicle miles traveled increased about fourfold between 1921 and 1929. The clogged roads felt the effects, and so did the whole economy. Car registrations, which stood at 630,000 in 1910, rose to more than 27 million in 1930, each representing a vehicle which needed highways on which to move, rubber for its tires, glass for its windows, and steel for its body. Massive demand stimulated growth in all the industries catering to the automobile.

The motor car, the refrigerator and the radio did not fit neatly into the categories Americans recognized when they thought of manufacturing. The process of making and distributing the new products resembled neither that of light industry, like clothing, or heavy industry, like steel. The clothing factory turned out coats and dresses in large quantities—undifferentiated, cheap and intended for a mass market. Its profits depended on high volume and speedy turnover sustained by style or fashion and by the need of consumers to buy at frequent intervals. The steel mill turned out rods, sheets and beams of which purchasers made machines, ships or bridges, all destined to last a long time and all used in further production. Since the number of buyers and sellers was relatively small, the market for steel was more predictable than that for clothing. Neither pattern, however, fitted the autos and the other new commodities. Like coats and dresses they went to thousands of individual consumers, yet were too expensive to be discarded after a season or two. They were consumer goods, yet durable; and none of the old manufacturing and sales methods applied to them. Success in this field rewarded entrepreneurs who developed novel techniques for manufacturing and distributing vast quantities of the new goods.

Henry Ford, calculating mechanic, in the first decade of the century worked out one solution in auto making—high volume, low price. Not for him the expensive land yachts hand-crafted in shiny brass by the best European and American manufacturers. He advanced to a high level of efficiency the techniques of mass production in which Eli Whitney had pioneered a century earlier. Each car consisted of thousands of parts, all replaceable, and all brought together for assembly at a line manned by an unskilled and therefore cheap labor force. The system adapted to new conditions enabled him to turn out Model T's at a price millions could pay. Concentrating on a single model, he organized the entire plant around the assembly line which carried components to workers, each of whom performed one of scores of small tasks of which the production process consisted. The ability to regulate output by the speed of the moving line drastically reduced costs. Ford's Model T went from $900 in 1909 to $360 in 1917 and to $260 in 1925, while annual sales rose from 18,000 to 785,000. To keep the staggering expense of inventory from devouring his profits he moved the cars expeditiously to their purchasers, mobilizing a national network of dealers, each with a sales quota to maintain a constant flow in good times and bad. Millions of identical Tin Lizzies poured from the factory out across the American landscape.

Ford, however, thereby locked himself into dependence upon the continued popularity of his Model T. He was helpless when shifts

in consumer preferences reduced demand for his product. Any change-
over, as in 1927, required closing down the whole plant for a year and
the dismissal of thousands of employees.

Ford's innovations never departed from the old assumption that
the way to sell was to lower price by lowering costs. Other manufacturers who modeled their production techniques on his nevertheless
experimented with quite different approaches to the problem of finding
purchasers. Instead of struggling to keep the price down, they tried
to manipulate tastes in the hope of eliminating caprice and hazard
from buying patterns. The aim was to influence the market so that
it would operate on a predictable plane.

The owner who held his vehicle until it was no longer repairable
was an impediment to planning; there was no knowing, when he drove
his new car away, how long it would be before he returned to buy
another. In the 1920s automakers more alert to the issue than Ford
learned that annual model changes and facilities for trade-ins encouraged consumers to return regularly to the showroom, while used
cars, sold to people who could not afford new ones, spread the habit
of ownership. Obsolescence according to plan permitted gradual al-
terations of design and made drastic, total changeovers unnecessary.

General Motors adapted to the new situation as Ford did not.
The founder of the firm, William C. Durant, a flashy financial manip-
ulator, lost control in 1920. Then the DuPonts moved in—an old
firm, but far from complacent, well armed with capital from wartime
gunpowder profits and deep enough in chemicals to be aware of the
utility of new scientific methods. They encouraged Alfred P. Sloan,
a sophisticated engineer, to reorganize the GM management. The
central administration of the corporation supervised the allocation
and efficient use of resources; but autonomous divisions competed
against one another, offering consumers a variety of choices at every
price level. Aggressive merchandizing methods sold style as well as
transportation, so that new models tempted the buyer even while his
old one was still usable. Credit terms spread payments over a number
of years; the percentage of cars bought on installments climbed steadily until in 1929 fully 70 per cent of automobile sales were thus
financed. The same practice spread to other durable consumer goods.
Debt of this sort amounted to more than $3 billion in 1929.

The novel features of the new industries significantly altered
both the patterns of consumption and the organization of production;
and both changes influenced the course of the depression. Early in
the century, the great majority of the population with annual earnings
of less than $2,000 expended 80 to 90 per cent of their incomes on the

day-to-day costs of food, clothing and shelter. In 1929 these items still accounted for 67 per cent of retail sales; but the remainder went almost entirely for motor vehicles and their accessories, for furniture and for household appliances. In hard times people cut back less on food and clothing than on consumer durables. Faced with a choice on how to spend the shrinking pay packet or salary check, they did without the new automobile or radio, particularly when they still owed installments for previous acquisitions. No matter how shiny the new model, fearful families were slow to trade in the old one. In the decade down to 1939, expenditures for food, fuel, clothing and shelter fell by less than 7 per cent; those for durables by more than 27 per cent.

An economy increasingly dependent upon the production and distribution of consumer durables felt the loss of purchasing power at once. Keenly sensitive to fluctuations in credit-financed volume sales, these branches of industry laid off hands as demand slackened after the panic of 1929. The spread of unemployment further diminished purchasing power.

Yet, restoration of demand through government pump-priming did not bring a full complement of hands back to the assembly line. Instead, it stimulated a higher level of mechanization. The automobile industry by 1937 had regained the output of the 1920s, and in 1939 surpassed it. The number of radios produced in 1939 had mounted to 10.7 million, so that by then 27 million families tuned in. Yet expenditures on durables that year had still not regained the level of 1929. Lowered prices achieved through improved technology accounted for the increased output. The labor force employed did not grow correspondingly; and the expanded production of cars and radios failed to soak up significant numbers of work seekers. This advanced sector of industry could no more turn the tide of unemployment than could the backward branches or the country's chronically feeble agriculture.

Changes in manufacturing as well as the impact of the depression emphasized the need for the sweeping economic reorganization which Herbert Croly and Theodore Roosevelt had demanded early in the century. Franklin D. Roosevelt in 1932 returned to the theme they had enunciated in the call for a New Nationalism. As long as expansion had opened equal opportunity for all, he explained, the "business of government was not to interfere but to assist in the development of industry." In the twentieth century, however, the nation had reached its last frontiers; "there was no more free land and industrial combinations had become great, uncontrolled and irresponsible units of power." The industrial plant was built, the President asserted, perhaps overbuilt. The country's task was not discovery or exploitation of natural resources, or producing more goods, but the soberer, less dramatic one of administering what was already in hand; and that required control by a central authority. Such statements evoked widespread assent in the 1930s; the issue was how to exert that authority—through public ownership, or through centralized planning, or through administrative regulation of enterprise.

Political considerations influenced the choice among competing strategies. Roosevelt's mandate for action was potent, particularly in the disorganized weeks when he first entered the White House. But even had he been clear in his own mind about which course to follow, he had to take account of divergent opinions. Reform could not run against the grain of popular opinion. Conservatives still argued that the fault lay in misguided tampering rather than in failure of the system; and, after the euphoric early months of the new administration, a dubious Congress scrutinized Brain Trust programs with care. Above all, Americans were not ready for a total social revolution; they wanted relief from hard times but in ways that preserved their roots in the past.

Economic reorganization was therefore always subsidiary to recovery from the depression. The schemes adopted reflected not the assertion of a single forceful political will but the compromises required by the process of enactment. At best, New Deal measures had anodyne effects. Some of them rectified earlier manifest abuses. Others created the potential for later reconstruction. Still others were damaging or altogether ineffective. But whatever their consequences, the frantically devised reforms fitted into no coherent reorder of the economy. Ironically, some of the most important changes were the unforeseen results of hasty improvisation.

Control to Roosevelt did not mean government ownership, the radical solution espoused by some workers and middle-class intellectuals. Many writers and artists had always resented the tone of the Big Business era—materialism crowding out every spiritual value. Capitalism, they believed, was dying for it was unable to operate an industrial system that depended upon mass production; and it deserved to die because it failed to distribute equally the wealth created by modern technology. Exhilarated by the collapse of what they considered a stupid, gigantic fraud, journalists, ministers and academics took comfort from their own ability to carry on while the bankers took a beating. The solution was clear: transfer the means of production to the people so that men of the mind would sit at the managerial desks. Thus it was that the Soviet Union averted crises.

But most Americans shied away from any suggestion of putting politicians in charge of the economy; the likelihood of a gain in efficiency from doing so seemed as slim as that for a decline in corruption. Without serious dissent, the railroads had reverted to their private owners as soon as the First World War ended. Whatever feeble enthusiasm municipal socialism had commanded earlier in the century faded in the 1920s and 1930s. New Dealers, aware of public sentiment, disavowed any intention of having the state take over. They proceeded on the assumption that enterprise would remain private, although subject to more oversight by the state than in the past.

When Roosevelt in 1932 spoke of control by a central authority he had vaguely in mind a realignment of the American economy to permit the unified planning of production. That concept had important ideological sources in two generations of thinking about conservation, evolution, engineering and law. Since the late nineteenth century, the number of Americans concerned about the conservation of natural resources had grown. Some, out of esthetic anxiety about changes in the landscape, wished the government to preserve wildlife and wilderness conditions. The depletion of petroleum, coal and timber resources worried people of a more utilitarian bent. Although new oil discoveries and a vast increase in the output of electricity were reassuring for the moment, conservationists shifted their forebodings to the future and continued to demand enlargement of the public role in the economy. By 1920 all the elements favoring conservation, for whatever reasons, had combined into a potent force. Forty states and the federal government had begun to act through conservation commissions of various sorts. Although these agencies generally faced the issue in a simple form—whether to withhold natural resources for the future or use them up at once—they all assumed that resources were limited and required centralized planning.

A more general strand in American thought regarded planning as the use of intelligence, applied through social science. William James and John Dewey insisted that men were not helpless victims of the environment. Lester Ward, C. H. Cooley and Thorstein Veblen argued that evolution was not a blind, purposeless process; there was room within it for human will exercised through planning. Professional engineers agreed; conscious of their status as a group and impatient with the mechanisms of the free markets, they believed that the systematic thinking with which they solved particular problems could equally well apply to the whole economy. Their hardheaded social engineering verged on the utopianism of Edward Bellamy but also drew support from changing concepts of law and psychology. Louis D. Brandeis and Oliver W. Holmes had suggested that law was an instrument of social change: judges and legislators were not merely to discover and apply eternally valid principles such as the right to property and contract but rather were to devise rules appropriate to social needs. Meanwhile J. B. Watson and others investigated the means of manipulating human behavior and opinion, which, they insisted, depended not on immutable instincts but on responses to external stimuli. Furthermore, the experience of the First World War provided evidence to sustain the faith in planning. The War Industries Board had pulled together the uncoordinated elements of the productive system; and standardization had produced measurable economies persuasive to people conscious of costs.

In the 1920s, all these sources fed the conviction that planning was the next economic stage in the United States. Self-conscious technocrats taught the value of a single over-all national plan; and trade associations sought to organize whole industries to eliminate waste, a kind of planning which had the incidental effect of reducing competition. The corporation then seemed to develop into a planning instrument. The old trust-busting hostility subsided and there were few prosecutions under the Clayton Act. In 1920 the Supreme Court refused to order the dissolution of the United States Steel Corporation, holding that mere size or command of a large part of the market was not itself evidence of restraint of trade. New mergers and consolidations followed; some states permitted branch banking; and chain stores increased the number of outlets—the A&P from 5,000 in 1922 to 17,500 in 1928.

Influential books justified the trend. John Maurice Clark's *Social Control of Business* (1926) explained that the day of laissez faire was over. Yet monopoly was not a danger because the large, organized interests of the country balanced one another for the general welfare. The spread of stockholding had divorced ownership from management, and mergers consolidated enterprise into a relatively few large units capable of cooperating harmoniously with the state.

The divisive issues of the 1930s dissolved the certainty of concordance between public and private interests. But the depression nevertheless emphasized both the need for national planning and the opportunity to institute it while the old order was in disarray. Raymond Moley and Henry Wallace were among the influential New Dealers who wished to erect a wall around the economy within which they could make rational estimates of resources, needs and future programs.

Furthermore, overseas experience seemed to validate the concept. Few Americans approved of the ideology or practice of Communism and Fascism. Yet many believed that the Soviet Union had taken a major step forward in its five-year plans to control the economy. Italy under Mussolini and, later, Nazi Germany also seemed to demonstrate what could be done with the new techniques. The United States had to move in the same direction, although in its own way. "A new world is within our reach if we can organize and act to take possession of it," proclaimed the final report of the National Planning Board (1934).

The prospect of developing a planning mechanism pleased those businessmen who, since early in the century, had searched for ways of adjusting production to the market without running afoul of the anti-trust laws. Wartime control had been an eye opener in its furtherance of efficiency and profit. The emergency had also blunted the edge of the Clayton Act; the newly created Federal Trade Commission was lenient in allowing industry to contrive arrangements for the sake of the war effort. The wartime practices persisted. Between 1919 and 1933 numerous trade associations collaborated with the Commission, through stipulations and conferences, to exchange information and to define agreements on fair practices that would not expose participants to conspiracy charges. Talk about planning as a cure for the depression revealed the possibility of systematizing these arrangements under the auspices of government.

The National Industrial Recovery Act of June, 1933, created the machinery for self-regulation, price fixing and planned production. Roosevelt challenged employers to "band themselves faithfully in these modern guilds" so that millions of workers long unable to earn their bread could raise their heads again. Industry had long insisted that, given the legal right to act in unison, it could do much for the general good. Now, the President announced, it had that right. In each industry, councils representing government, management, labor and consumers adopted codes enforceable at law which regulated all the terms of production, fixed prices and allocated quotas to each firm. Launched with enthusiasm, the N.R.A. immediately spawned more than five hundred industry groups under the leadership of such promoters as in more prosperous times arranged mergers. When they drew upon the experience of strong trade associations already in existence, when they had the cooperation of labor, and when they used recognized enforcement techniques, the codes were effective. But more often than not, they failed dismally, so that there was some sense of relief when the Supreme Court threw the whole scheme out as unconstitutional (May, 1935). The Bituminous Coal Conservation Act, which attempted to plan for a single industry, met the same fate.

A creaky mechanism was responsible for the perceptible difficulties of the N.R.A. Factionalism divided many councils, prevented agreement and encouraged violations, especially since few of them possessed the information to make adequate decisions. The central authority under General Hugh Johnson lacked the means of reconciling differences in clashes over what seemed good for a single industry and what seemed good for the whole country; and the federal administration grew impatient when it could not impose its wishes upon the voluntary trade associations.

The New Dealers' view of the economy as a stable, mature system no longer capable of growth made matters worse. Since the sum of rewards would not increase, the planning process involved the allocation of shares of a fixed total and the gains of any group were necessarily at the expense of others. The alternative to cutthroat competition was an amicable sharing of what was available. In effect, therefore, N.R.A. planning resulted in cutbacks in production or in other restraints upon output, attempts to control the market which, even in the absence of sinister conspiratorial motives, usually injured consumers.

Beyond the difficulties peculiar to the N.R.A. were more general problems that impeded any planning effort in the United States. Neither the theoretical nor technical means were available for the precise measurements needed to manage the whole productive system or any substantial part of it. A later generation armed with sophisticated computerized concepts had trouble enough understanding the economy. In the 1930s, American and foreign economists were only just beginning to break away from the neoclassical concepts to propose modern analyses of fiscal policy and to suggest the function of deficit spending. But scholars by no means agreed on these matters or on fresh interpretations of monopolistic competition, of international trade and of business cycles advanced in that decade. Meanwhile, the Census Bureau, the Departments of Commerce and of Agriculture, the Temporary National Economic Committee, numerous administrative agencies and private groups like the Brookings Institution (1928) and the National Bureau of Economic Research (1919) produced reams of statistics. But attempts to define the gross national product as a standard of measurement were as yet in an early stage.

The McKesson-Robbins Case of 1938 revealed the fallibility of accounting standards in informing a corporation of its own affairs. Could the nation be sure that the array of numbers before it was more reliable?

Above all, administrators and congressmen lacked the power to use what information they had, in imposing discipline upon the unarticulated segments of the economy. Planning was an abstract good. Hard-pressed manufacturers, laborers, working people threatened by layoffs, consumers with reduced incomes all indeed desired a more orderly mode of creating and distributing wealth. But that common longing did not of itself create a harmonious alignment of interests or draw people to a policy acceptable to all. Nor was any group strong enough to force its wishes upon the whole society through control of the government.

Americans lacked the political will for rigid controls. Great as were the fears of economic collapse, the fears of a single, all-encompassing state apparatus were greater still. The preference for regional rather than national projects reflected a wish to restrain the role of government. The Tennessee Valley Authority, the most successful planning venture of the decade, was a quasi-governmental body free of political interference. Like the Port of New York Authority and a few other similar agencies, it was local, posed no serious threat to private interests and pursued laudable social goals—flood control, the generation of power and regional development.

With the N.R.A. dead, the New Deal made no further effort to revive national planning as a technique either for economic reorganization or for solving the problems of depression. Since Roosevelt shied away from drastic measures and was unwilling to impose a unified policy upon the whole administration, a variety of different, sometimes contradictory, impulses throbbed through the federal government.

The desire to adjust aggregate supply and demand persisted as a durable vestige of the planning impulse because it spawned politically attractive relief measures. The great stocks of surplus agricultural and industrial commodities and the millions of families unable to buy what they needed lent plausibility to the diagnosis that the depression resulted from a gap between production and consumption, which government action could narrow.

Only it was not clear whether to seek the balance by limiting output or by stimulating purchasing power or by both policies.

The war on overproduction aimed to cut back every piled-up

surplus, notably in agriculture; agricultural adjustment acts limited the acreage farmers could plant, set up a two-price system for foreign and domestic sales and stored excess commodities in an ever-normal granary to smooth out the disparities between fat and lean years. Basic to the policy was the determination to reverse the trend of falling prices and to guarantee farmers parity, that is, the purchasing power they had enjoyed between 1909 and 1914. The New Deal showed no such solicitude for manufacturers; the bankruptcy of weak firms neatly reduced output without active government intervention.

The surpluses of farm or factory did not disappear, however. In industry, the collapse of some companies simply allowed others to expand, so that the flow of goods did not perceptibly decline; and in agriculture, the law in effect subsidized marginal producers, rather than forcing them out, so that huge quantities of grain and fiber accumulated in the hands of the government.

The failure to reduce the supply element in the equation spurred on efforts to increase the demand element by adding to the consumers' power to spend. Humanitarian considerations alone justified measures to feed the hungry. For eleven days in 1932, when no relief funds for food had been available in Philadelphia, people lived off spoiled vegetables and dandelions—or starved. In the rural countryside, evictions for debt drove tenants onto the roads, to drift away without resources. F.D.R. needed little urging to do something for these Americans. But while welfare and works programs put money into the hands of the aged, the indigent and the unemployed, and had other unanticipated effects, they did not end the hard times. Nor were they steps toward developing a planning process.

The assumption that free competition was the surest guarantee of efficiency still found influential supporters. Old Populists and Wilsonians responded emotionally to the anti-monopoly cry and, once the N.R.A. was gone, took up the pursuit of the trusts in the expectation that unstifled market forces would restore the nation's productive health. Both hostility to bigness and solicitude for small business were responsible for laws in 1936 and 1937 forbidding manufacturers to discriminate among dealers and limiting the ability of chain stores and other large distributors to cut prices. The Temporary National Economic Committee launched a massive study of monopolistic practices, and the Antitrust Division of the Department of Justice readied itself for vigorous prosecution.

Rejection of centralized planning also shifted attention to the development of effective means of regulating economic activity. The aim of furthering fair competition and protecting the consumers justified expansion of the jurisdictions of old agencies like the Interstate Commerce Commission and the creation of new ones like the Civil Aeronautics Authority. Boards sprang up to govern, subsidize or control the rates and output of shipping, power, communications, security and commodity markets and much of agriculture. State and local authorities also had a voice in shaping the conditions under which enterprise functioned.

The drastic growth of the federal bureaucracy, which leaped from 588,000 in 1931 to 1,370,000 in 1941, gave the appearance of a vast increase in the power of government over the productive system. But the appearance belied the reality. The web spun in Washington through the decade inhibited the regulators as well as the regulated.

In practice, the administrative agencies operated within very vague guidelines set by the intent of legislators as interpreted by judges. It was relatively easy to police the morals of businessmen when it came to violations like fraud or misrepresentation which were criminal by earlier, widely accepted statutes. But cases which involved judgments of conspiracy or of fairness in competition and rates called for more delicate decisions. Neither the language of the statutes, calling for balance between the interests of consumers and investors, nor judicial requirements of due process and reasonableness informed the bureaucrat what to do with the specific problem before him, but left him only the consciousness that any action might lead to years of litigation and possible reversal in the courts. As a result, administrators tended to rely upon pragmatic, *ad hoc*, arrangements, sealed in consent decrees, which mediated particular conflicts but established no general principle. Over the years, the process of bargaining, conducted by lawyers for both sides, developed a sense of limits beyond which neither the government nor the enterprises would push one another. Over the years, also, the exchange of personnel between agencies and business created an informal structure of mutual understanding about what would get by without government reprisal and what would not.

Anti-trust and regulation, like licensing, inspection, patents and municipal building codes—whatever their original purpose—slowly evolved into mechanisms for establishing orderly relationships within the economy. The threat of intervention from some uncontrolled political force remained; but day-to-day operations proceeded under the assumption that businessmen could plan their own affairs with some margin of security within the constraints of selective inspection and enforcement set by the administrative agencies. While sometimes, as in the case of railroads and urban transit systems, those constraints were so narrow as to stifle growth, in most industries entrepreneurs bore the burden lightly and even profited from it. Through the decade, the intent of finding a means for centralized planning had unintentionally developed into a mechanism for decentralized order.

Likewise, the New Deal's agonized wrestling with the depression without forethought laid the foundation for control of the economy through monetary policy. The immediate crisis of the spring of 1933 turned on credit. Roosevelt took office with the banks closed and the security exchanges in disorder. Prompt legislation helped him restore confidence so that the system could function once more. The weaker banks never reopened; those which did carried the assurance that a federal corporation guaranteed the safety of depositors' funds. The pathetic runs on banks were over; the long, anxious lines would never again wait desperately to retrieve savings and avert ruin. The Securities and Securities Exchange acts also eliminated some of the other causes of panic by providing mechanisms to police the stock and commodity markets and to warn against potential speculative collapses.

Bolder voices called for more radical manipulation of money and credit. The old Populist faith that easy money would raise farm prices, help debtors and put purchasing power in the hands of consumers still had numerous influential supporters, among them the Reverend Charles Coughlin, the radio priest. The President, never wholly converted to this view, nevertheless dabbled with inflation for more than a year. In April, 1933, he deserted the gold standard and set the value of the dollar in specie at 59.06 per cent of its former worth; and extensive purchases of silver aimed to raise commodity prices and to win Western mining support.

These maneuvers, however, had little effect upon the depression. But together with other measures they gradually defined the government's role in managing credit. Abandonment of the gold standard freed the government to raise or lower the amount of currency in circulation and thus indirectly to affect the pace of business. The power of the Board of Governors of the Federal Reserve system to set the rediscount rate and of the Federal Open Market Committee to alter the reserve requirements of banks influenced the flow of funds to borrowers. Few politicians, as yet, understood the potential of the instrument they shaped in the effort to blunt the effects of depression; but manipulation of fiscal policy would later exert forceful effects upon the economy.

Other attempts to restore confidence also had future consequences. In the dire months of 1933, millions of Americans lacked the means of subsistence and looked for support to their counties and municipalities, which unfortunately were also destitute. To feed the hungry, the Roosevelt administration set aside constitutional scruples and gave federal funds to the localities for welfare. The money thus passed along enabled penniless consumers to reenter the market as purchasers and restored some demand for the products of agriculture and industry.

As important were the fumbling efforts to find employment for those without jobs in industry. At first, the problem seemed temporary, susceptible to solution through incidental provisions in laws for other purposes; the statutes establishing the Civilian Conservation Corps (1933) and the N.R.A. had thus made some provision for public works. But in 1935, when unemployment had not disappeared, the Works Projects Administration assumed the task of providing jobs. In the seven years of its existence, it expended well over $10 billion on public buildings, roads, bridges, airports, housing and slum clearance and paid wages at its peak in 1938 to about 3,800,000 people.

Roosevelt began with no abstract commitment to public works or indeed to the social security and unemployment insurance systems which also began to sustain the purchasing power of the destitute. These measures stimulated business activity by putting dollars in the hands of people to buy the excess products of the farms and factories. New Deal pump-priming in that respect broadened Hoover's strategy of encouraging industry to expand through the Reconstruction Finance Corporation's loans to banks, railroads and large manufacturers.

The kaleidoscopic array of New Deal programs was expensive. Direct outlays by federal agencies, grants to the states, and the swollen bureaucracy drained the budget. Borrowings, not taxes, met the needs rising government expenditures created. The federal debt had climbed from about $1 billion in 1915 to the postwar peak of 26.5 billion in 1919, after which it declined during the 1920s to 16 billion. The depression shortfall in income after 1930 raised the national debt to 22.5 billion in 1933; and in 1940 it soared to 48 billion. The deepening deficits exerted some inflationary effect on prices. But since $20 billion of the debt came from banks, thus diverting funds from normal lending channels, the debt also tended to dampen private credit. What immediate effect debt had upon the economy remained unclear. The government had acquired the ability to influence fundamental choices about the allocation of capital resources and had begun to share with individual investors, banks and large corporate entities the decisions about which risks would be taken. But purposeful use of the national debt was still decades away.

The New Dealers did not understand the implications of manipulating either public works or the debt, although the ideas of J. M.

Keynes crossed swiftly from England to America during the 1930s. Roosevelt, who had entered the White House with a promise to reduce expenditures, tolerated deficits for want of an alternative and, when conditions improved early in 1937, cut back on spending to balance the budget. Recession followed. He did not realize that he had unwittingly hit upon an important tool for managing the economy. For the time being, compensatory spending was a useful political and social tactic rather than a fully developed strategy.

The New Deal had erratically stumbled upon the use of fiscal policy as a means of directing the productive system. Intervention by the government to ease the flow of credit and spending financed by deficits partially revived business. But the Roosevelt administration had neither the skill nor the political will to employ those instruments consistently.

All along, discussions of regulation and planning skirted the issue of control. Where would the power to decide reside? Blueprints did not come into being of themselves. The existence of a design implied the existence of a designer. Who?

Certainly not the politician! Even voters loyal to the New Deal who idolized F.D.R. carried about a negative image of the elected official and feared any increase in his power. Not the remote Washington bureaucrat or Brain Truster. Nor yet the capitalist, victim as he was in a long tradition of social excoriation—avaricious, wasteful, materialistic, and nonproductive. Nor yet the expert! Edison or Burbank could get things done because they were plain, comprehensible and commonsensible, hard-working men, unlike the engineer or scientist who spoke a language of his own and moved in mysterious ways his magic to perform. Honest common men, perennial gulls of the greed of others, alone were trustworthy; yet it was no easy matter to translate their wishes into action through a cumbersome political system, much of which still reflected rural origins, some of which still reflected eighteenth-century social assumptions.

The succession of practical compromises which impeded clear-cut resolution of the problem of control had nevertheless evolved into a pattern of accommodation by 1939. Although there were no important formal constitutional changes, the Congress, the courts, the President and the state and local authorities arrived at a working arrangement in which each respected the legitimacy of the powers claimed by the others. The new bureaucracy in government found leadership in administrators who sometimes possessed professional qualifications but who, in any case, functioned as brokers feeling out their way toward decisions that commanded acquiescence and still got something done.

American social and economic groups remained conscious of their diverse interests. The depression and a decade of experiment with novel policies sensitized farmers, laborers, bankers and manufacturers to the implications of government action for their welfare, but also evoked a dawning awareness of their mutual interdependence and of the costs of civil conflict.

The agricultural bloc retained its strategic political position. But industrial development in the South and the Midwest forced it to yield up a share of its power; and the decline of the total rural population foreshadowed a further shift in influence. Politicians and romantic writers still paid rhetorical homage to the rustic virtues of the family farm; and programs like rural electrification added convenience to virtue. But the statistics told another story—of sons departing, of holdings growing larger, of the increasing disparity between the great landowners who thrived through heavy investment of capital and little ones whose desperate labor did not slow their downward slide. The mule could not compete with the tractor.

Big business also changed. A few table-thumping individualists continued to fume at the interference by Washington in their affairs. But newer, more adaptable types gradually moved into the board rooms and into influential executive positions. The process of separating ownership from management in the great corporations had begun early in the twentieth century, but had accelerated after the First World War. The sons of the founders rarely took the places vacated by their fathers; more often professional administrators stepped in— engineers trained to deal with the technical aspects of production; experts in sales; and lawyers familiar with the complexities of negotiating with the government. The tendency to merger and concentration, which peaked in the 1920s, furthered the separation by combining small and moderate firms dominated by old-fashioned owners into large ones run by more distant managerial types. The diffusion of stock ownership in the 1920s had the same effect.

Business objectives shifted subtly. Since impersonal enterprises did not identify their welfare with that of an individual possessor, the clash of personality less often than formerly intruded upon decisions, the goals of which increasingly became autonomy, stability and the opportunity for long-term growth. The people most capable of directing such organizations were those most adept in accommodating without costly conflicts the play of political and social forces around them. They talked of the public character and responsibilities of the corporation and were less likely to confront government as an enemy than to treat with it as a potential collaborator. They also perceived the wisdom of recognizing the legitimacy of the interests of other groups in the society.

The transformation was slow, and often grudgingly accepted; but the trend was clear. The decisive test came in the concession—however reluctant—of the right of labor to organize and to bargain collectively.

The gains of factory workers during the First World War had proven temporary. The dominant attitude of businessmen had not changed since the turn of the century; good management kept payrolls, like other costs of production, as low as possible. With peace came a determination to return to the situation of 1914; and the failure of the steel strike of 1919 opened the way for an employers' counter-offensive which drove down union membership through the next decade. Steel, autos, aluminum and the other great new industries remained totally unorganized. As a result, the depression bore harshly not only upon the unemployed but also upon the defenseless employed. All who worked or wished to work felt the effect of narrowing opportunities, of declining rates of upward mobility and of the accompanying tensions in the competition for place.

Only a few industrialists before 1933 had begun to question the wisdom of squeezing labor costs as low as possible. Enlightened self-interest persuaded some employers that the gains in efficiency from satisfied workers, scientifically managed, more than compensated for the additional costs. Out of such calculations and out of the desire to inhibit unionization some corporations paternalistically offered their employees stock-ownership and profit-sharing plans, cafeterias, group insurance, medical services and vacations.

But the emergence of labor as an autonomous force capable of defending its own interests nationally was sparked by the determination to organize the mass industries with the support of the federal government, which legitimized collective bargaining in the Wagner National Labor Relations Act of 1935. Victory did not come until after bitter and sometimes bloody battles; but the auto makers finally yielded to sit-in strikes in 1937. The Committee for Industrial Organization then proceeded to enlist millions of workers. Union membership rose and American wage earners were in a position through politics and through industrial action to make their influence felt in the decisions that affected their welfare.

Substantial elements in the population remained voiceless—the marginal elements in the rural population that worked for others or farmed on shares and the unaffiliated, unskilled urban laborers. But the new breadth of representation gave a variety of groups the ability to balance one another in struggles for control; and that, in time, imparted unexpected order to the economy.

12

The Constraints of War

*N*ever was war more costly. Unceasing destruction, from the first tread of German tanks upon the Polish plains in 1939 to the final settling of the cloud over Nagasaki in 1945, took a tragic toll in lives and goods. A world scarce recovered from a lesser conflict two decades earlier, and still reeling in depression, could ill afford the price.

The end. The decline of the West set in, or seemed to; the shattered landscape where cities once stood validated Spengler's warning of the 1920s.

Yet desolation was not only an end but also a beginning. The ashes nurtured thirty years of economic growth.

The war had both immediate and long-term effects upon the American economy. In 1939, the United States became again the supplier to the combatants. Demands upon its productive capacity took up the previous slack, wiped unemployment away and raised incomes. More important, ultimately, were radical structural changes which unfolded only slowly, yet were as decisive in.altering the old order as the depression had been.

Between September, 1939, and December, 1941, the war did not directly involve the fortunate Americans. They manned the arsenal of the democracies, as repeal of the neutrality laws removed restraints upon transactions with the Allies, and suffered few casualties. A flood of orders from England and France got the assembly lines moving. Workers found jobs and brought home wages. Once more they became buyers and their revived demands hastened the spin of the wheels of industry. Pearl Harbor propelled the United States into the thick of the fighting and shifted a good part of the cost of the conflict to the shoulders of Americans. But all-out war yet further stimulated the economy. Demand soared and the farms and factories worked at full speed. At once, good times were back. The recession that had begun in 1937 swiftly came to an end. Employment rose and then continued to rise; and output increased steadily. The gross national product in 1940 had just about regained its level of 1929—about $100 billion; in 1945 it stood above $211 billion.* In the same five years, the labor force swelled from 45 to 64 million. Every other index measured the same happy change. The slow times of the 1930s receded into memory.

By conventional chronology, the war lasted from 1939 to 1945. But after the defeat of Germany and Japan there was no reversion either to peace or to the conditions of the 1930s. Instead, a quarter-century of limited war followed. The United States then dedicated a good part of its energies either to fighting or to the preparation for fighting. The pressure toward change persisted, sometimes easing, sometimes tightening, always there.

The long-term effects surfaced slowly. For a half-century or so impulses toward change had nudged the economy away from its nineteenth-century course. Now the movement accelerated; the national emergency dissolved the inertial forces of habit, interest and law so that the productive system, uninhibited, veered off in the direction toward which it had hesitantly been turning for years.

Americans did not bring to this war the illusions of easy victory that had lulled them in 1917 or 1898. They expected severe damage to the economy. Battle conditions were not compatible with business as usual or with the planning that permitted the fruitful use of resources. War dissipated resources; it destroyed goods and people, diverted energies into unproductive channels; tanks, bombers and submarines consumed rather than generated wealth. Mobilization furthermore removed from the labor force large numbers of men and women who became a drain upon the rest of the society; at its high point, at least 16 million Americans were in uniform, sustained by the work of others.

* In current dollars which take no account of inflation or deflation.

Dislike of waste and of disrupted routines had contributed to conservative hostility to foreign involvements in the 1920s and 1930s. Industrialists were prominent in the isolationist movement and resisted entry into Europe's conflict until the very last moment. And even those who were interventionists acknowledged that the war, however necessary, was inevitably destructive. After Pearl Harbor they accepted the need to fight but also believed they would have to pay the price for the economic disaster that would necessarily follow.

The boom touched off in 1939 seemed at first the frenzied activity of people caught in a hurricane—working harder, doing more for dear life, knowing that the luckiest who survived would still have to clean up in the aftermath. But the fighting had the additional effect of imposing on the country unexpected economic adjustments. All those men and women, dashing about, learned to behave in an organized way. War, irrational and wasteful, for a time at least imposed upon Americans obligations of rationality, prudence and order contrary to their former preferences, indeed sometimes contrary to the law. The change accelerated the development of agriculture and industry.

War supplied what the New Deal lacked, a sense of common purpose and the political will to act. What had earlier been unthinkable became necessary in the name of national defense. The fact of Pearl Harbor eliminated all questions about whether to fight and left only the question of how to win; any stinting of means was intolerable. The character of the enemies, their brutal assaults upon civilized values and the genuine danger they presented to the United States united every sector of the society. Even the Communists became patriots once the Germans attacked the Soviet Union; and pacifists maintained a discreet silence.

The willingness to spread shares of political power to all economic and social groups strengthened wartime unity. The government substantially expanded the hesitant steps it had taken in the 1930s to involve the formerly passive or hostile in decisions that affected them; and the depression experience readied many to respond. The unions which now spoke for labor thus represented far wider constituencies than those of 1917. The degree of unanimity thus achieved dissolved many institutional and political obstacles to action. There could be no dithering over choices while war raged around the world.

In a period of total mobilization, neither officials nor citizens hesitated to cross the line between public and private. Modernized plants and new equipment sprang into being—whatever the means or the expense. Often the government underwrote the cost to be sure of the necessary production. It accumulated stockpiles of strategic materials to ease manufacturing costs. It entered upon joint ventures with private firms, as when it agreed with Freeport Sulphur to operate a nickel plant in Cuba. In 1945 it owned more than 50 per cent of the capacity for making synthetic rubber, aircraft, aluminum, and machine tools and more than 3,000 miles of oil pipelines. Where it did not pay the price directly, it guaranteed loans and made substantial tax adjustments to aid industrial expansion. Direct involvement was not always necessary; a secure contract from the Army or Navy to purchase the output of a factory still on the blueprints was enough to bring together the capital for construction. The vast new buildings and the equipment they housed would remain when the shooting stopped.

The craggiest businessman could not deny the government's obligation to provide rubber for the wheels of bombers or the propriety of a subsidy at public expense to build the tire factory, entirely apart from any advantage he may himself have derived from aid to his own enterprise. But then neither could he deny the need, in gearing the economy to national defense, to expand the role of government in ways he found uncomfortable. Measures which a decade earlier were denounced as intrusions into the private sphere now became commonplace and sensible. With government prodding, Standard Oil of New Jersey in 1942 agreed to share all its rubber patents, royalty-free, with its competitors, postponing the question of compensation until after the war. Various chemical, plastic, carbide, titanium and magnesium producers did the same. There was no doubt after 1941 that political controls would guide the economy. The only relevant issues were where to locate the levers and which hands would operate them.

Yet the government did not take over—not even the railroads as in 1917, or the industries in which it held title to most of the plants during the Second World War. The experience of this wartime strengthened corporate management, which served a national purpose that was patriotic as well as profitable. The busy factories, operated by private companies even when publicly owned, restored the confidence of entrepreneurs. A sense of achievement dissolved the defensive feelings of frustration of the 1930s; fears that the economy had arrived at a plateau and was doomed to stagnation had now proven groundless. Manufacturers, aware of the pent-up spending power of consumers who had long been postponing purchases, looked forward to a waiting civilian market once military requirements eased. A sudden reversal in the trend of the birth rate gave them further cause for optimism; the decline of the previous decade halted in 1942, when the numbers turned upward, promising an expanded buying population for the future.

A sense of opportunity restored animated society. With men and women in demand in the armed forces, in the factories and the fields, each body acquired worth. People long without work found themselves courted. Those long stuck in lowly jobs found chances to be foremen. Expectations for the future soared—for education, for careers in the professions, for positions in management. Although the crust of prejudice was far from gone, increasingly the old patterns of discrimination seemed pointless, nay, contradictory to the objectives of the war.

Americans nevertheless did not lose themselves in a speculative orgy as they had in 1918 toward the end of an earlier war. Investors who remembered the depression were wary, especially since goods and capital were scarce and some branches of the economy were vulnerable. The railroads, for instance, earned substantial profits, but deteriorating equipment and declining efficiency suggested trouble ahead. A sober sense of the possibility but not the certainty of growth animated the process of strengthening the economy for the postwar decades.

During and just after the war the American productive system developed a structure which was new, although its elements had long been present. The tendencies toward bureaucratic management, toward the swift incorporation of new technologies and toward active manipulation of fiscal policy had asserted themselves early in the twentieth century and had moved to the threshold of implementation during the New Deal. The war crisis pushed them across that threshold.

The fact that the government became the largest single consumer in the economy profoundly affected the administration of all enterprises. Even in New Deal days, federal expenditures had not risen above $8 billion a year; during the war they zoomed above $100 billion. Planning and a system of priorities to allocate scarce materials and manpower were essential to meet military requirements, which could not wait upon the hit-and-miss methods of the free market. The War Production Board and the Office of Price Administration enlisted vast staffs to direct the flow of goods to civilians and to the armed services.

Public and private, military and industrial officials participated in a common process of making decisions. People who worked together toward a common end learned to find ways to agree. Too much depended on the outcome to permit endless bickering; and the imperatives of war took the edge off conflict. Furthermore, accelerated transfers of key officials among corporate, military and civil government offices raised the chances for mutual understanding among all of them.

The intermingling of personnel changed the character of business leadership. The individual entrepreneur, already old-fashioned in 1939, was anachronistic in 1945. The administrator who did well was one capable of finding his way through intricate bureaucratic labyrinths, equipped to assimilate and comprehend increasingly sophisticated statistical measurements, and knowledgeable enough about the law to handle complex tax, financial and contract problems. If he was familiar with foreign countries and foreign languages, so much the better. The top posts in industry, government, and law went to such people.

Rationing, price fixing and other wartime controls disappeared soon after the peace; and a rash of anti-trust suits seemed to presage the revival of an adversary posture between government and business. But though the formal wartime machinery of collaboration vanished and although administrative agencies differed about what should replace it, the interdependence of the polity and the economy endured, along with the apparatus for measurement and for the diffusion of information that gave private enterprise a rational, bureaucratic and political aspect.

The war stimulated the application of advanced technology to industry. In some cases, the process was direct and straightforward. The advances in electronics and aviation demanded by the military and paid for by the government promptly found applications in civilian life and became the bases for expanding branches of manufacturing.

In addition, the war significantly shifted emphasis in the ways in which new discoveries affected the economy. Innovations in the past had spread by imitation within the boundaries of an industry as engineers and managers learned from their rivals. In the emergency, the government forced the transfer of new methods to totally unfamiliar territory for the sake of efficiency. The effect upon the manufacture of aircraft was instructive. At the beginning of the war, President Roosevelt had casually set as a goal the production of 50,000 planes a year, a figure far beyond existing capacity, far beyond the experience of any of the companies then in operation. None were prepared or even knew how to prepare. Nor was there time to let them learn on their own. The War Production Board therefore arranged to transfer an army of technicians and manufacturers from the auto makers to the aircraft makers. The newcomers knew nothing about flying, but they did know about assembly lines and mass production and they attained the goal set by the President.

The broadened conception of the uses of technology heightened the willingness to invest heavily and generally in research and development. The Bell System, Eastman Kodak and a few other large enterprises had already perceived the advantage of moving beyond a narrow view of product improvement in the scientific investigations they sponsored. Wartime experience taught many other administrators not only that research could enhance profits, but also that the chance of success was greatest when research was defined liberally.

The war also provided decisive evidence of the fruitfulness of collaboration among industry, government and organized science. The Manhattan Project, which produced the atom bomb, was the most dramatic example, enlisting the Army, university scientists and a cluster of private companies. But the planning and design of other complex weapons also required the command of vast arrays of skills, resources, money and equipment. The future leaders of American enterprise learned in this school the lessons they would apply through the next three decades.

Finally, the war was instructive about the impact of fiscal policy on the economy. What the depression President did hesitantly, inadequately and inconsistently, the war leader out of necessity did boldly and unrestrainedly. When it came to battle expenses, F.D.R. accepted no limit. With survival the issue, the budget went out the window.

Military needs pushed total federal expenditures to unprecedented heights. No questions asked while fighting men and women died. Taxes met part of the staggering expenses. The levies on incomes and on excess and undistributed profits rose from $2.1 billion in 1940 to $35.1 billion in 1945. Yet the mammoth increase evoked no protest; the nation was at war. The immediate result was some restraint on inflation and some redistribution of income since taxes affected increased wages less than increased dividends. The long-term result was a galloping annual deficit which rose from $3 billion in 1940 to a peak of $55 billion in 1943. The total national debt therefore climbed from $48 billion in 1940 to $252 billion in 1945, with few complaints and little debate.

The sale of bonds directly to the public and to banks kept inflation within reasonable limits. The $45.5 billion in savings bonds outstanding in 1945 drew out of circulation funds that, had they gone into immediate spending, would have raised commodity prices. The amount thus withheld would be used after the peace for expenditures deferred until goods were available.

Like the troops in distant lands, the decision-makers in the offices of state and business fixed their attention on the task at hand.

But in turning out tanks and planes, they were also creating relationships, developing modes of organization and settling into habits of action that would permit them to resolve problems which had troubled the American productive system since the beginning of the twentieth century.

The modes of behavior developed under war conditions influenced the ways in which Americans dealt with the old difficulties of agriculture, of international trade and of a labor force in manufacturing perennially victimized by unemployment.

As in earlier wars, the demand for agricultural products rose. Restored purchasing power at home and urgent needs abroad expanded the market for American staples. The armed forces around the world and battle-scarred civilians in allied countries and in captured enemy territory all depended heavily upon shipments from the United States. Prices and output went up so that wheat and cotton growers, stock raisers and dairymen had cash in their pockets. The loss of manpower and the availability of capital in the hands of large farmers renewed the emphasis on mechanization and efficient processing. The government still held surpluses to even out fluctuations in the market, and the question lingered in 1945 whether another depression would follow this boom. But agriculture was set to take advantage of markets wider than seemed conceivable to people who had lived through the constricting conditions of the preceding two decades.

The enormous flow of shipping during the war primed international trade for revival. The United States had to send goods to its own overseas forces, to allies in Europe and Asia, and to the United Nations Relief and Rehabilitation Administration, formed in 1943. Exports grew steadily, as did the size of the merchant fleet.

Similar increases in 1917 had left many Americans a sour taste in the morning after of the 1920s when economic nationalism had stifled commerce and had choked off hopes of movement toward one economic world. The Roosevelt administration hoped for a different outcome from this second, greater war; and it aimed to heighten the consciousness of interdependence and of the obligation to share the tasks of reconstruction through loans and other forms of assistance. The United States determined also to help reform the international monetary system, which had been in disorder since the 1920s. The Bretton Woods conference in 1944 laid the foundation for the World Bank and for the International Monetary Fund, which freed trade both from the dependence on specie which had shackled it before 1932 and from reliance upon the bilateral barter deals of the 1930s.

The key element in the new currency arrangement was the American guarantee of a constant relationship between gold and the dollar at $35 an ounce. All nations could thereafter settle their accounts in dollars. While the world's currencies were still in confusion there was no telling how the system would work; in fact, it would endure for a quarter-century, breathing new life into the concept of a one-world economy open to the flow of commerce unrestrained by political barriers.

Expanding trade widened the markets of industry as well as of agriculture and provided jobs for a steadily growing labor force. The goal of 60 million places seemed fanciful when enunciated in 1945; the United States would soon reach and pass it.

The kind of unemployment which had been characteristic of the depression and which, indeed, had been endemic in the whole industrial past of the United States came to an end. The level of joblessness would fluctuate from year to year, but would not again in the next three decades rise to 10 per cent, much less to the 25 per cent of the 1930s. Furthermore, it became increasingly clear that government, if it wished, could regulate the level; whether unemployment rose above 6 per cent or fell below 5 was a matter of choice. The employment act of 1946 grew out of an awareness of the existence of that choice and of the ability to make it. The law stated that full employment was a necessary and desirable condition of American life and that it was the responsibility of government to assure work to all who wished it. The law established the Council of Economic Advisers to appraise the state of the economy and from time to time suggest measures that would sustain the required level of productive activity. The use of experts to mobilize information and to clarify issues demonstrated the acceptance of public responsibility for the economy. The future would reveal to what extent government would use its power to meet that responsibility.

In 1946, there was still cause for trepidation about the consequences of the end of the fighting. People who remembered the aftermath of an earlier war feared that a depression would again follow, with no jobs available for returning G.I.s. The planning for demobilization which began shortly after the defeat of Germany therefore aimed to limit the adverse effects anticipated. The program·called for gradual demobilization and the retention of controls lest inundation of the labor market by returned veterans create vast unemployment. The scheme collapsed, however; the pressure to bring the boys home speeded up discharges so that fewer than 2 million men remained in the Army at the end of 1946. Production, price and wage controls also vanished in the face of demands for business as usual. Wage earners and manufacturers alike wished and secured relief from wartime restraints. Rationing quickly disappeared and a black market in consumer goods thrived. Legally or illegally, prices rose; and strikes put muscle into labor's demands for pay increases.

Inflation followed, but not depression. Peace did not bring a collapse into stagnation. On the contrary, it opened into a period of rapid growth. The mass of consumers had the means to absorb the output of industry; and the wartime capacity to produce was intact, available at low cost for conversion to peaceful purposes. The wheels could still turn, the assembly lines still move, after 1945 as during the war. The country was poised for a quarter-century boom during which its wealth and productive power rose to undreamed-of heights.

Americans ascribed their good fortune of the moment to stored-up demand and to the need for reconstruction. For a while therefore they were cautious rather than speculative in estimates of the future. They did not at once understand the ultimate economic effects of a rising population and of the increased rationality of their productive system. Only slowly did they refocus their thinking. For more than three hundred years, they had been concerned with the management of scarcities within a relatively stable, relatively closed system. Too many little pigs, too much cotton had disoriented them. They had dealt with surpluses in the 1930s by efforts to restore scarcity, although thousands of potential consumers had then lacked food and clothing. Now, when they began to absorb the evidence of their economy's unexpected capacity for generating abundance, they began to play with the prospect of unlimited growth, to dream of wealth increasing so rapidly as to satisfy the wants of all.

13

The Meanings of Affluence

Promises fulfilled; reward withheld. Americans learned the bitter taste of success. After the long struggle toward it, aridity at the destination.

Because arrival for so many years seemed a hopeless dream, it acquired fanciful, dreamlike features. If it be only pie in the sky, let it be perfect, people thought; and then, having found the dream come true, were dismayed at its imperfection.

In the 1970s the means are finally at hand to end want in the United States. Only then do the questions arise: What is want? And what is life without wants?

Awareness slowly dawned that the economic recovery achieved under pressure of war endured. Historic problems that only a few decades earlier had seemed intractable now vanished, to be replaced by new, unanticipated difficulties.

The economists by midcentury used a measuring stick for the productive system more precise than any available before. The concept of gross national product provided an increasingly reliable way of assessing the country's total output of goods and services.

Measured in constant dollars,* that is, adjusting for and taking out of account the effects of inflation, the gross national product of the United States on the eve of the war had been about $170 billion,

---

* 1958 values. These figures therefore differ from those on p. 223.

having edged upward since the depth of the depression. In 1945, on this scale the GNP had risen to $270 billion. Then it soared, the rate fluctuating from year to year, but maintaining a constantly rising trend. In 1950 it was $355 billion, in 1960, $487 billion, in 1970, $722 billion. In about a quarter-century, the value of the GNP in real terms had almost tripled. The per capita figure for the United States was substantially greater than that for any other large country.

Other measurements traced the same course. Industrial production rose markedly between 1947 and 1955 and then again in the 1960s; using the level of 1957–1959 as 100, the index reached 160 in 1966. Productivity, employment and incomes also climbed. These trends certainly ran counter to the pessimistic expectations of 1945. The economy for the time being had eliminated the cyclical features characteristic of the eighteenth and nineteenth centuries. Year by year it served up an ever bigger pie, so that there was always more to share.

A surprising increase in population contributed to economic expansion. The 90 million Americans in 1910 had gone up to 130 million in 1930. But the most scientific projections during the depression demonstrated that the country would never have more than 150 million residents. The case seemed clear. The slackening in the rate of increase between 1930 and 1940 proved that the birth rate had fallen permanently. And gone were the factors that had generated the phenomenal increases of the previous two centuries—the availability of land and immigration from overseas. Without those exceptional forces, the United States was bound to stop growing, as other advanced countries had. Yet to the surprise of the demographers, the nation's population zoomed to 180 million in 1960 and to 210 million in 1973.

The causes which produced the dramatic rise in population after 1940 were not the same as those responsible for the growth earlier in American history. Neither the push of peoples from Europe nor the pull of vacant lands caused the reversal of the trend in the postwar decade. Immigration—largely of refugees—never regained the levels of the years before 1925; nor did a new frontier offset the steady drift away from the land.

The increase of the 1940s and 1950s came through the unexpected fall in the age of marriage and a rise in the birth rate, trends which continued without interruption until 1957 and which were not reversed until late in the 1960s. The will to form families and to rear children sprang from the war, which restored a sense of purpose to millions of men and women and, despite the sacrifices entailed, left them confident. A future worth fighting for was one worth living for, one worth rearing a new generation for.

The rising population of the United States was not a drag on the economy as it had been in nineteenth-century Ireland, as it was in twentieth-century India. For the moment, at least, Americans possessed the social, political, and economic capacity to use the new numbers to create wealth. The increase was stimulating because a growing percentage of the population found productive employment on terms which enabled it to consume the goods of the farms and factories. The total labor force grew to 63 million in 1950, to 72 million in 1960, to 85 million in 1970 and to 89 million in 1973. Furthermore, the hours worked were more productive and more remunerative than formerly. The amount of labor expended in agriculture declined drastically, while that in manufacturing went up moderately, and in services, professions, finance and government jumped sharply, thus shifting effort from low- to high-yield employment. In addition, all areas gained in efficiency, and within most of them the number of white-collar jobs increased while blue-collar ones did not.

These changes raised per capita income and correspondingly increased purchasing power. Americans were still far from any equality of conditions. Some 20 per cent in the 1960s were poor by current definitions, that is, lacked enough for necessities without assistance; another 20 per cent were somewhat better off though the cost of rent and food left them little leeway in their spending. Fully 60 per cent enjoyed incomes large enough so that they were free to make discretionary purchases. Together, rich and poor mobilized enormous buying capacity. The complexity of the relationship between poverty and the economy emerged in the experience of Tunica County, Mississippi, which held an unenviable record; it ranked lowest in level of well-being in the United States. In 1960, fully 80 per cent of its households fell below the poverty level; yet more than 50 per cent possessed television sets, more than 45 per cent, automobiles and more than 35 per cent, washing machines. Even the very poorest elements in the population were within the army of consumers who expanded the internal market for American agriculture and industry. In 1970, in the per capita number of cars, television sets and telephones, the United States was far ahead of any other country.

Foreign buyers crowded into the same market. In the first few years after the peace, philanthropic and political considerations overseas further stimulated the American economy. Former allies like Britain and France, former foes like Germany and Japan lay in ruins and, torn by war, looked for aid to the one modern productive system which had survived intact. Furthermore, even before the peace, and long before 1946 when Winston Churchill sounded the alarm about the Iron Curtain that had descended across Europe, many Americans

understood that they would have to help overseas lest the ironic outcome of their victory be the replacement of one totalitarian regime by
another. Poverty was the breeding ground of Communism; and countries which failed to get to their feet promptly might collapse entirely
and yield to the Soviets. The intention to deliver such aid culminated
in the Marshall Plan, which provided the means for European reconstruction.

At the same time Americans were impelled to help the newly
independent nations of Asia and Africa which seemed unprepared
to stand alone. Partly because the United States had pressed its allies
to liberate their colonies, partly out of fear of the spread of Soviet
influence, the country accepted the obligation to aid the formerly
dependent areas in the optimistic expectation that all would shortly
follow the Western course of modernization. For good measure, it
was politically expedient to count among the beneficiaries of assistance the Latin American countries which had been independent for
a century or more.

An assumption of breath-taking boldness, product of pure American faith, enabled policymakers to crowd into a single category the
Brahmins of India, the sheiks of Arabia, Congolese tribesmen and
Argentine cattlemen. The category, underdeveloped, implied that all
countries would ultimately unfold in the same way: any society, any
culture, any political order, with just a friendly shove in the right
direction, could evolve a self-sustaining industrial system.

President Truman's Point Four program reaffirmed the intention
to help, later implemented by the Agency for International Development, by Food for Peace and by the Alliance for Progress. The substantial sums that flowed abroad rarely achieved the permanent reforms enunciated in the rhetoric. But they had at least a palliative
effect in regions subject to much suffering.

Although military considerations after the outbreak of war in
Korea tended to extend some aid programs indefinitely, the basic
purpose remained that of building a structure of international economic relationships that would encourage the free flow of capital
and goods. Between 1945 and 1951 the United States delivered to
other countries some $118 billion in goods and service and received
in return some $69 billion. About 60 per cent of the deficit went as a
gift, the remainder on long-term credit. And in Europe and Japan,
when the survivors had cleared away the wreckage of war, rebuilt
their factories and restored their fields, the links of commerce thus
formed remained, indeed gained in strength. At the suggestion of the
United States, twenty-three nations in 1947 joined in a General Agree-

ment on Tariffs and Trade (GATT) to reduce international barriers. The number of participating countries grew and successive rounds of bargaining produced perceptable relaxations of the restraints upon world trade.

The evolving global economy expanded the markets for American goods. It also reopened opportunities for investors.

After the long stoppage of the 1920s and 1930s, the international flow of capital slowly resumed. American businessmen at first shied away from new foreign adventures except in Canada and Latin America. Opportunities were abundant at home and some people still nursed unhappy memories of prewar expropriations. Conditions were unstable everywhere in Europe, China and Japan; there was no telling what regimes would take power or when recovery would come. Furthermore, in the initial stages at least, manufacturing costs were higher overseas than in the United States. Subsidiaries and affiliates already establish might reinvest their earnings; but there was no rush to plant additional good American money in alien soil. Oil, mining and airline companies had to take the risk; others did not.

After 1950, however, foreign investment displayed more attractive features. The government of the United States, eager to involve the private sector in development, made useful concessions as, for instance, in exempting from tax those profits earned abroad until brought home. The return of stability to Europe and Japan eased anxieties about the security of property rights. New consumer markets broadened out; and, as before, entrepreneurs, ready to take advantage of low foreign labor costs, or unwilling to risk tangles with the antitrust laws, or eager to defend their markets against the effects of tariffs or exchange controls, perceived the utility of foreign manufacturing branches. Above all, the guarantee of a fixed relationship between the dollar and gold gave American corporations leverage abroad. The command of dollars enabled them to acquire overseas subsidiaries and to set up foreign branches on favorable terms. In 1968 the book value of direct investments outside the country had risen to $65 billion, distributed much as before 1914—about 30 per cent in Canada, about 30 per cent in Europe, about 17 per cent in Latin America and the balance in Asia, Africa and Australia. In 1970, the total had risen to $78.1 billion with some $26.8 billion more held in portfolios.

The flow was by no means in one direction only. Increasingly European, Canadian and Japanese firms established or acquired branches in the United States; the value of such direct investments in 1968 amounted to $11 billion, in 1970, to $13 billion. In addition, many foreign individuals held $18 billion in shares in American corporations.

The flow of capital into the country and out of it gave new life to the concept of the multinational corporation, operating through subsidiaries in many parts of the world, recruiting management, labor and funds everywhere, its attention focused on global rather than local concerns. In 1972, Union Carbide—a large but by no means the largest company of its kind—produced over eight hundred different chemicals and numerous types of plastics, gases and batteries in addition to managing some nuclear establishments for the United States government. It owned majority shares of subsidiaries in Canada, Belgium, Germany, Greece, Sweden, Australia, Hong Kong, India, Indonesia, Japan, Malaysia, New Zealand, Pakistan, Philippines, Iran, Ivory Coast, Kenya, Sri Lanka, Argentina, Colombia, Costa Rica, Ecuador, Mexico, and Venezuela; of two different enterprises each in France, in Italy, in Spain, in Singapore and in the United Kingdom; of three each in Rhodesia, Norway, Brazil and Ghana; and of four in South Africa. In addition, it owned up to 50 per cent of five companies in Japan, of two each in France, the United Kingdom and Thailand, and of one each in Belgium, Spain, South Africa and Sweden. In the United States it employed 51,000 persons directly and 15,000 more on behalf of the government; abroad the payrolls of its subsidiaries bore more than 59,000 names.

Operations such as these grew in complexity and intricacy. The overseas subsidiary managed by local personnel acquired an identity of its own, reached out for its own raw materials and fought for its own sales where it could find them, sometimes establishing offshoots of its own. The foreign branches of a single parent company might well battle on another for customers in third countries—Ford-Dagenham against Ford-Köln in Switzerland, for instance. Only control over basic capital decisions from headquarters in the United States held these widely scattered branches of empire together.

The central place of the dollar in these wide-flung transactions spurred the rapid development of the international activity of American banks. The number of overseas branches and subsidiaries of members of the Federal Reserve System grew slowly in the 1950s, then leaped spectacularly in the next decade. In addition, some American banks formed holding companies in partnership with European firms for joint operations in the international currency and credit markets. In 1970, more than fifty major institutions were thus involved in financing trade and investment. Moreover, even medium-sized firms far from the principal financial centers now joined in consortia for operations outside the country in procedures made possible by the Edge Act of 1919 but little used until the 1960s. In all, in 1970, the 536 overseas branches of United States banks controlled assets of $52.6 billion and much of that sum was free of effective regulation by any authority. These institutions provided the usual financial services and, in addition, were sensitive locators of funds available for investment in their corporate clients.

The spread of investments abroad demanded domestic adjustments. Along with the flow of dollars went advanced technology, management and marketing methods, so that firms in the United States occasionally found it advantageous to import goods purchased abroad from their own subsidiaries; and sales from foreign affiliates to third countries sometimes diminished the market for American-made exports. Some trade unions resented the transfer of technology which, they believed, deprived their members of jobs. The Opels sold in New York or Mexico City seemed to take wages away from General Motors workers in Detroit. But the case was by no means that clear. The Opel competed not with the Cadillac or even Chevrolet but with the Volkswagen or Fiat; and the corporation was only covering its flanks against competition it could not avoid. The enterprises which could not make it were those which depended upon low labor costs, and even tariffs and quotas rarely saved them. Offsetting any potential losses to the national economy were two important sources of gain— the reverse movement to the United States of branches of advanced German, Japanese and British firms and the income Americans derived from foreign investments, which climbed until it stood in 1968 at $8 billion.

On through the 1960s, the voyagers among the continents carried, along with their bulging attaché cases and their worries about jet lag, the vision of a single global economy inherited from an earlier business generation. During the Second World War, an immensely popular book had described One World, free for trade and peaceful intercourse among all people, which, its author believed, would spring from the ashes of battle. For the moment, the Soviet Union, China, and their satellites stood apart, but someday even they might make a deal and participate in the universal market.

The domestic economy was ready to compete.

Increasingly, the world depended upon farm products from the United States. Agriculture, after limping along for a half-century, entered upon a flourishing new era in the 1960s. At first the markets opened in the immediate postwar years by the needs of Europe and Asia seemed to offer only temporary relief, as they had in 1918 and 1919. Braced for a recurrence of old problems, the government continued to guarantee income at parity and to export or store excess commodities. But the vast increase in population everywhere left hordes of would-be buyers who looked to the United States for food to stave off hunger, for cotton and hides with which to manufacture clothing. The period of surpluses ended; that of shortages opened.

All producers of primary materials gained, but especially the American growers of grains and fibers who were in a strategic position to take advantage of the dramatic expansion of markets by virtue of their flexibility and efficiency. A generation of government subsidies had provided small producers either with the means to sell out and retire or with the capital to expand and mechanize. The farm population declined from almost 25 million in 1950 to about 10 million in 1966, and the number of farms went down from about 6 million to about 3 million in the same period. Meanwhile the average size rose, as did productivity.

Agriculture adjusted successfully to changing domestic food habits and to the appearance of new synthetic fibers; mechanization transformed cotton cultivation in the Southwest; new patterns of stock-breeding based on genetics met the soaring demands for meat; pesticides and chemical fertilizers increased yields per acre; and new processing methods brought fruits, vegetables, dairy products and poultry to consumers. Technology became central to farm operations, not only for the contract growers of tomatoes and chickens, geared to the factory, but also for those who raised wheat and corn and even cherries. The rising output and improved strains of sorghum for forage demonstrated the adaptability of Great Plains farmers. The prominence of the soybean was even more striking. That source of oil and meal had become known in the United States in the late nineteenth century but only in the 1920s had effective processing methods developed. In the late 1960s Illinois, Iowa and Indiana were annually raising, on 40 million acres, about a billion bushels (two-thirds of the world's total) worth $2.6 billion.

Everywhere else in the world, the amount of grain available for export shrank. In America it grew eighteen-fold. The United States in 1974 raised 2 per cent of the world's rice; but it supplied 25 per cent of world exports.

Vast improvements in distribution added to the competitive strength of the domestic economy. The national highway network and the airfreight system sent goods swiftly and cheaply to computerized warehouses; and even the ailing railroads effectively modernized their non-passenger services. Supermarkets and discount houses transmitted food and manufactured goods to consumers efficiently enough to keep the cost of living from rising as steeply as in other industrialized countries.

The structural transformations which enabled American industry to compete effectively in world markets had roots back in the early decades of the twentieth century, but developed fully after 1945. The great corporations of the 1970s differed significantly in size, form and spirit from their predecessors. Capitalization of more than a billion dollars was no longer exceptional, as it had been at the foundation of U.S. Steel in 1900. Many companies registered annual sales of more than that amount.

Organizations of such scope drifted into new patterns of behavior. The tendency toward industrial concentration, which had fallen off during the depression and the war, regained force in the 1950s and the 1960s, but no longer through the spread of a single productive enterprise either vertically or horizontally. In 1952, Royal Little, head of Textron, which had thrived through the war in the manufacture of yarns, worried about the limited opportunities for expansion in textiles and began to pick up small firms in a variety of fields, electronics, cement, aluminum, paint, plywood, leather and aerospace, many of them stagnant but subject to rejuvenation under new management teams. Other entrepreneurs followed, though not always in the same way. The corporation had long since ceased to be identified with an individual; now it ceased also to be identified with a static product. Instead it became a device for manipulating investment capital, often combining disparate activities in vast conglomerates.

These complex aggregations sometimes pushed their constituents to new levels of efficiency, sometimes provided a cover that long concealed costly inefficiencies. In the one case, external oversight and control shook up ingrown bureaucracies and smashed routinized habits in the interest of improved performance. In the other, a rule book imposed from the top inhibited initiative, delayed decisions and covered up failures within the organization so that it took a violent purge to effect any change.

Whether they did well or poorly, the conglomerates altered the character of the risks of enterprise. The book publishing and car rental firms acquired by RCA reduced its dependence on the sales of television and radio receivers and on the revenue from broadcasting. On the other hand, the company could absorb the losses from a daring and disastrous venture into computers. The promise of both stability and long-term growth attracted investors, particularly the mutual and pension funds and the institutions, which in 1970 held about 40 per cent (in value) of the shares listed in the New York Stock Exchange and which were not primarily interested in a quick killing.

Whether it generated its own capital resources on the security markets or turned for aid to banks and insurance companies, no great enterprise could afford to sink into pachydermatous lethargy, lest it be overtaken and devoured by a ravenous outsider. Growth was the only means of survival and growth called for sensitivity to opportunity and responsiveness to change.

Mechanization—long since familiar—took a new form when the technological side effects of the war sank in. Mechanization no longer involved simply the replacement of skilled and unskilled labor. It now called for controls automatically triggered and for machines which electronically received information and instructions from stored data and which therefore functioned without human intercession. Often new petrochemical plants used little labor, skilled or unskilled, other than that of technicians who monitored the machines.

Heavy expenditures for research and development lay behind the appearance of sophisticated new products in electronics, computers, and nuclear power. In addition, some great corporations learned to depend upon subcontractors and gained in flexibility by encouraging small feeder firms which could experiment with new techniques. It was therefore relatively easy for young men with bright ideas to attract venture capital and develop peripheral products. The dominance of the computer field by a single large firm, for instance, did not curtail the ease of launching new devices—hardware and software—for the input, handling and display of information.

New small companies tended to follow the management style of the large established ones. The tough entrepreneur, frugal saver, daring risk-taker, who ran at the fringes of the pack hoping to tear off a prize as proof of personal prowess was a vanishing species. The great rewards now lay in a subcontract or in takeover by a big outfit, earned by the same qualities which brought advancement within the firm—by the ability to work efficiently and unassertively as part of a group. The objective of orderly, predictable growth replaced that of the spectacular haul.

The trend toward rational organization had a beneficial side effect on the use of the country's human resources. Wasteful warfare between labor and capital subsided; strikes in the new era were tactical instruments in a collaborative bargaining process rather than bitter-end weapons wielded by enemies out to destroy one another. The United

Mine Workers, once among the most belligerent of unions, now cooperated with employers to mechanize the coal fields in the face of competition from rival fuels.

Racial and ethnic prejudice appeared anachronistic in this context. Slowly but steadily old patterns of discrimination crumbled and ceased to close off desirable places in the labor force. The pool of talent from which managers were drawn also broadened. Some individuals still climbed to prominence through inherited wealth, through lucky windfalls or through speculative gains. But increasingly the top corporate executives moved up by competition through a graded hierarchy. In 1899, 60 per cent had started as independent proprietors, in 1960, only 15 per cent; the family and group connections which had helped Carnegie's generation were far less important in the business bureaucracy. The ideology of equal opportunity, reinforced during the war, and the needs of large global enterprises for merit-based leadership combined to speed up the rate of social mobility in the whole society.

The nineteenth-century conception of a clear line between what was public and what was private could not stand in the face of the war, of industrial concentration and of the interrelations between enterprise and government. The weight of political influences and altered character of enterprise limited the operations of the free competitive market, and modified, although they did not altogether destroy, the distinction between the public and the private sectors of the productive system.

Once the government assumed the responsibility for providing work to all who wished, it had to intervene in the economy and its primary instrument was fiscal policy. The New Deal compromise over control was still effective after the war so that the banks, fearful of inflation, and the government, fearful of unemployment, continued to check one another. A running feud between the Federal Reserve Board and the Treasury enlivened the effort to establish the optimal balance from 1945 to 1951, when an open confrontation finally produced a silent understanding. However much the administration wished to encourage expansion, the Board could raise interest rates to check inflation. On the other hand, budgetary deficits and the Treasury's open market operations could offset restrictive credit policies when the administration desired.

The outcome was moderation in both unemployment and inflation down through the 1960s. Government action kept joblessness from rising much above 4 per cent of the labor force. With the end of the immediate postwar shortages and the rise in industrial output, supplies caught up with demand and inflation moderated. The consequences were expansive. Rising prices tended to diminish the value of fixed incomes and of safe bonds and savings accounts. The real returns from such investments shrank, encouraging the shift of capital into more productive although more risky channels.

Government action, however, did not lock Americans into rigid centralized planning. Widespread acceptance of the principle of economic management did not lead to the concentration of power at any single point of control. True, the President annually delivered an economic report which presumably set forth the appraisal and recommendations of the whole administration. But, in fact, the Treasury, Commerce, Defense, Labor and Agriculture departments operated with their own specal models of the economy, as did the Federal Reserve System and the regulatory agencies. In addition, the Joint Economic Committee of the Congress had its own staff and expressed its own views which affected, but did not always determine, legislation and appropriations. Then too, banks, universities, the Brookings Institution and the National Bureau of Economic Research generated a mass of intelligence which supplemented, ran parallel to, or challenged that emanating from government sources. Economists conveyed information and ideas from one office to another as they shuttled among public and private agencies; but that compounded rather than eased the difficulty of adopting and executing any policy. On the other hand, looseness and tentativeness made the planning apparatus sensitive to change and responsive to opportunity.

Direct controls over prices, wages, profits and commodities such as had served during the war seemed undesirable. The government only rarely used the extensive power it had received in the Taft-Hartley Act (1947) to intervene in labor negotiations, but preferred to act as broker, mediating between the national unions and the employers to arrive at bargains which would not outrage consumers. The regulatory agencies also took a limited view of their responsibilities. The Interstate Commerce Commission, the Federal Trade Commission, the Food and Drug Administration and the Environmental Protection Agency assembled vast and growing bureaucracies, remote from popular control or responsibility. Every company of any size and every trade association maintained its embassy in Washington to negotiate with administrators as well as to put its case before congressional committees and to fend off assaults from labor, consumer and self-styled public-interest groups. Constant activity in the national capital left a sense of the omnipresence of government and of the weight of its role in the economy. But the administrative agencies rarely expanded their roles beyond the resolution of conflicts among contending interest groups. Immense obstacles frustrated the occasional efforts of zealous officials to take the initiative or to assert positive policies of their own.

The government continued to dispense subsidies for research and development of the aircraft industry and of other enterprises of military value. It also aided the failing railroads, not by ordering rate increases but by out-of-pocket payments from tax revenues. It maintained commodity stockpiles not only to help out farmers and miners but also to guard against interruptions of supplies. These transactions and purchases for foreign aid, for Vietnam aid for direct military and space consumption took large chunks out of the free market so that it became increasingly futile to pretend that government activity was confined to a discrete, circumscribed public sector of the economy.

What then was private about the corporation? Not the operation of industrial enterprise, thoroughly intertwined as that was with judgments of government about capital, prices and profits. In the 1960s the courts withdrew from the effort to disentangle what was private and what was public in these relationships. Insofar as it served or professed to serve the general welfare, insofar as its performance affected the whole economy, insofar as it drew together vast amounts of capital and employed thousands of wage earners, the corporation was public, and subject to the scrutiny and control of government. What was private was the right of investors in it to a return upon their capital. Other than the privilege of annually sending their proxies in to ratify the decisions of management, the holders of common stock differed from the holders of bonds in the same company or in public authorities in one respect only. The return shareholders expected was risk-rewarding appreciation of values, rather than a fixed dollar amount.

Ambiguities in the continuing redefinition of what in the economy was public and what private long confused policymakers. What was good for General Motors was good for the nation—in a way, but not quite or altogether, so that the mere assertion was either a truism or a challenge. Recognition of the social role and responsibilities of the corporation did not in itself advance decisions; it did not, for instance, resolve the conflict between those who justified concentration on the grounds of efficiency and planning and those who criticized it as a mask for monopoly. Mergers and acquisitions continued to expand the scale of enterprise; but hostile critics were always ready to attack, through the Senate Antitrust and Monopoly Subcommittee when Estes Kefauver took over in 1957 or through the

Justice Department when Richard McLaren headed its Antitrust division in 1969. Now and again a giant, stumbling over the regulations, came crashing down.

Through the 1960s the monopoly issue—like that of fiscal policy and like that raised by every aspect of the impact of government action on the economy—smoldered unresolved. Continued growth then put some gains within the reach of all and took the edge off disputes. Although individuals and groups pulled in different directions, everyone argued from the same premise, accepting the logic and desirability of growth.

Toward the end of the decade two related difficulties threatened the economy. By 1970 inflation and energy had become intractable problems, largely because dramatic shifts in social values raised questions about the ultimate worth of growth.

At first the monetary difficulty affected mostly business people concerned with foreign exchange and tourists worried about the rates at which they cashed their traveler's checks. For a quarter-century the dollar had stabilized a large part of the world's currency and had also been the primary instrument for financing international trade and investment. The burden on the United States grew heavier in the 1960s as prosperity everywhere in the West and in Japan increased the volume of commerce, of investment, and of money in circulation. The fund of dollars overseas, and especially in Germany, Canada and Japan, grew larger. By the spring of 1971 some $100 billion in obligations were thus outstanding, much of them presentable at the United States Treasury for conversion into gold at $35 an ounce. American gold stock dwindled as foreign holders lost confidence in the dollar and cashed in their paper for the metal, which rose steadily in value.

The weakness of the dollar, the standard by which all other free currencies measured their worth, was a threat to all the trading partners of the United States. But none was eager to help. Resurgent nationalism narrowed the sights of many Europeans and Japanese who had, in any case, grown accustomed since the war to shifting the cost and responsibility for international economic order to the United States. Yet, without the cooperation of other nations, unilateral efforts to check the flight from the dollar would have had inflationary consequences within the country.

The Americans gained a respite by thrusting drastic measures upon their partners. The United States devalued the dollar slightly, thereby quietly emphasizing how dependent other currencies still were upon its stability. Agreement to separate the gold traded in the free market from that used to settle international accounts and to supplement the latter by the Special Drawing Rights of the International Monetary Fund further protected the dollar against speculative assaults.

On the domestic front also, government action temporarily braked inflation. Restrictive fiscal policy in 1968–1969 thus locked the valves on credit, the money supply and federal spending, and held down prices at the expense of a slight rise in unemployment; with the subsequent release of controls, the economy lurched forward once more.

But in the 1970s, worldwide demand, fueled by economic development, sent commodity prices soaring. The success in raising output in Europe and Japan gave new millions the discretionary purchasing power that made them competitors with the Americans for primary goods, which suddenly became scarce and expensive. In most respects, the ability to satisfy many of its own requirements for food fibers and minerals shielded the United States from the full consequences. In one respect it was vulnerable—the increasing dependence upon foreign sources of energy.

Suddenly the awareness dawned of the relationship between energy requirements and the capacity of the economy to grow. Despite the mournful predictions of conservationists early in the century, a bountiful providence had always seemed to provide Americans with plenty, so that the consumption of energy mounted steadily, doubling between 1950 and 1960 and then continuing to rise. However swiftly industry and individuals drew upon the stores of power, more was available and at reasonable cost—until the 1970s.

New sources and improved techniques again and again mocked the pessimists who predicted the approach of the day of total depletion. When the nineteenth-century standbys, wood and coal, ran short, water power, petroleum, natural gas and nuclear fuel supplied the deficiencies. At any given time, the proven oil reserves covered the needs of only twenty years. A presidential commission predicted in 1952 that consumption would double by 1975. It did not matter, as long as fresh fields continued to come in. Furthermore, the level of demand and of price markedly influenced supply. The forests did not give out after all, because it paid the lumber companies to replenish the stands depleted. When the cost of oil rose, the drillers went back to the dry holes with more expensive equipment and also launched their platforms offshore. After 1950, strip- and deep-mining machines —mammoth augers, supergiant shovels, conveyor belts and bucket-wheel excavators—dug coal out of sites once considered not worth bothering with.

Government policies were therefore haphazard, excessively responsive to popular fads and consumer pressures. Low natural gas and oil prices discouraged the use of alternative fuels, reduced the incentive for additional discoveries, and increased the dependence upon imports from abroad. Solicitude for the environmentalists limited offshore drilling, prevented the erection of new refineries and blocked the construction of the pipeline to bring in the yield from Alaska's northern shelf.

In the fall of 1973 a politically motivated cutback in oil deliveries by the Arab countries and a staggering price rise managed by OPEC, an international association of oil producing nations, swiftly raised energy costs and burst the restraints which until then had kept inflation within reasonable limits. Yet nationalism long prevented agreement upon a common policy among the Americans and their trading partners.

How the United States would respond was still unclear a year later. A political crisis which had dragged itself out for two years and forced the resignation of the President had destroyed the capacity for effective action. Divisions between his successor and Congress, itself divided, continued to deprive the nation of leaders able to make decisions.

But beyond the confusion left by Watergate lay deeper causes for concern. Americans were by no means as sure of themselves as they had been a decade earlier. Having reached the goals set by their predecessors, they now wondered whether the effort had been worthwhile. Even had the means for action existed, the uncertainty would have remained about what action was desirable.

Economists were no longer as sure as they had once been that progressive refinement of techniques would infallibly lead to correct solutions. Awkward questions intruded. Could their science be value-free? Could they make statements about the increase of national income without prior assumptions about its distribution? Could they assert general principles about the allocation of resources without a previous commitment to political and ethical premises?

In translating theory into action, they and the officials they advised repeatedly tripped over inconvenient practical obstacles. People in a position to influence or determine policy generally accepted the concept—vaguely associated with J. M. Keynes—that fiscal policy could regulate the pace of the productive system. But agreement in principle was not enough to win support for specific proposals to raise or lower taxes. In 1962–1963, a cut seemed desirable; President Johnson finally got it in 1964. Two years later, an increase seemed equally desirable, but the President had lost his arm-twisting capability and could not get it from Congress.

The political process no longer shaped decisions through compromise and through the willingness of minorities to accept the rule of majorities. As the decade drew to a close, politics more often than not became the arena for confrontation and conflict, with Vietnam the glaring, but not an isolated example. Everything flew apart. Congress, reluctant to accept presidential leadership, nevertheless lacked the unity to formulate policies of its own on energy, transportation, food, cities or international relations. Judges who agreed to decide public-interest suits on behalf of consumer or environmental groups appropriated functions theretofore considered legislative. The number of bureaucrats grew, as agency multiplied upon agency. The F.C.C., F.T.C., E.P.A., and F.A.A., Interior, Agriculture, and Justice each performed important functions; but in the absence of firm central control, each went its own way and internecine rivalries flourished. Enterprises caught in the whipsaw of competing policies floundered helplessly through to the courts. The railroads set the pace. Their rates were fixed by the I.C.C., yet they were forced by the states to maintain unprofitable passenger traffic and prevented until too late by the Federal Antitrust Division from combining for the sake of efficiency. They plunged toward bankruptcy, and foreshadowed the fate of airlines, power companies and other regulated businesses.

While the productive system increasingly depended upon government action, the government was less capable of acting than for decades before. Almost no one could get anything done because almost anyone could bring anything to a stop.

The paralysis that crept through the organs of administration and legislation was only in part due to party disputes or to ideological uncertainties. More important was the loss of that sense of purpose and of that will to act which had been a product of Pearl Harbor and which had survived the end of the war for two decades. The glare subsided; and though no all-clear sounded, as Korea and Vietnam showed, with the passing years people, believing the emergency over, put off the uniforms and dispersed along their separate ways. And behold, they did not lapse into the want of the thirties but wandered toward abundance, so that they forgot where they were. Or why.

Lengthy welfare rolls, urban housing on the way to deterioration from the day of completion, pockets of rural misery in Appalachia and of urban misery in Harlem, and the grim plight of the dependent elderly were evidence that, despite economic growth, problems remained almost a decade after the country had declared war on poverty. But these were not the problems which exercised the great majority of Americans who were not poor.

"People in this country are starving," said a Tennessee jewelry store owner in 1973.

Starvation had many meanings in the United States. Once, and not so long before, it meant literally the lack of anything to eat. Later, it referred to improper diet, malnutrition.

In 1973, however, it also meant something different to the Tennesseean. "People in this country are starving for something to do," by which he meant not work, but play. In that year, some 6.5 million families owned trailers, campers and other recreational vehicles, sales having mounted from 83,500 in 1961 to 740,000 in 1972. A society trained to consume, expanded the definition of its needs in order to continue to consume. Ten years after the end of the Second World War, more money went into automobiles, television sets, household gadgets and other consumer assets than went into capital for productive purposes. The trend continued. The advertisements referred often to the problem, what to give the man (or woman) who had everything.

The man (or woman) who has everything. What does he (or she) feel? Sometimes boredom, ennui, purposelessness—what's the use?

Sometimes too, guilt. Guilt drew some into compensatory or justificatory action. They shared their much with the less fortunate or proved in the manner of its use their right to have it.

Others eased guilt with a diffuse sentimental sense of obligation to all not as privileged as they—the blacks and chicanos, yes, the poor and the prisoners, yes, the Biafrans and the Bengali, indeed yes. But also the endangered species, the animals deprived of rights in zoos and the pets cheated by tins stuffed with cereal instead of beef chunks. And something, too, for the psychologically underprivileged doomed to discontent whatever their possessions. Sympathy indiscriminate obscures differences; the leopardless forest and the death of half a million people are alike faults of a plundered planet. The psychological pauperism of the middle classes and the material pauperism of the incomeless register alike on the scale of deprivation. The distinctions count for little in assuaging guilt; they count for much in decisions about the allocation of resources. The ability to make choices demands the ability to distinguish differences.

Premonitory signs in the 1960s pointed to the effects on the economy of ennui and guilt. The bored, avid for the big thrill, lapse into sensate hedonism, in which each gratifies the impulse of the moment and satisfaction of the ego is the measure of all good. Work, if it is not diverting, is a horrid chore for those who have forgotten its link to their daily bread; incentives drop for the competitive race when everyone deserves a prize; and less energy goes into cooperative effort when each regards his own well-being only. Productivity on the assembly line, in the shop, and in the office, suffers.

Guilt spreads confusion. The affluent and their children learn systematically to denigrate their society and its achievements. Demands never cease for American action to help in Israel and Cyprus, to correct injustices in South Africa and Chile, to press reform upon Korea. Yet present wars, but past ones too, are exercises of a stupid and corrupt military machine—*Catch-22*. The Mafia is just another kind of business—*Godfather*. Intellectuals joyously discover sickness all about them; the media, avid for cashworthy sensation, take up the cry. It seems all to have been a mistake from the first despoiling of the continent to the most recent assault on the environment. Turn it back to where it was before vile man's intrusion. The counter-culture prattlers exhort the readers of *The Atlantic* to abandon western science and instead learn "their proper place in nature from American Indian lore, Zen, and Tantra." The birth rate plummets. Growth is evil.

So, how come Brezhnev turns up in this market with his shopping list, and also emissaries of the venerable Mao? And the residents of the Sahel and Bengal, their environments unspoiled by modern pollution—where do their eyes turn for succor? Could there be some merit in an economy which, year by year, and even in the recession of 1974, provides livelihoods to ever more people, which steadily raises their standard of living, which rebuilt Europe and for three decades poured aid overseas?

These are questions not asked. In the dissonant clamor, each yells for advantage or to hear the sound of his own voice or to escape the effort of listening to others.

Yet even though the answers are not simple the questions need asking.

The communities of farmers, merchants and artisans which two hundred years earlier brought the nation into being are gone beyond retrieval. The hustling men and women who built its industrial structure in the nineteenth century have moved off stage. The elaborate enterprise they left behind, infinitely intricate, composed of innumerable interdependent parts, spins on. But whether the pieces will long remain in place without guidance or purpose—that is the ultimate question.

Perhaps economic growth was but a temporary episode in human history and Americans would do well to prepare for its end, as the gloomsayers urge. In that event, it would be best to reckon the cost of narrowing expectations—not only the shrinking portions for everyone that a smaller pie would provide but also loss of the dynamic power that, in the past, expanded opportunities for freedom and equality.

The sense of space running out and of resources exhausted often enough in the history of the United States swept through some sectors of society. Again and again, too, moralists bemoaned the absorption of their fellow citizens in the pursuit of material gain. The forebodings and the criticism did not matter much before 1970. They may matter more in the 1970s when they express the discontent not of isolated aristocrats and intellectuals but of the affluent majority.

Back in the 1840s a historian, pondering the meaning of the American wealth amassed in his day, commented on the opinion that the pursuit of material goods was a low, base, groveling occupation fatal to the dignity and virtue of man. He ascribed that view to the prejudices of persons whose intellects were out of proportion to their capacity for action. To set himself straight he copied out the phrases of an ancient Puritan ecclesiastic:

> Inasmuch as a righteous life presupposeth life; inasmuch as to live virtuously it is impossible unless we live; therefore the first impediment which naturally we endeavor to remove is Penury and Want of things without which we cannot live.

Having moved beyond that first impediment, Americans cannot forget the importance of having removed it. Nor can they disregard the importance of growth in removing penury and enabling some to live virtuously. In the painful effort to discover the meaning of a righteous life they must consider whether there is any alternative to growth as a means of spreading the benefits to all and of averting a relapse to want.

Suggestions for Further Reading

An abundant literature deals with the problems treated in this book. Apart from the works in economic history narrowly construed, the subjects here considered have also profited by the analyses of local, social and political historians, and of biographers. The reader who wishes to go farther will find a plethora of material.

The notes which follow make no pretense to completeness. They are selective and perhaps idiosyncratic since they reflect the preferences of the authors, and to some extent also a prejudice in favor of books which are literate and readable.

Some of the institutional economic histories of the United States written in the nineteenth century still have value, among them, William B. Weeden, *Economic and Social History of New England, 1620–1789* (2 vols., Boston, 1890) and P. A. Bruce, *Economic History of Virginia in the Seventeenth Century* (2 vols., New York, 1896). But a series of volumes under the auspices of the Carnegie Institution of Washington, entitled *Contributions to American Economic History* (Washington, 1915–1933), established the basic canon in the field; many titles remain essential. Other general works of value include John R. Commons, *History of Labour in the United States* (4 vols., New York, 1918–1935), which is much broader in scope than its title; and Joseph Dorfman, *The Economic Mind in American*

Civilization (3 vols., New York, 1946–49) which is somewhat narrower in scope than its title. *The Economic History of the United States* edited by Henry David and others (9 vols., New York, 1945–1951), is a more recent series. The most useful single volumes of this material are Edward C. Kirkland, *A History of American Economic Life* (New York, 1969); and Ross M. Robertson, *History of the American Economy* (New York, 1964). The essays in *The Reinterpretation of American Economic History*, edited by Robert W. Fogel and Stanley L. Engerman (New York, 1971), provide an introduction to the newer quantitative economic history.

On the colonial period, we still like Weeden and Bruce. Wesley F. Craven, *The Southern Colonies in the Seventeenth Century* (Baton Rouge, 1949) is good. There are handy treatments of commerce in Bernard Bailyn, *New England Merchants in the Seventeenth Century* (Cambridge, 1955); Bernard and Lotte Bailyn, *Massachusetts Shipping, 1697–1714* (Cambridge, 1959); Frederick B. Tolles, *Meeting House and Counting House* (Chapel Hill, 1948); and Richard Pares, *Yankees and Creoles* (Cambridge, 1956). Other excellent accounts on special subjects include Abbot E. Smith, *Colonists in Bondage* (Chapel Hill, 1947); Curtis P. Nettels, *The Money Supply of the American Colonies before 1720* (Madison, 1934); Converse D. Clowse, *Economic Beginnings in Colonial South Carolina 1670–1730* (Columbia, South Carolina, 1971); and W. T. Baxter, *The House of Hancock* (Cambridge, 1945). On the English background we liked particularly the thoughtful and provocative analysis in Joel Hurstfield, *Freedom, Corruption and Government in Elizabethan England* (Cambridge, 1973).

Curtis P. Nettels, *The Emergence of a National Economy* (New York, 1962) and John A. Krout and Dixon R. Fox, *The Completion of Independence* (New York, 1944) are useful surveys of developments in the early republic. Samuel Eliot Morison, *Maritime History of Massachusetts, 1783–1860* (Boston, 1921); and John G. Clark, *New Orleans 1718–1812: An Economic History* (Baton Rouge, 1970) are exceptionally good regional studies. Also enlightening are: Robert A. East, *Business Enterprise in the American Revolutionary Era* (New York, 1938); and Joseph S. Davis, *Essays in the Earlier History of American Corporations* (2 vols., Cambridge, 1917).

On agriculture and the frontier one still begins with Frederick Jackson Turner, *The Frontier in American History* (New York,

1920). George W. Pierson, *The Moving American* (New York, 1973); and David M. Potter, *People of Plenty* (Chicago, 1954) go on from there. R. C. Buley, *The Old Northwest: Pioneer Period, 1815–1840* (2 vols., Indianapolis, 1950); and E. W. Bidwell and J. I. Falconer, *History of Agriculture in the Northern United States, 1620–1860* (Washington, 1925) are packed with information. Maldwyn A. Jones, *American Immigration* (Chicago) is a good brief introduction; and Paul W. Gates, *The Farmer's Age* (New York, 1960) is a competent survey of agriculture between 1815 and 1860. Katherine Coman, *Economic Beginnings of the Far West* (2 vols., New York, 1925) is detailed and interesting. John G. Clark, *The Grain Trade in the Old Northwest* (Urbana, 1966) is an exceptional monograph.

A wide variety of works deal with issues connected with the role of the state in the early nineteenth century. Douglass C. North, *Economic Growth of the United States* (Englewood Cliffs, 1961) treats the development of commerce, on which there is also a good deal of material in a very different book, Robert G. Albion, *The Rise of New York Port, 1815–1860* (New York, 1939). Oscar and Mary F. Handlin, *Commonwealth* (Cambridge, 1960) and Louis Hartz, *Economic Policy and Democratic Thought* (Cambridge, 1948) treat Massachusetts and Pennsylvania respectively. George R. Taylor, *The Transportation Revolution* (New York, 1951) is a general account; and Nathan Miller, *The Enterprise of a Free People* (Ithaca, N.Y., 1962) deals in detail with the experience of New York State, 1792–1838. Bray Hammond, *Banks and Politics in America,* (Princeton, 1957) is a nice introduction; and Thomas P. Govan, *Nicholas Biddle* (Chicago, 1959), is a sympathetic biography of the president of the Bank of the United States.

On the early industrial experiments, monographs are best, among them: Caroline F. Ware, *Early New England Cotton Manufacture* (Boston, 1939); Oscar Handlin, *Boston's Immigrants* (Cambridge, 1959); and Vera Shlakman, *Economic History of a Factory Town* (Northampton, Mass., 1935). Constance M. Green, *Eli Whitney* (Boston, 1955); and Allan Nevins, *Abram S. Hewitt* (New York, 1935) deal with important entrepreneurs. Norman J. Ware, *The Industrial Worker* (Boston, 1924) is more general. Stephen Salsbury, *The State, the Investor and the Railroad* (Cambridge, 1967) is a model case study. Edward C. Kirkland, *Men, Cities and Transportation* (2 vols., Cambridge, 1948), is a splendidly written account of the

New England transportation system in the nineteenth century. John F. Stover, *American Railroads* (Chicago, 1961) is a concise summary. Among the more useful histories of particular industries are Arthur H. Cole, *American Wool Manufacture* (2 vols., Cambridge, 1926); and Peter Temin, *Iron and Steel in Nineteenth-Century America* (Cambridge, 1964).

The basic work on Southern economy remains L. C. Gray, *History of Agriculture in the Southern United States to 1860* (2 vols., Washington, 1933). The account of U. B. Phillips in *American Negro Slavery* (New York, 1918) and in his *Life and Labor in the Old South* (Boston, 1929) has been challenged by Kenneth Stampp, *The Peculiar Institution* (New York, 1956). Eugene D. Genovese, *The Political Economy of Slavery* (New York, 1965) and his *The World the Slaveholders Made* (New York, 1969) present another interpretation. Oscar Handlin, "The Capacity of Quantitative History," *Perspectives in American History*, IX (1975) criticizes the novel thesis of Robert W. Fogel and Stanley L. Engerman, *Time on the Cross* (2 vols., Boston, 1974). Kathleen Bruce, *Virginia Iron Manufacture* (New York, 1930); and Broadus Mitchell, *William Gregg* (Chapel Hill, N.C., 1928) describe the problems of the factory in the Old South. Valuable monographs which treat other aspects of the Southern economy include: Herbert Weaver, *Mississippi Farmers 1850–1860* (Nashville, 1945); and Anthony M. Tang, *Economic Development in the Southern Piedmont* (Chapel Hill, N.C., 1958). Harold D. Woodman, *King Cotton & His Retainers, Financing and Marketing the Cotton Crop of the South, 1800–1925* (Lexington, Ky., 1968) is an especially valuable monograph. There are general surveys of the period after the Civil War in C. Vann Woodward, *Origins of the New South, 1877–1913* (Baton Rouge, La., 1951) and in Broadus and George S. Mitchell, *The Industrial Revolution in the South* (Baltimore, 1930).

Fred A. Shannon, *The Farmer's Last Frontier* (New York, 1945); and Harold U. Faulkner, *The Decline of Laissez-Faire, 1897–1917* (New York, 1962) survey agriculture after the Civil War. Walter P. Webb, *The Great Plains* (Boston, 1931) is a sensitive analysis of relations between culture and environment. Everett Dick, *Vanguards of the Frontier* (New York, 1941) treats the Northern Plains and the mountains. There are sections on this period in B. H. Hibbard, *A History of the Public Land Policies* (New York, 1924) and in Roy N. Robbins' *Our Landed Heritage* (Princeton, 1942). Everett

Dick, *The Sod House Frontier, 1854–1890* (New York, 1937) contains a good account of the social conditions of frontier life. Kenneth W. Duckett, *Frontiersman of Fortune* (Madison, Wisc., 1955) is a candid biography of Moses M. Strong, who speculated unsuccessfully in land, railroads, lumber, mining and politics. More modern analyses of agriculture include Allan G. Bogue, *Money at Interest* (Ithaca, N.Y., 1955); his *From Prairie to Corn Belt* (Chicago, 1963); James C. Malin, *Winter Wheat in the Golden Belt of Kansas* (Lawrence, Kansas, 1944); and Robert P. Swierenga, *Pioneers and Profits: Land Speculation on the Iowa Frontier* (Ames, Iowa, 1968). Harold Barger and Hans H. Landsberg, *American Agriculture, 1899–1939* (New York, 1942) is a technical study of output, employment, and productivity. Leo Rogin, *The Introduction of Farm Machinery in Its Relation to the Productivity of Labor* (Berkeley, Calif., 1931); Oscar E. Anderson, Jr., *Refrigeration in America* (Princeton, N.J., 1953); and Rudolf A. Clemen, *The American Livestock and Meat Industry* (New York, 1923); and Leonard J. Arrington, *Great Basin Kingdom* (Cambridge, 1958) are useful monographs. Ernest S. Osgood, *The Day of the Cattlemen* (Minneapolis, 1929) is a good general description; and in Andy Adams, *Log of a Cowboy* (Boston, 1931) and Doyce B. Nunnes, Jr., ed., *The Golden Frontier, The Recollections of Herman Francis Reinhart 1851–1869* (Austin, Texas, 1962) are interesting personal documents. Populism is most rewardingly examined through the studies of specific states; among the best are: James C. Malin, *Concern About Humanity* (Lawrence, Kan., 1964); Francis B. Simkins, *The Tillman Movement in South Carolina* (Durham, N.C., 1962); and Alex M. Arnett, *The Populist Movement in Georgia* (New York, 1922). Theodore Saloutos, *Farmer Movements in the South* (Berkeley, 1960) and Albert D. Kirwan, *Revolt of the Rednecks* (Lexington, Ky., 1951) handle other aspects. Some features of Western transportation are treated in Robert E. Riegel, *Story of the Western Railroads* (New York, 1926) and Oscar Lewis, *The Big Four* (New York, 1938), a stimulating narrative about the builders of the Central Pacific.

A general account of late-nineteenth-century manufacturing will be found in Edward C. Kirkland, *Industry Comes of Age* (New York, 1961). Edward Hungerford, *Men and Iron* (New York, 1938) is a history of the New York Central; and Alan Trachtenberg, *Brooklyn Bridge* (New York, 1965) suggestively analyzes the meaning of that structure. Ralph M. Hower, *History of Macy's* (Cambridge, 1943) and Boris Emmet and J. E. Jeuck, *Catalogues and Counters* (Chicago,

1950), the story of Sears Roebuck, treat aspects of retailing. Joseph F. Wall, *Andrew Carnegie* (New York, 1970); and Harold C. Livesay, *Andrew Carnegie and the Rise of Big Business* (Boston, 1975) are both good. On labor, Philip Taft, *The A.F. of L. in the Time of Gompers* (New York, 1957); Wayne G. Broehl, Jr., *The Molly Maguires* (Cambridge, 1964); Norman J. Ware, *The Labor Movement in the United States, 1860–1895* (New York, 1929); Henry David, *History of the Haymarket Affair* (New York, 1929); Rowland T. Berthoff, *British Immigrants in Industrial America* (Cambridge, 1953); and David Brody, *Steelworkers in America* (Cambridge, 1960) are suggestive. A. C. Littleton, *Accounting Evolution to 1900* (New York, 1933) treats a much neglected subject.

Samuel P. Hays, *The Response to Industrialism: 1885–1914* (Chicago, 1957); and Robert H. Wiebe, *The Search for Order: 1877–1920* (New York, 1966) are useful surveys. Alfred D. Chandler, Jr., *Strategy and Structure* (Cambridge, 1962) brings together thoughtful essays on industrial enterprise. Sidney Fine, *Laissez Faire and the General-Welfare State* (Ann Arbor, Mich., 1956); and Arnold M. Paul, *Conservative Crisis and the Rule of Law* (Ithaca, N.Y., 1960) contain solid accounts of the conflict in American economic thought after 1865. Morton Keller, *The Life Insurance Enterprise* (Cambridge, 1963) illuminates the whole problem. C. K. Yearley, *The Money Machines* (Albany, 1970) analyzes the changes in government and party finance, 1860–1920, and the implications for the economy. Sigmund O. Diamond, *The Reputation of the American Businessman* (Cambridge, 1955) treats Morgan, Rockefeller and Ford, among others. Robert W. Wiebe, *Businessmen and Reform* (Cambridge, 1962) is more general. Allan Nevins, *Study in Power* (New York, 1953) is a sympathetic biography of Rockefeller; Henrietta M. Larson, *Jay Cooke, Private Banker* (Cambridge, Mass., 1936) and Julius Grodinsky, *Jay Gould* (Philadelphia, 1957) are scholarly; Frederick L. Allen, *The Great Pierpont Morgan* (New York, 1949) is chatty; and John A. Garraty, *Right-Hand Man: The Life of George W. Perkins* (New York, 1960) is adequate. Edward C. Kirkland, *Dream and Thought in the Business Community, 1860–1900* (Ithaca, N.Y., 1956) is sympathetic; Robert G. McCloskey, *American Conservatism in the Age of Enterprise, 1865–1910* (Cambridge, 1951) is less so. Milton Friedman and A. J. Schwartz, *A Monetary History of the United States* (Princeton, 1963) is excellent although technical. Other aspects of finance are the subjects of Irwin Unger, *The Greenback Era* (Princeton, 1964) and Walter T. K.

Nugent, *Money and American Society, 1865–1880* (New York, 1968). Edward C. Kirkland, *Charles Francis Adams* (Cambridge, 1965) and Willard L. King, *Melville Weston Fuller* (New York, 1950) deal with influential figures in the development of government regulation.

Cleona Lewis, *America's Stake in International Investments* (Washington, 1938) and Mira Wilkins, *The Emergence of Multinational Enterprise* (Cambridge, 1970) are excellent. Leland H. Jenks, *The Migration of British Capital to 1875* (New York, 1927) also has a bearing on American developments.

George Soule, *Prosperity Decade* (New York, 1947) and Broadus Mitchell, *Depression Decade* (New York, 1947) together cover the years between the two world wars. Forrest McDonald's *Insull* (Chicago, 1962) deals with a figure representative of the mood of both decades.

Among the works which treat the international economic problems of the 1920s are: Joan Hoff Wilson, *American Business and Foreign Policy 1920–1933* (Lexington, Ky., 1971); Carl Parrini, *Heir to Empire: United States Economic Diplomacy, 1916–1923* (Pittsburgh, 1969); Harold G. Moulton and Leo Pasvolsky, *War Debts and World Prosperity* (New York, 1932); and John D. Hicks, *Rehearsal for Disaster: The Boom and Collapse of 1919–1920* (Gainesville, 1961). James Willard Hurst, *Law and Social Process in the United States* (Ann Arbor, 1960) examines some of the issues then prominent. Irving Bernstein, *The Lean Years* (Boston, 1960) treats labor during the depression; and Ellis W. Hawley, *The New Deal and the Problem of Monopoly* (Princeton, 1966) reviews the general evolution of economic policy.

On World War II and the period just after it, the material is spotty. We found Edward S. Flash, Jr., *Economic Advice and Presidential Leadership* (New York, 1965), a study of the Council of Economic Advisers, and L. H. Kimmel, *Federal Budget and Fiscal Policies* (Washington, 1959) helpful.

Leo Fishman, ed., *Poverty Amid Affluence* (New Haven, 1966); Ralph E. Freeman, *Postwar Economic Trends* (New York, 1960); Leonard S. Silk, *The Research Revolution* (New York, 1960); A. E. Holmans, *United States Fiscal Policy* (Oxford, 1961); and Harold G. Vatter, *The United States Economy in the 1950's* (New York, 1963); contain material on the most recent decades. Mira Wilkins, *The Maturing of Multinational Enterprise* (Cambridge, 1974), covers the ground from 1914 to 1970; and Mabel Newcomer, *The Big Business Executive* (New York, 1955), reaches back as well. J. K. Galbraith, *The Affluent Society* (Boston, 1958), and Robert Leckachman, *The Age of Keynes* (New York, 1966), are provocative. Peter F. Drucker, *Concept of the Corporation* (New York, 1946), and Eugene V. Rostow, *Planning for Freedom* (New Haven, 1959), analyze some of the central problems of the period. Lowell Mason, *The Language of Dissent* (Cleveland, 1959) by contrast contains an earthy description of the actual operations of a government agency.

Index